INK!

For Steve, Freddie and Ashtyn

FROM THE AGE OF EMPIRE
TO BLACK POWER

INK!

THE JOURNALISTS WHO
TRANSFORMED BRITAIN

YVONNE SINGH

The
History
Press

First published 2025

The History Press
97 St George's Place, Cheltenham,
Gloucestershire, GL50 3QB
www.thehistorypress.co.uk

British Library Cataloguing in Publication Data.
A catalogue record for this book is available from the British Library.

ISBN 978 1 80399 809 1

Typesetting and origination by The History Press
Printed and bound in Great Britain by TJ Books, Padstow, Cornwall

MIX
Paper | Supporting
responsible forestry
FSC
www.fsc.org
FSC® C013056

The History Press proudly supports

Trees for LYfe

www.treesforlife.org.uk

EU Authorised Representative: Easy Access System Europe
Mustamäe tee 50, 10621 Tallinn, Estonia
gpst.request@easproject.com

'Out of suffering have emerged the strongest souls; the most massive characters are seared with scars.'

Broken Wings, Kahlil Gibran, 1912

CONTENTS

CONTENTS

INTRODUCTION

'They didn't really care about our history. It wasn't really valued as such,' says the middle-aged Black archivist at the British Library as they apologise for the quality of the microfilm that I am handed. The film is one of four copies of a collection of the issues of the *West Indian Gazette and Afro-Asian Caribbean News* that exist in the UK – other incomplete runs of this newspaper are kept at the University of Oxford, Lambeth Library and the Institute of Race Relations.[1]

The film reveals a journal that is burnished ochre, torn and ragged around the edges, with vital sections missing. A dark cumulus of smudged newsprint occasionally deems the odd page unreadable. In its time this newspaper was the foremost voice among the Caribbean community in Britain, emerging from the embers of the Notting Hill riots in 1958 to serve its shell-shocked readers, the recently arrived Windrush generation. Under the auspices of its driven and talented editor Claudia Jones, this newspaper acted as a lifeline, a vital guide to those in the community, emphasising that they weren't alone in this new and often hostile world they found themselves in.

Considering that the *Gazette* was a fairly recent publication, the lack of care taken with regard to its keep is shocking, but unfortunately not unique. To date only one newspaper that served communities of colour in the UK in the twentieth century is digitised on the British Newspaper Archive, that of *The Keys* (1933–39). Una Marson edited some of its earlier issues.[2]

Similar circumstances confronted me when I searched for the work of the journalists of colour of the nineteenth century and early twentieth century – for this is a story that predates Windrush and indeed stretches back to the work of Robert Wedderburn, who published six anti-slavery pamphlets *The Axe Laid to Root or a Fatal Blow to Oppressors* in 1817. While researching the work of Samuel Jules Celestine Edwards and Dusé Mohamed Ali, I found that no complete runs of their newspapers existed in the UK. Print copies of some of Ali's paper – the *African Times and Orient Review* – went astray during my research, lost between two archives, a situation compounded by the British Library cyberattack of October 2023. The hunt for issues of *Fraternity* took me via email to the University of Illinois' History, Philosophy and Newspaper Library, which had thankfully preserved some copies on microfilm, including extracts from Edwards' now-lost logbook.[3]

Like the faded newsprint of their journals, the legacies of the journalists who worked so hard to produce them similarly eroded over time. Edwards was a fierce critic of the legacy of the slave trade and the British Empire when it was at the zenith of its powers, regularly sharing a stage with contemporary luminaries George Bernard Shaw and Annie Besant. However, unlike those two, you would be hard pressed to find Edwards' story in any historical record.

Newspapers are often cited as the 'first rough draft of history', but what does it mean when your history is not deemed worthy of preservation?[4] In his book *Black Ghost of Empire: The Long Death of Slavery and the Failure of Emancipation*, Kris Manjapra refers to the Pan-Africanist philosopher W.E.B. Du Bois, who stated that the 'problem of the twentieth century is the problem of the color-line'.[5] To Du Bois' articulation of an all-pervasive, inter-generational harm wrought by racial discrimination, Manjapra adds that the problem of the twenty-first century is that of 'the ghost line'.[6] He elucidates that: 'Because of slavery and colonialism, certain human groups have been made into '[phantoms] in other people's eyes.'[7] Quoting from Ralph Ellison's *Invisible Man*, he states 'they are told ... that their history is not substantive to remember and to call human history'.[8]

When your history is condemned to the spectral realm, when many of the UK's established institutions, libraries, museums and archives do not deem it worthy of space or commemoration, its ephemeral nature means it can be all too easily forgotten. It can also, in the current political climate (where the past is weaponised for political gain), be deemed

– like the phantasmagorical inhabitants of our imagination, the jumbies, wraiths and shapeshifters – unbelievable.

It pained me to read recently that the 1976 BBC programme, where the sociologist Stuart Hall interviewed the foremost Black intellectual C.L.R. James on his seventy-fifth birthday in May of that year, was destroyed, wiped before transmission because the BBC director general at that time, Aubrey Singer, stated in an internal memo: 'Sorry, but I have no interest in a 45' conversation with CLR James.'[9] A history unrecorded because of one man's choice. Or that the director Steve McQueen on the promotional junket for his 2024 film *Blitz* has to constantly explain that 1940s London was a cosmopolitan and diverse place, with 'a large Chinese community, there were a lot of Black people, Asian people'.[10] *The Keys*, in particular the photographs of the children's trips to Epsom funded by Harold Moody, immortalises in print a diverse, multicultural 1930s London. Likewise, Ali's Herculean attempts in the *Review* to continually highlight the contribution of the colonies to the First World War effort had a purpose. He knew back then that this story would be conveniently erased from collective memory. More than a century later, he has been proved right as few British people are aware of the contribution of colonial troops to both world wars, such as the 1.4 million Indian soldiers who served alongside British troops in the First World War, or that the country donated a significant amount to Britain's war chest (£146.2 million, approximately £14 billion in today's money).[11]

• • •

I have been a journalist for more than three decades, one of the very few journalists of colour on Fleet Street in the 1990s and early 2000s. During the course of my career, I have worked as a feature writer in the field, sometimes working with charities and reporting from conflict zones. I have also been employed as a senior backbench editor on a national newspaper. In the late 1990s, on my first shift on a national broadsheet, I noticed only one other Black journalist on that newspaper's floor. The other people of colour staffed the canteen or wielded a mop. It was something I was acutely aware of – who gets to tell which stories are amplified in the public sphere matters. The rise of the internet opened up a printed realm that was once the rigid preserve of a few privileged voices and the situation has improved somewhat, but is still wanting. A 2024 Women in Journalism report acknowledged a 'shocking' lack of diversity in a profession that is overwhelmingly white and upper middle-class.[12]

Throughout my career, I often pondered the fate of the journalists of colour that came before me, who worked at a time when the air was filled with prejudice and scorn for their ideas, and when the political classes and public at large were less than receptive to their cause. These courageous journalists were not afforded a seat at national newspapers. Instead, they operated on the fringes, working on shoestring budgets to produce their journals at times of great adversity. Consequently, their stories were often punctuated with personal tragedy and loss, and grievous tolls were taken on their mental and physical health.

The cast of seven remarkable men and women journalists that I have chosen to profile in *INK!* – Samuel Jules Celestine Edwards, Dusé Mohamed Ali, Claude McKay, George Padmore, Una Marson, Claudia Jones and Darcus Howe – all had a formidable role to play in the birthing pains of multicultural Britain. Their combined story arc covers a period, from when Britain's Empire spanned nearly a quarter of the globe to the heady start of the 1980s when seismic shifts in the British political, social and cultural landscape led to the Black British and Asian community asserting their voice.

Their personal lives laid bare rival any popular drama – Edwards' progressive movement was split asunder by forbidden love, jealousy and the untimely death of its charismatic founder; Ali lived in abject poverty in Edwardian England under possibly an assumed identity and survived by reciting Shakespeare to the upper classes; Padmore was interrogated by Göring's Nazi goons and deported to the UK for distributing *The Negro Worker* from Hamburg. Meanwhile, Marson, whose activism took her to the centre of the world stage, working as Haile Selassie's secretary when he made a plea to the League of Nations in 1936 against the fascist aggression of Mussolini's Italy, spent some of her final years incarcerated in a mental hospital, slowly undone, not just by the chicanery of global politicians but by years of insidious and blatant racism that had eroded her sense of self.

Nested within their stories are the rich social, intellectual and pro-gressive worlds of multicultural Britain, for this is also a tale of unity between races for the greater good. For example, the chapter on George Padmore will bring in the remarkable actors of 1930s Black Britain – Amy Ashwood Garvey, James and future Kenyan prime minister Jomo Kenyatta. Allies included those on the progressive left and feminist movements, such as the heiress Nancy Cunard and Sylvia Pankhurst (with the latter's anti-racist work straddling decades), and even Charlie Chaplin, a staunch ally of Claude McKay's journalism, makes a vaudevil-lian appearance. Similarly, the chapter on Darcus Howe will look at the remarkable individuals, groups and alliances, such as the Indian Workers' Association and the Bengali Housing Action Group, that fed into Black Power and the later Race Today Collective.

A number of these journalists operated during the 1920s and '30s, a time when race and global revolutionary politics were heavily entan-gled. Journalists such as McKay, Padmore and Jones aligned themselves to the Communist cause, which promised to serve as an international beacon of racial equality. Their own work was often stymied as a result of these allegiances and it may have dented their legacies. Nearly all the journalists I have featured were subject to constant surveillance by the secret services.

The publications that these journalists produced reacted to the hinges of history – the Scramble for Africa, the race riots following the First World War, the rise of Nazism and Fascism, the anti-colonial movement and the subsequent decades of active anti-racist struggle. Their paragraphs act as precious portals, charting the response of the global majority to these time-snaring events. A June 1960 editorial by Jones 'Freedom … Africa's Right' emphasises the tipped domino effect of the independ-ence movement on the continent. Under an illustration by Hugo Gellert of men and women breaking free from chains, she writes: 'Whereas a few years ago it was held by many that the struggle for African freedom would be a gradual one – everyone bids fair to revise estimates as the people of Africa in heroic struggle, supported widely throughout the world, move with seven league boots to their dawn of freedom.'[13] Two months later in an erudite piece entitled 'These are the facts: Behind the Congo Upsurge', Jones outlines how Patrice Lumumba's fledgling government was suffering downright attempts to 'sabotage its right to self-determination' from Belgium, its former colonial ruler.[14]

Such unique international perspective linked the struggles of the UK's non-white population to those of the global community, emphasising that their fight for equality in education, housing and employment was part of a much broader narrative.

The community that these radical journalists engendered should not be underestimated. The latter period of this book covers my living experience. I grew up in 1970s and '80s Britain, at a time of overt and blatant racism. I remember my father taking my hand as a small child and guiding me away from a National Front stall in Romford town square; one of the leaflets had photographs of people who looked like me and called for their repatriation. I recall the monkey chants that my sister and I endured on our way to school; and I still get chills thinking about when a complete stranger on a bus tried to set fire to my hair with his lighter while spluttering vindictively 'I want to kill all P—s'. These incidents were frequent and constant, and back then not deemed a crime. When a house fire claimed the lives of thirteen teenagers at 16-year-old Yvonne Ruddock's birthday party in Lewisham, the shock, terror and sheer anger in the community was visceral. As a 10-year-old, I witnessed how Howe's Race Today Collective and the New Cross Massacre Action Committee articulated this fury into direct action – such journalism as activism ultimately led to change and a better society for all.

Indeed, these pioneers ushered in social movements that transformed the course of British history and the global order. They ultimately believed in the power of their ideas to remake the world. In cramped offices, they performed alchemy, forging, weaving and moulding ideas that were disseminated across painfully nurtured networks. Their ink bore witness: through the words that flowed from their pens or issued from their typewriter ribbon, they endeavoured to analyse, comment and make sense of their environment. Taken as a whole, their journalism reflects the history of race relations in this country.

Like linked paper chains, their important presses unite and mesh across decades: Ida B. Wells credits Edwards' anti-lynching campaign with pressurising the US government and turning the political mood against these horrific acts – Wells herself was a pioneer of the US civil rights movement. Edwards' work was an inspiration for Ali, who later tutored a young Marcus Garvey, the leader of America's first Black nationalist movement. While McKay's 'wanderings' and writing influenced France's Négritude's movement, and its proponents, Aimé Césaire, Léopold Sédar Senghor and others, in turn influenced Black Power in the US and the UK. James, Padmore's boyhood friend and erstwhile political companion in 1930s Britain, is a constant presence throughout the book, reoccurring again when he moves into the flat above the Race Today Collective offices in south London in later life, his ideology influencing much of his nephew Howe's and that group's important work.[15]

The majority of the seven journalists I have chosen to profile have Caribbean origins; I too am a daughter of Windrush – my late mother was recruited by the NHS from Georgetown, Guyana, to work as a nurse in the UK in 1962 and my father came over on the boat-train from Trinidad in 1961. My choice of subjects reflects no bias on my part (well maybe a bit), but instead illustrates the legacy of enslavement, indenture and colonialism that exists between the UK and the Caribbean and how the British education system fostered a dual and conflicting climate: one of subservience to the so-called Mother Country but also one of rebellion reared by a deeply unequal society in the wake of emancipation. James argued that Black Caribbean intellectuals were afforded a unique perspective on the world, as in these small societies people of different ranks and classes intermingled. It was through this 'small conspectus' that these intellectuals gleaned 'a certain comprehensive view'. Hence those 'who come from those miserable scraps of dirt and really have some sort of impact upon the intellectual life of the world'.[16]

The fact that many established institutions did not deem this history worthy of space means that the void was often filled by the personal recollections and collections of our elders. I remain hugely indebted to the late historian Marika Sherwood, whose bookshelves in the rural Kent village of Oare strained with a rich repository of pamphlets, books and newspapers, such as the original first programme of the Notting Hill Carnival, that brought this history to vivid life.[17] I was fortunate enough to talk to Diane Langford, the Race Today Collective's Farrukh Dhondy, Leila Hassan Howe and Gus John, who all gave up their time to help me in the completion of this project. My father Eddie Singh (who occasionally visited the Black House and was a huge fan of the civil rights activist Roy Sawh) also helped me shade this world.

With limited funds, this book owes much to those authors and historians who spent inordinate time researching these worlds in intimate, scholarly detail: Stephen Bourne (who was generous with both resources and time), Carole Boyce Davies, Wayne F. Cooper, Dr Caroline Bressey, Robin Bunce, Ian Duffield, Dr Jacqueline Jenkinson, Peter Fryer, Paul Field, Delia Jarrett-Macauley, Marc Matera, James Procter, Carol Polsgrove and Dr Leslie Elaine James. The latter two authors provided me with invaluable facts about Padmore, whose absence in the archive was compounded by his own flexibility with dates and his compunction to torch his papers.

An acrostic in praise of Edwards appears after his death in 1894 in issues of *Fraternity:* 'Celebrity thou well didst gain/Endowed with gifts not spent in vain … Deeds of greatness live, and the voice from the grave will speak with greater force/Surely thy bright example deserves our imitation.'[18]

Sadly, Edwards' vision was never emulated, his story erased by the endless cruelties of time. It was only in 2020, more than 125 years after his death, that a blue plaque was erected in the city of Sunderland at the former site of the Assembly Hall, a venue where he was famed for his lectures. A forgotten legacy is shared by many of the journalists featured in *INK!*.

There is no way to remedy smudged newsprint, but *INK!* hopes to resurrect these long-buried stories for a new generation, centring these narratives, and revealing how the sacrifices and struggles of the past have shaped our present. As a community, we are used to operating from the margins in order to get our voice heard; what is not so well known is how deep the historical roots of this activism reach. By recounting the amazing lives of these historically marginalised characters, *INK!* seeks to paint a truer picture of who we are as a nation.

INK! is a story of *all our* history. It's a story that deserves to be told.

1

THE FORGOTTEN ANGEL OF HISTORY

SAMUEL JULES CELESTINE EDWARDS, stowaway, seaman, anti-racism campaigner and 'Britain's first black editor of note'
(*Lux*, 1892–94; *Fraternity*, 1893–94)

Raglan Hall, 16 December 1882. There had been many great acts at this venue: Harry Sansom, billed as the funniest man in London, had graced this stage, as had Professor Hotine's 'wonderful performing dogs and monkeys'.[1] Tonight's seasonal entertainment promised much and the large auditorium buzzed with anticipation. In the front rows, the long wooden benches were crammed with working men in stiff flannels and Derby hats. Some stamped their feet; others took up this percussion, rapping the wooden benches with their knuckles or clapping their hands. Young women in their most fashionable outfits, silk bustled gowns in nightshade and mazarine, leaned over the balcony of the upper circle, riling those below, the reflections from the mother-of-pearl buttons adorning their bodices sending a frantic moonbeam dance across the stage.

The warm-up act was the Primitive Methodists. They had secured a prime spot to deliver the message of Christ to an audience that lived in one of the most neglected districts in south London. This hall held more than 2,000 people. The young missionary who was about to take the stage first tonight was nervous – he had never faced such a large crowd before. The heavy velvet curtains provided a barrier he was not willing to dispense with just yet.

Slowly he edged forward, his eyes adjusting to the gloom. The rows of faces that greeted him reminded him of the ocean's vastness, for before arriving on these shores he spent many years at sea. In the gas-lamp light, the men's features at the front of the stage seemed to distort like watery moons, as their jaws moved frantically 'in a most extraordinary manner'.

The missionary walked to the centre of the stage but before he could open his mouth 'a hail of brown, pulpy substance of objectionable odour saluted him'. His fellow missionaries gasped, as he was driven several steps backwards by the pellets' onslaught. 'Go and teach your brother n——s in your own country,' growled a voice. The front row stamped their feet. Raucous laughter rippled across the hall and built to a crescendo. The missionary wiped his face with his jacket sleeve, staggered forward and attempted to address the audience again. The front row gobbed and hoicked once more. He slipped backwards in the snail-like mucin that bathed the stage. The heckling continued, brutal and vicious, criticising his appearance. 'Look at his black face, go and have a bath'; 'Get off. Off, off, off. We don't want the likes of you here.' His white brothers from the mission emerged from the curtains, and flapped their arms, desperately appealing for calm, but the front row again showed their vehement disdain. The hall had now descended into pandemonium: the women in the gallery started to indulge in 'profane dances'. A sound of splitting wood came from the rear. The audience was now 'a wild and savage beast'. Surely the young man had lost this crowd? A flash of inspiration came to him, 'recollecting that music hath charms to soothe the savage breast', he quickly seated himself at the harmonium, reached tenderly for the keys and played the hymn *Cut it Down*.[2]

Years spent at sea, at the mercy of its swell, and having to deal with a variety of life-and-death situations as a child and then as a young man, had more than prepared him for the vagaries of the Victorian music hall audience.

A fellow missionary spoke later of that night: 'He had a marvellously beautiful touch upon the instrument and a sweet, powerful voice.' The room quietened. When Samuel Jules Celestine Edwards finished, he took off his top hat and solemnly bowed to the crowd. The stunned audience pleaded with him for yet another hymn.[3]

• • •

Seven years later, Edwards' reputation had grown considerably and people flocked to see the popular lecturer at Hackney's Victoria Park. Here he would make speeches at the Forum, a makeshift stage situated in the shadow of the ornate Gothic Burdett-Coutts fountain. On 26 May 1889, the first of that year's open-air lectures, he was presented with a new podium, a great honour, as the list of those who had spoken at what was commonly known as 'People's Park' read like a roll call of famed orators – George Bernard Shaw, William Morris, Annie Besant and Ben Tillett, as well as speakers from the Independent Labour Party – all had graced its stage.[4] According to historian Charles Poulsen, the golden age of the Forum was between 1890 and 1914 – for this was 'the school in which the intelligent young men and women of the East End learnt about the society they lived in, their place in it and how it could be changed for the better'.[5] In fact, the Forum was where people got their news and entertainment of the day.

An extraordinary story exists of Edwards' ability to captivate. At one of his lectures in the park, career criminal Joseph Wailey threaded his way through the human tangle that had thronged to see Edwards. Wailey, in his shabby frock coat and tilted cap, saw in this avid crowd the rich pickings of leather wallets, moleskin purses and pocket watches. At nearly 80, he boasted a lengthy criminal CV of unusual talents – his early years pickpocketing had led to smuggling and gangs, and he had even spent his best years as a horse thief in the United States. Old age had brought him back to a familiar stamping ground, a place where he could make, in his own words, thousands of pounds. Newspaper reports described him as a man who 'could have given a few hints to "Fagin"'.[6]

As Wailey's fingers encircled a watch chain, the speaker began to preach, on 'reason and godliness' and an almost ecclesiastical hush descended over the crowd. Wailey, his curiosity piqued as to who could demand such rapture, looked up to see a tall, elegant Black man in a top hat, frock coat and tails, framed by the limbs of a cherry blossom tree, speaking on the open-air platform.[7]

Charmed by this extraordinary figure, whom he later found out was Edwards, from the Christian Evidence Society, Wailey renounced his lifetime of crime there and then, and up to his dying day would tell anyone who cared to listen that it was Edwards and his lecture that had set him on the straight and narrow path. As Edwards ended his speech and made a special appeal for funds to provide breakfasts for the poor children of the district, Wailey found himself reaching for any loose change in his pocket as the collection tin was passed around.[8]

A 'marvellous personality'

Edwards' mesmeric qualities were well documented. 'His was truly a most marvellous personality,' wrote R.V. Allen, a friend and colleague. 'The bright and merry twinkling of his piercing eye, the motion of his head and limbs, the erectness of stature, every one of them silently t[old] volumes and len[t] to his words an irresistible charm.'

His ability to 'take up the threads of an opponent's argument, and unravel, disentangle and expose them, recorded another admirer, 'caused him often to be greeted with a wild and frantic cheer of triumph and delight'.[9]

He was handsome, always smartly dressed in a top hat and frock coat, the lapel boasting a boutonnière (once the famed coat and hat had been stolen at a talk in Sunderland, arousing such anger in Edwards that he threatened to 'knock the dust' out of 'the prig'), while the newspapers of the day were extravagant in their praise of Edwards' rhetorical alchemy, with the words 'eloquent', 'assured' and 'witty' peppering reviews.[10]

On one occasion, Edwards' magnetism led to a crush in Landport, Portsmouth, with the floor giving way, and about fifty people falling 7ft into the cellar below. The local paper reported: 'So closely had the people been standing together that they fell in one block and filled the cellar so completely that there was no room even to fall down.' It continued to report 'fainting and hysterical' ladies among the injured.[11]

At the point of the Portsmouth crush, in 1893, Edwards, 34, was a lecturer of huge renown, the editor of *Lux*, the Christian Evidence Society journal, and soon-to-be editor of *Fraternity*; roles that, according to the journalist and author Peter Fryer, earned him the title of 'the first black British editor of note'.[12]

The manner in which Edwards had reached this elevated national profile was unconventional to say the least. He was born in the village of Burns, Dominica, probably on 28 December 1858, the youngest of nine children.[13] Edwards' grandparents were both enslaved and Edwards' father was born into slavery, although his parents later secured his freedom. The family were poor but 'not the poorest' and were devout Catholics. His father held for years a small appointment with the French government, and also worked for Sir Benjamin Pine (who was governor of Antigua 1869–71) and Edwards' mother did much of the running of the home. Edwards was spoiled by his five older sisters and mother. He wrote effusively in letters: 'A woman should be like an invisible enchantress, drawing out what is noblest and best in a man's nature ... The noblest women have been such – *this I have seen in my mother*.'[14] In later life, he would promote female writers and intellectuals in his publications, no doubt inspired by the women of his childhood.

The multicultural crews that would dock in Dominica's ports held an endless fascination for the young schoolboy. He made friends with lascar sailors at every opportunity and would never tire of listening to their stories of far-off places. He wrote of these encounters: 'I got them to tell me about the different countries they had seen. Hearing the sailors' yarns made me want to go to sea so much that I made one or two attempts to run away.'[15]

When his father worked in Antigua, Edwards was placed in a Wesleyan Methodist School on that island aged about 9. At this school he received a comprehensive Christian education: studying the New Testament, attending Sunday school and joining the chapel choir; he also became a Methodist and expressed hopes of becoming a missionary. The school's teachers did not shy away from teaching about the unjustness of colonialism and it might have been here that Edwards became first aware of the subject. An influential teacher at this school was the Reverend Henry Mason Joseph and the two would cross paths again in England when Edwards' fame was at its height. Joseph would come to England seeking financial help for the Wilberforce Institute in Chatham, Ontario, a school for children of African Americans who had escaped from slavery on the Underground Railroad. He would later become an enthusiastic supporter of *Fraternity*.

The sudden death of his father in 1869 crushed any hopes Edwards had of becoming a Wesleyan missionary. He returned to Dominica to support his mother and rekindled his friendships with the sailors on the docks. A year after his father's death, at the age of just 11, he decided with a schoolboy companion to go to sea, taking only a bundle of clothes. This time he was successful, slipping on board a vessel bound for Guadeloupe with a friend and hiding in the ship's hold. Another schoolboy had seen the pair and informed Edwards' mother, but by the time she had reached the wharf, the ship was departing. Edwards recalled seeing her from a porthole, standing on the wharf, and calling at the top of her voice 'Come back! Come back!' – the words puncturing him 'like an arrow into my heart'.[16]

The stowaways were found and the children were forced to work for their passage, scrubbing the decks and washing the *jhulis* (the webbed hammocks suspended from beams that made up the lascars' sleeping quarters). Worse was to come, as when the boat did eventually dock in Guadeloupe, the two boys were carted off to work in a hotel. Their plans to 'go everywhere and see everything' faded abruptly, as they were 'cooped within the walls of a hotel, deprived of their liberty and compelled to work hard for little pay'.[17] Eventually, they escaped their landlocked plight. Edwards was employed by a Martinique vessel and once he acquired his sea legs, his usefulness as an interpreter (he spoke both French and English) gained him the respect of his superiors.

Edwards wrote of the pleasures of the calm waters and of watching 'the wonderful objects – the whales, porpoises and the flying fish' – when they came into sight. There is no doubt that these early years at sea equipped him with a worldly intelligence far beyond his years. Living, working and sleeping with an international crew that spoke *lascari*, the language of the sea, would also have given him a unique insight into other cultures.[18]

Occasionally the lessons he learnt were harsh. When the ship he had sailed on for four years retired in New York and discharged its crew, a teenage Edwards found himself wandering the streets of the big city with a not inconsiderable amount of money on his person. In his own words, he encountered 'a land shark', a man who offered him friendship and lodgings, but ended up stealing his money and leaving Edwards only with the clothes he stood up in. It was around this time that he became aware of the different treatment accorded to those whose skins were not white in the United States. The news that the abolitionist John Brown was hanged for inciting a failed slave rebellion in Harpers Ferry, Virginia, in 1859, profoundly affected Edwards and the incident was something he would refer back to in later years. He acquired a strong sense of social justice, rebelling on board a Liverpool-owned vessel, where the poor pay and tyrannical captain almost caused the sailors to mutiny.[19]

At the age of 17, and on the verge of adulthood, Edwards found himself in San Francisco. He became associated with 'a motley crew of gold-diggers, miners and other Bohemians, who observed no Sabbath and spent all days alike in a godless, reckless fashion'.[20]

While he was hanging out with this unorthodox crew, an incident of horseplay escalated into a fight. A pistol was pulled on Edwards, with the bullet narrowly grazing his right ear. The episode prompted a reckoning for the teenager and his next employment on a vessel where the captain and his wife were both devout Christians led to him renewing his faith, especially when a friend, a Finnish sailor, fell to his death from the crow's nest before he had time to repent.[21]

Despite numerous attempts to get back to Dominica, Edwards found himself in England, in the port of Hull briefly before relocating to Edinburgh in 1877, where he worked as a labourer. The city's medical school attracted a number of West Indians and Africans and was in many ways a nascent multicultural community, which could be perhaps why Edwards settled here.[22] Edwards did not join a union, but joined the Hope Lodge of the Order of Good Templars, perhaps spurred by having witnessed the ravages of drink on his fellow sailors.[23]

His first public speech was on the evils of drink and showed his gifts as a natural orator. He would spend all day working as a builder and then devote his evenings to delivering temperance addresses. Insecurities he had about leaving formal schooling at 11 meant that he devoted an inordinate amount of time to study and 'every spare copper to books'.[24]

From Edinburgh, Edwards went to Sunderland and spent time as an insurance agent. However, he left this situation because he 'could not tolerate' the business practices of his superior, stating that, 'as a Christian, I found it difficult to reconcile the methods of obtaining insurances with my conscience'.[25]

At the time of the 1881 census, Edwards was boarding at 57 Square Street, Tottington, Lancashire, and he gave his main occupation as a lecturer, an employ that would earn him nationwide fame. In time he began to vary his lectures, giving talks on his sailing adventures, and also talking about life in the Caribbean. It was reported that 'very frequently he held spellbound many an audience'.[26]

Controversial Subjects

His reputation was such that Edwards entered into a short, successful mission in the East End, with the Reverend J.F. Porter of north Bow. Here he found the duel of words that took place at Victoria Park's Forum a powerful lure. He became a frequent speaker there, combining these talks with a hectic schedule of public lecturing for the Primitive Methodists.

He was not afraid of broaching controversial subjects. In an 1884 address to The Society for Propagating the Gospel Among the Heathen in Bishop's Waltham, where his audience was predominantly upper middle class, he admonished the 'white civilisers who go to Africa for what they can pocket'. In a later address in the August of that same year to the Balloon Society of Great Britain, which met at the Royal Aquarium, he challenged the notion that the 'black man was lazy and would rather be slaves than free men'. Citing his own family as an example, particularly his grandfather who had toiled and bought the liberty of his own children, he stated: 'I believe the Negro is capable of higher and nobler things than you give them credit for, and when trained for as many years as you have been will make a nobler race and a better people than the present generation.'[27]

In the same address, despite the boos from some of his audience, Edwards spoke about the 1865 Morant Bay rebellion in Jamaica and the 'despicable actions of that monster Governor Eyre'. He was able to show that any fears of a Black revolt were unfounded and Eyre's actions at the time had been entirely disproportionate.[28]

In the hostile world of late Victorian Britain, Edwards was not one to shy away from controversy. Nearly a decade later, in a December 1892 article for *Lux* entitled 'The Negro Race', Edwards took scientific racists to task by correctly identifying that the discovery of increasing numbers of hominin fossils implied all humans had a common origin, with equal capacity for intelligence, civilisation and humility. At the time, spurious ideas about craniology reflecting intelligence and even moral capacity promulgated by scientific racists such as James Hunt, the president of the Anthropological Society of London, were gaining traction and being used to justify a new era of colonialism.

While his star was ascendent, audiences of all classes clamoured to see him. '… [When] conferences are discussing how to get people to church,' marvelled one of his auditors in Bristol, 'Mr Edwards is filling a hall with 1,000 people five nights in the week and a much larger one three times on a Sunday.'[29]

Edwards' activity attracted the attention of the Bishop of Bedford, who employed him in the early summer of 1885 on a good salary of £80 a year as Christian Evidence missioner for London's East End. This was a highly trusted role and illustrated the value that the Church placed on Edwards' work. It was not an easy posting: the capital's East End suffered from a particular deprivation – Charles Booth's multi-volume study *Life and Labour of the People in London* had identified that one third of the East End's 900,000 inhabitants lived at or below the poverty line. Booth wrote that: 'their life is the life of savages … their food is of the coarsest description and their only luxury is drink. It is not easy to see how they live.'[30]

At around this time, Edwards left the Primitive Methodists and joined the Christian Evidence Society (CES) as the head of the east London branch. Many of his lectures mirrored the society's objectives, which were to actively promote Christianity and to controvert atheist and secularist ideals.

The Christian Evidence missioner salary paid for further training and he embarked on a theology course at King's College London in 1887. He earned the 'diploma of associate' but 'refused the gown', even though he had prepared for holy orders and received a definite promise of a curacy after he had qualified for his duties. Illustrating his strength of attachment to the community and the works he was undertaking, Edwards strongly believed that he could be of more use to the people out of the church than in it.[31]

While he was studying at King's College, he lived with three medical students, including Wilfred Grenfell, an upper middle-class Englishman. The deeply Christian Grenfell had met Edwards through the church. The men had acquired lodgings in Palestine Place, Bethnal Green. Grenfell wrote of their very basic accommodation: 'We had no furniture and little spare cash so the first week or two was lived in perpetual picnic. And as the snow was on the ground, and the frost severe, we generally took our meals in our overcoats and hats.'[32]

Gradually the residents sourced furniture: armchairs plumped by sackcloth that regularly did the splits, a pair of exercise bars and a bath that Edwards, who was nicknamed Skipper by his housemates, ingeniously 'plumbed in himself'. Grenfell described how a hole through the side of the house served to empty the bath, while a hose from the tank on the roof coming in at the window filled it. The friends recalled Edwards' 'bright and happy nature, his ringing laugh ... qualities which served not a little to enliven one who spent nearly 12 hours a day at the East End London Palace of Pain [referring to the London Hospital]'.[33]

They were a 'cosmopolitan set', who still lodged with Edwards when the household broke up in 1889 and he moved to 50 Tudor Road, Hackney. Grenfell wrote: '[We consisted of] an Indian from Madras, an African, an Anglo-Indian, now in Australia; two southerners, and one north country Englishman and at times a Russian Jew; yet I never remember a dispute and I look back to these days as a time of uninterrupted happiness.'[34]

Grenfell chided Edwards for overwork, noting that his flatmate would, following his studies at King's College, preach nearly every evening and read into the night. Edwards also became interested (possibly influenced by his flatmates) in treating the body as well as the soul. In 1889, he enrolled as a student of the London Hospital, but the fees were a serious drain on his finances and he had to work harder than ever to meet their claim.

This often meant lecturing in provincial towns around the country, and he started travelling by night mail to cram in even more speaking engagements. When visiting a town for the first time, Edwards would build an audience, lecturing night after night for a fortnight until the halls were full. After he left a town, Edwards left behind him a branch of the CES, consisting of around 50 to 200 people, a visible representation of his skills as an orator and the passion with which he held his religious duties. He sincerely believed that addressing issues such as temperance would alleviate poverty among the working classes and he began to identify as a Christian socialist.

He started producing penny pamphlets as another way of spreading the gospel and producing much-needed funds. His prolific output included *Atheism a Failure* and *Theosophy Old and New*. In 1891 he authored a 164-page book entitled *From Slavery to a Bishopric: The Life of Bishop Walter Hawkins*, chronicling Hawkins' escape from a life of slavery in Columbia, Maryland, to become the superintendent of the British Methodist Episcopal Church in Canada. Edwards would later go on a national tour with Hawkins.

All the while his reputation at the London Hospital grew. He visited patients after-hours and his kind and gentle manner endeared him to the gruffest of East Enders. One newspaper report stated that: 'The poor people used to ask for the Black Doctor.'[35]

In the spring of 1891, his studies were interrupted by a serious illness, most likely tuberculosis, and he was advised by Sir Andrew Clark, his supervisor at the London Hospital and also William Gladstone's personal physician, to take time off from his medical studies. Despite being warned against over-exertion, Edwards continued to lecture as he had no other means of subsistence. He wore out shoe leather again on a hectic national lecturing schedule in the autumn of 1891. This 'Anti-Infidel Crusade' for the CES took in the towns of Derby, Sheffield, Manchester, Liverpool and Oldham. On tours such as these, Edwards would charge 1*d* for admission, a proportion of which would go towards hall hire and advertising, so despite reaching large audiences, such lecture tours were hardly lucrative.

Antidote to Atheism

The idea of a weekly Christian Evidence paper, *Lux*, was mooted by the CES, as there was clearly a hunger for such literature in these towns. Edwards published a circular as a means of gauging the extent of support for such an initiative, stating that, 'It is humiliating to confess that while organised Atheism has two weekly papers which find their way among the working classes ... there is not one Christian weekly paper acting as an antidote to their deadly poison.'[36]

He proposed forming The Lux Newspaper Company Ltd, with a capital of £2,500 in 2,500 shares. The company was to have a board of managing directors, each of whom would hold more than fifty shares. In order to ensure a wide circulation of *Lux*, Edwards stated that he would go on tour in the provinces for six months in the autumn and winter following the paper's launch. On his enforced break from the London Hospital, Edwards launched *Lux*, a sixteen-page weekly, on 6 August 1892, declaring that he hoped fellow Christians would support the initiative.

Lux appeared every Thursday and sold for a penny through a variety of national agents boosted by CES networks. Initially agents were focused on the capital, with twenty-three in Fleet Street and in the area around Victoria Park and Hackney while a similar number (twenty-one) covered the rest of London. This soon expanded to include national stockists and by March 1893 the paper was stocked by forty outlets in Manchester, fourteen in Liverpool and also boasted vendors across a number of regional towns including Sunderland, Bolton and Norwich, and Southampton and Portsmouth in the south. Edwards was optimistic about circulation: by September 1892 he was claiming a weekly circulation of 15,000, which he hoped would soar to 100,000 by Christmas with further promotional pushes.

As editor, Edwards penned the leading article, 'Our Conviction', which appeared on the front of the paper: in the first issue he bemoaned 'the spirit of unbelief that was sweeping through Christianity' and laid out the need for *Lux*.[37] The paper followed a distinct format, with pages two and three devoted to reports from local CES meetings, reviews of lectures and a list of Edwards' forthcoming speaking engagements; there was also a regular woman's page – 'From a Woman to a Woman', written by Helen Sillitoe – near the front. James Marchant, former president of the West Ham secular society, was a regular contributor, with articles including 'Jesus and Morality and Observations on Atheism'; while R.V. Allen, John W. Clayton and William Brandle also contributed articles with a theological bent. The paper also featured creative writing such as two or three-page morality tales and poetry by Leo Atwin and Albert J. Treolar. In the Christmas 1892 issue, Marchant contributed a story, 'Christmas Stockings', featuring Herbert Holman, an atheist Scrooge-like character.

Other regulars were Letterbox (which often included examples of fevered debate following one of Edwards' lectures), and Flashes and Sparks, a series of news titbits. The format was popular. In its second issue, under the leader 'Lux at Last', Edwards reported on the paper's favourable reception despite supply issues.

Brodie's Imperial Hair Dyes, Fitchetts Paraffin Soap, the Densmore Typewriter and Singer sewing machines were among the paper's regular advertisers and, in a nod to Edwards' Quaker supporters, Fry's cocoa. There was also a regular published appeal for the Field Lane Ragged Schools and Refuges and the paper's staff advertised Bible classes.[38]

On a number of occasions, Edwards used the paper as a mouth-piece to plead for racial justice, reiterating one of the central tenets of Christianity, that all men are created equal, if only all would abide by it. In the leader for the 10 December 1892 issue under the banner 'The Negro Race: An appeal for justice ...', Edwards did not just take the scientific racists to task but also called for equal treatment of all races.

On 18 February 1893 Edwards used 'Our Conviction' to chart European imperialist intentions from the New World (the Americas and the Caribbean), where native races were slaughtered, to India, Australia and New Zealand. He stated that imperialists were turning their atten-tion in Africa from British colonies in the south to West Africa and Uganda in the east. In the three-page leader, Edwards shone a light on British government policy in the Niger Delta in the 1880s, a period that launched the Scramble for Africa among colonial powers. He used the consular returns to illustrate that gin, rum, gunpowder and lead were being imported into the country to devastating effect. He decried: 'Is it just to take advantage of these creatures, steal their country – for it is nothing short of the three-hand card trick – and make those whom we pledged to protect slaves to vices worse than their native savagery.' He continued: 'We are a powerful nation today; but unless we use that power legitimately and wisely ... the British Empire will come to grief unless it changes its method of dealing with aboriginal races.'[39]

Edwards was becoming more stridently anti-imperialist in his calls for action, and this thinking went beyond his Christian and temperance views. He was an admirer and subscriber of *Anti-Caste* magazine – a slim but mighty four-page journal founded in March 1888 in Street, Somerset, by Catherine Impey, a Quaker editor. The magazine took its name from the caste system that perpetuates in India (to this day), a hierarchical system decreed at birth and which promotes a segregated society. However, Impey's focus was wide: the masthead declared the journal advocated 'the brotherhood of mankind irrespective of colour or descent'.

Impey was privy, through her Quaker connections, to a number of transatlantic and international anti-racism networks. She had travelled to the US as part of the Templar movement in 1878 and 1886, and had seen the unjust nature of post-slavery societies at first hand. She had written to the great American abolitionist Frederick Douglass in February 1883, explaining that during her first visit she had been 'awakened' to the 'colour question' and wanted to be of more use to Black Americans. She also outlined the need for a society that 'must take the front in the cause of human equality'.[40]

As a subscriber, Edwards admired Impey's work, and her affinity with racial justice. Impey was particularly horrified by the practice of lynching, where men, women and children could be accused of crimes without evidence, taken from their homes or jail cells and murdered. She wanted to raise awareness in the UK of these horrific crimes in order to put pressure on the US government to halt this terrible practice. Her campaign gained traction – reports of the gruesome murder of Edward Coy, who had been accused of raping a white woman and was burnt alive in front of a crowd of 5,000 in February 1892, in Texarkana, Arkansas, were carried in the *Manchester Courier*, *Sheffield and Rotherham Independent* and *Belfast News-Letter*.

In January 1893 Impey made the brave decision as a British female editor to publish a powerful and affecting front cover showing 'A lynching scene in Alabama', qualifying the picture with: 'Many hundreds of similar lawless scenes (AND WORSE) are enacted every year in the southern states of America – and NO ONE IS PUNISHED. How long will the callous nation look on!'

The cover was a reproduction of a postcard sent by attendees of a lynching to boast that they were there. Such gruesome souvenirs were common practice. In the postcard Impey used, children stand in the front row, evidence of a new generation being indoctrinated into the warped ideals of a white supremacist society.

A year before the historic lynching cover, Impey had met a young journalist and fellow activist, Ida B. Wells, on a return visit to the US. Wells' best friend Tommie Moss, the owner of a grocery store, had been lynched along with his fellow business partners in Memphis a few months earlier for no other reason than a disagreement with some white men. Impey was determined to bring Wells over to the UK: here was an articulate young woman who had personally been affected by lynch law and segregation and could convey its horrors to British audiences.

Impey's anti-lynching campaign had attracted the attention of the Scottish novelist Isabella Fyvie Mayo, a friend of Leo Tolstoy and Mahatma Gandhi, who published under the pen name Edward Garrett. Mayo lent her not inconsiderable celebrity to the cause, utilising her networks in Scotland and beyond to help raise funds for Wells' passage. She also co-edited with Impey the March and April issue of *Anti-Caste*, which focused entirely on the United States and lynching.

In April 1893, Wells arrived in the UK and launched her six-week speaking tour of the UK from Mayo's drawing room in Aberdeen. Edwards joined Wells for the English leg of her tour, which included Liverpool, Manchester, Newcastle, Darlington, Sunderland, Birmingham, Sheffield, and Portsmouth, as well as the village of Street in Somerset. When they spoke at the Friends Meeting House in Newcastle on 9 May, so many people arrived that the audience was divided into two halls, and Wells and Edwards tag-teamed across.

Their talks made a deep impression on English audiences, with Edwards and Wells being hailed as wonderful speakers and the audience reception hugely sympathetic. A report in the *Newcastle Chronicle* on 13 May 1893 stated:

Miss Wells, who is a young lady with a strong American accent, and who speaks with an educated and forcible style, gave some harrowing instances of the injustices to which members of her race are subjected in the Southern states, of their being socially ostracised and frequently lynched by mobs on mere suspicion, and without any form of trial ... she was listened to attentively, and loudly applauded, as were also Miss Impey and Mr Edwards.

Pledges were put forward at these meetings with the aim of calling on the US government to put 'a stop to these lawless deeds'.

Edwards and Wells co-edited what would be the final issue of *Anti-Caste* in May–June 1893, stating in the prescient editorial, 'There never was a time when all peoples should combine more to stem the tide of injustice than the present.' Wells' final stop was the capital, which she toured between 23 and 28 May, before setting sail from Southampton. Her tour had been such a success that Edwards started making preparations for her return.

Wells' visit had galvanised a sense of hope that racial prejudice, wherever it existed, could be challenged in all its forms. It also heralded a revival of a transatlantic movement to promote racial justice, the likes of which had not been seen since pre-abolition. A new anti-racism movement was proposed, eventually named the Society for the Recognition of the Brotherhood of Man (SRBM). Signatories included the MPs Alfred Webb and Dadabhai Naoroji; Douglass; Thomas Fortune, editor of the *New York Age*; Ellen Richardson, who had helped raise money to purchase Douglass' freedom; William Edward Axon, a senior editor at *The Manchester Guardian*; and many high-profile British Quakers.

Brotherhood of Man

In Edwards, Impey saw someone with a charisma and reach who could take *Anti-Caste* forward. In June 1893, she proposed a new monthly paper, called *Fraternity*, to promote the society's ideals of 'freedom, equal opportunity and brotherly consideration'. Edwards was to be its editor.

In the first issue of *Fraternity*, which was launched in July 1893, Edwards commended Impey's work in a leader column entitled 'Unity our Aim', proclaiming: 'For more than six years *Anti-Caste* has been doing a quiet work in England, slowly and surely permeating society and winning the hearts of good men and true women to the causes of the helpless races in America, India, Africa and Australia.'

In order to capitalise on the momentum following Wells' tour, Edwards continued a hectic lecture pace, promoting *Fraternity* and the newly formed society. In July, he was in Bristol, Manchester and London, addressing a crowd of thousands on 'American Atrocities'. On 12 August, he took his campaign of Christian socialism to working men, joining a list of speakers addressing a trade union march in Portsmouth, pushing in his speech for better working conditions. That month he also spoke in Newcastle to an audience numbering in the thousands at Ginnett's Circus. He continued this pace throughout August and early September, introducing the SRBM to audiences nationally.

On the ground, a network of several branches of the SRBM, which had been established in London and major English towns following Wells' tour, worked in tandem with Edwards, distributing free copies of *Fraternity* to public libraries, hotels and reading rooms. Impey's west of England branch raised enough funds to send about 18,000 free copies to India, China, South and West Africa and Europe and several hundred copies to the US and Caribbean.

This groundwork paid dividends and *Fraternity* built its circulation at remarkable speed. From an initial subscription list of 3,000, the sixteen-page journal had a regular readership of 7,000 by mid-September. In order to save costs, *Fraternity* shared its publishing offices with *Lux* at 18 Paternoster Row in London and also utilised that paper's existing distribution networks. The times were favourable for launching such an organ – New Unionism was in full flow, and would climax with the emergence that year of the Independent Labour Party, and the Indian National Congress had recently established its British commit-tee. Edwards spoke in the December issue of *Fraternity's* popularity: 'In one week the Editor has calls for it from West Africa, the West Indies and even Norway wants it.'

The paper carried similar adverts to *Lux*. *From Slavery to a Bishopric* was also advertised regularly, along with a collection of Wells' UK speeches entitled *United States Atrocities* (Douglass had written the foreword) that Edwards had organised to be published under the Lux publishing company. This book is widely noted as a precursor for Wells' famous *Red Record* published in 1895.

Global Snapshot

Fraternity boasted a much larger international scope than Impey's *Anti-Caste*. Edwards used its pages to express his proto Pan-African views, linking the anti-imperialist struggle of all colonised peoples across the Americas, Caribbean, Africa and Asia. Using a range of international sources, including the *New York Age*, *Colored American* and the Calcutta-based *Indian* and *Johannesburg Star*, its pages provided a unique global snapshot of racial injustice at the close of the nineteenth century.[41]

When the paper was issued in full in August, complete with a new layout for the cover price of one penny, Edwards clearly stated its aims:

> Thus in America we shall oppose lynching because it is inhuman and the spirit which prompts it is diabolical; in India we oppose caste; in Australia we must remind the colonists that Chinamen are their brethren; in this country, in every sphere, no one should be refused any opportunity in life on the ground of his nationality, nay, not only in this but in all countries.[42]

In the same issue, Edwards continued to promote Impey's anti-lynching campaign, printing a report of the murder of C.J. Miller in Bardwell, Kentucky, on 7 July. Miller had been accused of the horrific murder of two white girls, Ruby, 18, and May, 9 – which Edwards attributed to 'an unknown Jack the Ripper'. A vengeful crowd sought justice, even though witnesses claimed a white man had escaped into the cornfield following the double murder. Miller was accused of the crime, as he happened to be stealing a ride on a freight train going out of Missouri at the time. The article notes 'a log chain, nearly over 100 feet in length, weighing over one hundred pounds, was placed around Miller's neck and body' and he was led and dragged through the village followed by thousands of people. The baying, drunken mob then hoisted his limp and exhausted body from a telegraph pole, where he was hung until his neck broke and 'numberless shots were fired into the dangling body'. The corpse was then burnt, with the article concluding 'in a few moments there was nothing left of CJ Miller save a few bones and ashes'.[43]

Miller was later found innocent of the murder of Ruby and May.

Throughout his editorship of the paper, Edwards continued to push Impey's anti-lynching campaign, publishing statistics and articles about these gruesome murders. In March 1894, he published the statistics from the *Chicago Tribune* of 200 persons lynched in 1893. He stated: 'On such frivolous pretexts as these nearly two hundred men and women of the race have been murdered by lawless mobs during the past year without opportunity to defend themselves or prove their innocence.'[44]

In *Fraternity*, Edwards could stretch his journalistic limbs and produce in print a well-designed paper that replicated his oratory talents. The paper was a lively, informative and entertaining read. Its two or three-page leader columns, featuring Edwards' unmistakable voice, would be followed by an 'Around the World' round-up that boasted an international breadth rarely covered in other UK national papers. These included reports on the overthrow of Queen Liliuokalani, the last sovereign monarch of Hawaii; the Emperor of Japan; the treatment of Siberian prisoners in Russia; and the reduction of the rate in native wages in Johannesburg coal mines. Stories from the British Caribbean were also covered.

News items were not confined to people of colour. Also given space were regular references to religious and political oppression in Europe, such as the restrictions on Jewish life in Siberia, the massacre of Catholics in Poland and a disturbing report of children being enslaved in Sicilian mines.

Hajee A. Browne contributed a series of essays on Islam and the Brotherhood of Man, renouncing the prejudice and suspicion with which the religion was viewed in the west and expressing the common values of tolerance and equality it held with the SRBM. Occasionally there was fiction by Katherine St John Conway and poetry contributions, while a column by Katharine Davis Tillman in March 1894 focused solely on the work of Afro-American poets such as Josie Heard.

As in *Lux*, Edwards was keen to promote women writers – the majority of the branch secretaries of the SRBM were women, including the

Scottish anti-racism campaigner Eliza Wigham, and they regularly contributed reports on the progress of the society in their areas for *Fraternity*.

In 'Things as They Are and Should Not Be', Edwards again turned his focus to the States, where Jim Crow law, and social and economic inequalities post-abolition were all-pervasive. In October 1893, a story of two African American youths in Kentucky pleading guilty to a burglary just so that they could be sent to reform school featured; while anecdotal reports of the ejection of Black men and women from train carriages and sleeping cars were common. In April 1894 the column reported on a Catholic school for Black children in Tampa, Florida, which had been targeted by arsonists and burnt to the ground. Edwards balanced the rather grim nature of this column with 'Things That Are as They Should Be' and 'To Their Credit', which would feature positive, upbeat stories such as the Harriet Hayden scholarship, a fund for Harvard University students set up by a slave who had been freed by the Underground Railway; and a Black porter Caret Logan being honoured with a portrait for his many years of service for the Bank of Kentucky.

In October 1893, Edwards launched a new and regular column 'The Angel of History', in which he attempted to analyse the legacy of slavery and colonialism on British culture, identifying race antipathy with 'Anglo-Saxonism' and arguing that such 'evil' had 'paralysed' the social and economic chances of the population of the British West Indies.

Edwards stated that the inherent nature of Empire and its system of governing fostered 'a feeling of superiority existing in the mind of the English race over his darker brethren', which perpetuated a racial hierarchy in Britain and its colonies. He regularly reported on specific instances of racial oppression, reaffirming these views. In July 1893, the paper reported under the headline 'British Misrule in Bahamas' of 'whites wantonly clubbing and kicking innocent men, women and children' on the streets of the capital Nassau. The article continued: 'While England busies herself with the woes of Armenians, Egyptians and others, she will do well to overhaul the doings of her colonial constabularies, judges and governors.' In August, it reported on an attempt by South Australia and other Australian colonies to prevent Chinese immigration and in October a travelogue by George Pitt reported on the treatment of lascars by upper-class English passengers on a voyage to India. In April 1894, a shocking story of the whipping and torture of some Black Johannesburg residents by British settlers appeared in the paper. Their crime had been to use the footpath rather than the gutter. In order to instil 'the difference between the races into the mind of "the black", the unfortunate victims were not just flogged but had their flesh wounds salted' until they quivered in pain.[45]

Fraternity's radical stance on Empire was attracting dissenters as well as admirers, with Edwards forced to qualify in November 1893 that *Fraternity* has 'nothing whatever to do with any revolutionary or political party, its mission is purely humane and appeals to the whole human race, regardless of creed, to unite in one common brotherhood'.

Still these critics did not deter Edwards from making a brave pronouncement in December 1893 about the actions of Cecil Rhodes' British South African Company in Matabeleland, now Zimbabwe. The illiterate Zulu king Lobengula had been tricked into signing over the mining rights of his territory. The subsequent war would involve the first ever use of Maxim machine guns, which could fire 500 rounds a minute, by British forces in combat, and the results were horrific. In one battle 1,600 Matabeles were cut down by just four of these weapons. Edwards talked about 'the thirst for gold and dividends' being at the heart of this conflict, and urged the British government to intervene to stop the march of these speculators.

In the following month's leader, entitled 'Murder Will Out', Edwards could scarcely contain his rage at a public banquet that had taken place in Cape Town in honour of Rhodes. Edwards was incensed by this feting of a man who had indulged in a murderous campaign. He stated bitterly:

> By a curious coincidence in human nature, some murderers are hanged, others escape being hanged on the ground of provocation; but there are others who kill so many that, either through fear or favour, they are neither hanged nor transported, but are feasted by their compatriots as heroes ... Two hundred and fifty guests assembled, not to weep over the thousands of people killed in a war made for the express benefit of dividend-mongers, but to feast Mr Cecil Rhodes and laud him sky-high for the great victory which he had achieved.[46]

The actions of the British South African company divided British opinion, and a good number of the informed population at the time could see Rhodes' actions as morally indefensible. Agnes Pearson's letter to *Fraternity* in April 1894 from Edinburgh is typical. She stated:

> My idea is that it [Matabele war] was brought on by the purpose of plunder. To see the horrible cruelty that has been perpetrated by the consent of the British legislature is something awful … What are we doing but going into another man's territory and demanding his lands, houses and wealth? Because he is not willing to give up his own, we take it by force; and, more than this, we *murder* them.

However, there were signs even before *Fraternity*'s launch that Edwards' old health problems were beginning to flare. In February 1893, prior to Ida B. Wells' first tour, he had been unable to continue a lecture and had taken to his bed with fever. In September of that year, following the frenzied promotion of *Fraternity*, a news item appeared in *Lux*, stating that because of the sheer pressure of work: 'This is the first time in 59 weeks that the Editor has not signed Our Conviction.' The article added that 'the Editor left Plymouth stopped in London and then went on to Edinburgh and then on to Aberdeen', a distance of some 600 miles in twenty-four hours.[47]

A Classic Bind

Edwards found himself in a classic bind. His popularity had propelled *Fraternity*'s early boom but he needed to continue to tour to maintain the paper's success. He was also keen to bring Wells back for a second tour of the UK to help maintain the energy of the society. Ideas were mooted in December's issue of *Lux* to buy in a printing press to keep publishing costs down for both papers.

Sadly, an extraordinary combination of events was about to derail all plans. A row between Impey and Mayo, witnessed by Wells on the conclusion of her first tour, had split the society. One of Fyvie Mayo's boarders, a young Sri Lankan ophthalmic surgeon Dr George Ferdinands

— who had helped set up the society and the first tour — had received a letter from Impey declaring her love for him and that she wished for them to marry. The affection was not returned by Ferdinands, who was bemused by such a declaration. He showed the letter to Fyvie Mayo, who went ballistic, calling Impey a nymphomaniac and demanding her resignation from the movement and the destruction of the March 1893 issue of *Anti-Caste* that both of them edited. In a dramatic showdown, she urged Wells to choose between her and Impey. Wells wrote in her autobiography thirty years later that the scene 'was the most painful ... in which I ever took part ... To see my two ideals of noble womanhood divided in this way was heartrending. When it was demanded that I choose between them, it was indeed a staggering blow.'[48]

Wells sided with Impey, who, as she explained in her autobiography, had worked for many years for racial justice and she knew her intentions to be good. She added that because of this decision Fyvie Mayo cruelly 'cast her into outer darkness with Miss Impey and I never saw her again'.[49]

Without Fyvie Mayo's support and the Scottish side of the Brotherhood she represented, Edwards had to raise the funds for Wells' tour himself. This must have put him under considerable financial pressure and a later issue of *Fraternity* stated: 'The burden of this campaign fell mainly on our friend's shoulders, and it was his private purse which supplied much of the funds necessary for the carrying on of Miss Wells' work.'[50]

Over Christmas 1893, Edwards suffered an attack of the flu, so severe that he was dictating his leaders for *Lux* and *Fraternity* from his sickbed. In January 1894, he collapsed while giving a lecture in Brighton and again had to be confined to his house. *Fraternity* reported him suffering from 'nervous rheumatism' and an old affliction with his right lung — in all probability the consumption had returned. In March, Edwards issued an appeal for supporters to 'share the burden of the magazine's production', having been ill since Christmas. Readers were largely responsive, an Indian reader suggesting in April that a syndicate be formed, selling 3,000 shares at £1 each to support the paper.

On 22 March 1894, Edwards managed to accompany Wells when she spoke to a large audience at Hope Hall, Liverpool, on the first stop of her nationwide tour, but those that witnessed him speak after the American reported on his frail appearance and a truly dreadful cough that wracked his whole body. Witnesses wrote, '[No one] realised, until they saw him on the platform, that his state of health was so serious.'[51]

Funds of £206 10s 6d were raised by *Lux* subscribers to send him to Dominica, where it was hoped he would recover, but Edwards never did. He died on 25 July 1894, aged only 35, in his brother Albert's house in Portsmouth, Dominica.[52]

Before his death, the front of the July issue of *Fraternity* advertised a book *Hard Truth*, by the author Theodore Thomas, which the historian Douglas Lorimer has identified as a pseudonym for Edwards.[53] The book takes the form of a dialogue between Christ and Lucifer, and in it Lucifer announces a reckoning with the imperial mission: 'Here's my truth: Britain is the birth-place of the very essence of the seed of prejudice against the negro race ... the uncouth, rough shrub when transplanted from its mother country, grows into a great tree ...'[54]

British Protestant missionaries also came in for criticism by the author for aiding and abetting this prejudice with their 'civilising missions' across the Empire, a guise for further land-grabbing and exploitation. In this extraordinary book, Edwards asks, with remarkable foresight: why did the British government following abolition compensate the slave owners for lost capital with £20 million (approximately £150 billion in today's money) rather than giving this money to the enslaved? The same question would be asked a century or so later, in 2015, when it was discovered that British taxpayers had finally paid off the debt accrued following these reparations.[55]

There is no doubt that Edwards' early death plunged the fledgling SRBM into chaos. The division between Mayo and Impey became more pronounced, with Mayo writing 'The Female Accusation', an article in the August issue of *Fraternity* linking the 'diseased imaginations' of 'elderly, dowdy' women with the mental illness of white women that led to the charges of rape and subsequent lynching of Black men. She also used the journal to state that the south-west branch of the SRBM was under the charge of a discredited and mentally disturbed female.[56] If Edwards had been alive, it is unlikely these articles would have been sanctioned.

Mayo and the Scottish branch of the SRBM took over the editing of *Fraternity*, but it lacked Edwards' verve and was reliant on cuttings rather than original prose. The paper limped on until 1897, but even in these later issues acrostics, poetry and writings about its charismatic founder, who remained immortalised on the masthead, endured. Later editors, such as Carolyn Martyn and Frank Smith, were important figures in the establishment of Keir Hardie's Labour Party. *Lux's* last issue appeared on 13 July 1895, with a plea inside: 'Our Last Appeal – Is *Lux* to Live or Die?'. It was incorporated into *The Light of the World*, another Christian publication.

Hope and Optimism

Edwards' voice had encapsulated the hope and optimism of New Unionism and the various progressive racial justice movements of the late nineteenth century. In his last speech, made in Liverpool before his journey to Dominica, Edwards' socialist position was evident; he stated: '... a revolution must come when the labourer will receive not only the equivalent of his labour, but also participate in the profits derived'.[57]

Despite his newspapers folding, Edwards' legacy lived on through the many lives he'd touched. Grenfell, who wrote a touching eulogy in *Fraternity* 'To My Friend' after Edwards' death, was knighted in 1927 for his medical services to Inuit communities in Newfoundland, Canada. Edwards' last act, the funding of Wells' anti-lynching tour, paid dividends: MPs and signatories such as Tillett, Eliza Wigham and Sir Edward Russell, the editor of the *Daily Post*, swelled the ranks of a newly established Anti-Lynching Committee set up in 1894 by the activist and future suffragette Florence Balgarnie. In her autobiography, Wells, who later became a prominent civil rights activist, credits the British tour with the decline of lynching in the southern states.

Edwards' old teacher, the Rev. Henry Mason Joseph, who had joined Impey and Edwards at the founding meeting of the SRBM in August 1893, became secretary of the African Association, formed by the Trinidadian lawyer Henry Williams. The association convened the first Pan-African conference in London in 1900, over 23–25 July. This 'remarkable movement in history', according to the *Westminster Gazette*, boasted an illustrious thirty-two representatives from all five continents, including W.E.B. Du Bois, Naoroji and the composer Samuel Coleridge-Taylor, all calling for an end to racial injustice.[58] In fact, it was Du Bois' famed proclamation at the conference 'To the Nations of the World', which declared: 'The problem of the twentieth century is the problem of the colour line.' It was a powerful statement that would resonate well into the next century.[59] It is unlikely that the conference would have happened without the assiduous networking Edwards had established in the years leading up to it.

The conference's momentum, though, was difficult to sustain, particularly with a jingoistic Conservative government now in power. In the closing years of Victoria's reign, the political currents that had buoyed Edwards' *Fraternity* were now flowing the other way as the Liberals languished in opposition. Plans to convene the conference every two years floundered, with its newspaper, the *Pan-African*, folding after just a few issues. It did not meet again until nearly two decades later in Paris.

Post-1900, when the memories of that first Pan-African conference had faded and just a faint echo remained of Edwards' strident, entertaining voice that had so moved the Forum's Victorian audiences to whoops of delight, it was his writings in *Fraternity*, the ink from his pen, that endured and stirred an Egyptian actor and radical journalist to take up the mantle of racial justice and publish a newspaper devoted to 'the coloured races of the world'. According to Dusé Mohamed Ali, the editor of *Fraternity*'s influence on him was profound. He stated that Edwards' journalism belonged in the same high-quality canon as Du Bois', Booker T. Washington's and Edward Wilmot Blyden's, arguing that Edwards was 'the most progressive full-blooded West Indian negro to make his mark on England'.[60]

Edwards' identification of colonial policies as the root of racial discrimination found a welcome home in Ali's progressive journal, ensuring that the indomitable and remarkable spirit of Samuel Jules Celestine Edwards lived on well into the twentieth century and beyond.

A LIFE IN THREE ACTS

DUSÉ MOHAMED ALI, actor, bon viveur and crusading newspaper journalist (*The New Age*, 1909–11; *African Times* and *Orient Review*, 1912–20; *The Comet*, 1933–44)

In spring 1905, the actor and budding playwright Dusé Mohamed Ali was at his lowest ebb. For several years he had been living a hand-to-mouth existence as a jobbing actor and occasional penny-a-line journalist, a lifestyle that had placed him on the cusp of extreme hardship. With his trademark fez and cut-glass English accent, Ali was well known in theatre circles – the profession had awarded him status and the occasional brush with royalty – but the success and fame he craved was proving tantalisingly elusive.

Aged almost 40, he had travelled to Liège, Belgium, as part of a troupe known as the Extreme Orient, his designated role being that of the 'Amorous Sultan'. Six-month tours like this were well paid and Ali was desperate for the money this gig would bring. Calamity beset the tour from the very beginning: the cast of twenty-five thespians arrived from London at the city's exhibition grounds following an arduous boat and train journey only to find a building site. Ali noted with grace that at least 'the roof was in place' of the half-completed theatre.[1] Their play was part of Liège International, a world fair marking seventy-five years of Belgian independence and forty years of Leopold II's reign. Twenty-nine countries were in attendance from Europe and the Americas with various stalls and several dignitaries set to attend. However, the fair's grand billing failed to live up to expectations, with even *The Times* noting that: 'As in most undertakings of this kind, neither buildings or exhibits will be complete on the opening day.'[2]

Rehearsals took place the next day on a stage surrounded by lumber, cement and building tackle. The din of hammers was so great that Ali could not hear himself speak, let alone think, his headache exacerbated by an ornate and cumbersome turban. The diverse cast, including Chinese jugglers and acrobats, Indian fakirs, Egyptian dancing dervishes and fire-eaters, magicians and artisans, had its fair share of squabbles.

Ali, who had started to produce his own plays with limited success, was scathing about the show's content and its creator – the rehearsals were 'sketchy'; and the producer and author of the show 'a champion clog dancer without the faintest knowledge of dramatic technique'. He reserved his greatest ire for a scene where he had to seduce the leading lady, a former member of the Tiller Girls, a troupe of dancers that toured the English music halls:[3]

> As an amorous Sultan, I was expected to … surrender my fabulous wealth for the love [of] this very charming 'dam-sell' and throw my jeweled [sic] turban at her none-too dainty feet. A miracle worker was needed to perform this onerous feat and I never, in my wildest imaginings, pretended to be a miracle worker.[4]

Ali pleaded with the producer to revise the scene but his protestations fell on deaf ears. The production limped on, failed to attract an audience and died, in Ali's own words, 'an inglorious death'. The only highlight of Ali's stay in Liège was being mistaken for the Shah of Persia on account of his red tarboosh (the country had a stall at the exhibition) and being hailed by an 'immense' crowd while riding in a two-horse cab with his friend.

In his autobiography, Ali recalled how the pair continued the ruse, with his friend showering centime pieces on the expectant throngs: 'We drove off to the race course amid the acclamations: "Vive Le Shah" and the unsuppressed laughter of my companion.'[5]

This jubilant scene masked the truth. Before Liège, Ali was penniless, hungry and destitute in London. He had spent the last two decades ricocheting from bit-part to bit-part, scraping journalism work here and there. He could not have imagined that in less than a decade he would be at the helm of a crusading anti-racist newspaper feted at the heart of government, and would mentor the future Black nationalist leader Marcus Garvey.

At the nadir of his career, he had performed in a 'back-alley slum theatre' in Liverpool, where he was given the bird and pelted regularly with leftover fish and chips, after failing to get regular work at the *Liverpool Post*. In one of the plays the company performed, *Uncle Tom's Cabin*, he was paid 30 shillings a week for the lead role of Uncle Tom. In another, Boucicault's play *Jessie Brown, or, The Relief of Lucknow*, he was given the part of Nana Sahib, a role of 'a cruel, lecherous Muslim'. Numerous times he would play the part of 'Nubian slave', and once an 'Arab Slave Dealer' in *Secrets of the Harem*.[6]

Undoubtedly, these stereotypical parts gnawed away at Ali, and he was becoming more and more disillusioned with the profession.

Ali wrote in his 1937 autobiography that it was real-life events that had reduced him to this nomadic lifestyle. In florid prose, he described how he was born in Alexandria, Egypt, on 21 November 1866, the second child of Egyptian army officer Abdul Salem Ali and his Sudanese wife, Ayesha (little information is given about his mother), and had enjoyed a relatively comfortable childhood. His father, despite being from a *fellah* (peasant) background, had benefited from the reforms of moderniser Khedive Ismail, which had opened up the military to all, regardless of ethnic and social background. His older brother followed his father into the army.

The family moved in establishment circles in Alexandria and his father had strong ties to Colonel Urabi Pasha, a nationalist leader with a similar background. Abdul Salem, who had served in the foreign legion and had received an education from the French Military Academy, was eager for his youngest son to receive a European education. To this end, Ali was sent to England at the age of 9 to study under the care of a friend of his father, a French officer, Captain Dusé (again little information is given about his guardian), and Ali later adopted his guardian's name.[7]

In April 1882 at the age of 15, Ali was recalled by his father from his studies to Alexandria. The nationalist movement against British and

French occupation in the country was gaining pace, with Urabi at its helm. Urabi wanted to end the absolutist regime of Khedive Tewfiq, who was subject to European influence. Ali recalled Urabi as 'a frequent visitor to my father's house during those stirring times',[8] but regretted not being able to converse with him: 'My residence in England had all but bereft me of my knowledge of Arabic, and as Urabi spoke no European language, I was placed at a disadvantage which I have always regretted.'[9]

A month after Ali returned to Alexandria, a heavily armed Anglo-French fleet cruised off the coast. Their presence 'to protect European interests and to restore order if necessary in the name of the Khedive' added to tensions in the city, between nationalist forces and the large European and Christian population. On 11 June 1882, these tensions ignited when an Arab donkey driver El Ajjan was stabbed by an unidentified Maltese passenger after an altercation over a fare in the European quarter of the city.[10]

In the ensuing riot, 50 Europeans and 125 Egyptians were killed, with the British admiral Beauchamp Seymour narrowly escaping the mob. Later reports stated that the riots were premeditated (either by Urabi or the Khedive as a false flag operation).[11] Following the riots, Europeans left the city in their droves and the Egyptian nationalist forces began to barricade their forts in anticipation of an attack.

After issuing an ultimatum, British gunboats (under the command of the 'fire-eating Admiral Seymour')[12] bombarded the city on 11 July for eleven hours, eviscerating the forts that lined the harbour. Ali recalled in his autobiography:

Shells fell fast and furious not only in the forts, but about the city – especially in the native quarter. The engines of war reaped a rich reward in carnage, death and conflagration. All through that day ... And extending far into the night, there was one long procession of maimed and mangled, passing from the forts, and the groans of the dying were punctured by the staccato service of the artillery. Hell with all its furies were let loose upon us.[13]

Ali's mother and sisters had fled to Sudan before the bombardment and his brother was killed during the assault on the forts. Further tragedy was to come. In September 1882, in Urabi's last stand at the Battle of Tel al Kabir, Ali's father was killed.

Desolate and alone in this now charred and blackened city, and unable to locate his mother and sisters, a teenage Ali had lost any sense of family, and he returned to England, and the only home he knew.[14]

This was a tragic backstory and, if taken at face value, must have in many ways informed key decisions in his later life. Ali, to all intents and purposes an orphaned youth, now depended on his wits and opportunity to get by – a default position that he was to rely increasingly upon.

Ali stated that his late father had wanted him to attend medical school and become a surgeon in the Egyptian army, but he professed later in the *Nigerian Times* that 'suffering from a weak stomach with no special penchant for blood-letting or human dissection, I decided upon my return to England to change the lancet for the pen and the operating theatre for the rather doubtful plaudits of the playhouse'.[15]

Ali approached Wilson Barrett, a leading actor-manager at the time, after he won plaudits at school for his performance as the Prince of Morocco in *The Merchant of Venice*. His first part was a Roman slave in *Claudian*, a Roman drama at the Royal Princess Theatre, London, which was staged between December 1883 and December 1884. The bit part opened doors and Ali went on a tour of America with the company. Following that tour, according to his memoir, he was able to secure a lucrative engagement touring theatres in the States as 'The Young Egyptian Wonder Reciter of Shakespeare', with the lecture agent Major Pond; Pond represented a number of famous figures, including Mark Twain and Harriet Beecher Stowe, and the tour netted Ali $2,000, a not inconsiderable sum. The buoyant young actor returned to the UK and took on various theatrical engagements along the south coast in Miss Sarah Thorne's stock company.

It is here that aspects of his backstory fall apart. According to historian Jacob S. Dorman, Barrett's company did tour America in 1886 and it was a significant event of the American theatrical calendar. The company arrived on the ship *Wyoming* but Dorman's analysis of the sixteen-member cast suggests that there was only one person close in age to Dusé Mohamed Ali, and it was a William Rand, whose age is given as 21. Dorman's analysis has found no record of a Dusé Mohamed

Ali conducting a lecture tour in America, however, a 'Rev William Rand' did lecture on Egypt at the YMCA in Worcester, Massachusetts, in February 1888: a newspaper reported Rand displayed a large number of lantern slides 'giving one a clear impression and vivid impression of the wonders of the pyramids, tombs and ancient inscriptions'.[16] Later in life, Ali, dressed in full balloon harem pants and turban, would give similar slideshows like this on Egypt, as a side hustle.

The questions posited by Dorman are these: was Dusé Mohamed Ali an identity created by Rand to shield him from the horrors and state-sanctioned racism of Jim Crow America and the colour bar in Britain? Was the backstory in Ali's autobiography a confection to hide the fact that he hailed from somewhere in the West Indies? In his book *The Princess and the Prophet*, Dorman has written extensively on the adopted biographical identities of a number of African Americans in the Gilded Age who were fascinated by the Orient and used the guises of fakirs, 'Hindoo' mystics and Arabian acrobats. These identities were not just a 'magic pass', granting these individuals special status in a world where they were seen as second-class citizens, they were a way of identifying with the East and religions such as Islam, which preached racial tolerance. As such, these assumed identities had dual psychological and political purpose.

Dorman further points out inconsistencies in Ali's accounts of his childhood. Most Egyptian children received an Arabic education and schooling in the Quran from the age of 4, meaning that he should have been able to converse with Pasha. The fact that no relatives or friends survived to corroborate Ali's story adds further mystery to his origins.

In England, Ali clung to this Egyptian identity. The siege of Alexandria, whether he had borne witness to it or not, had awakened his political consciousness and he fired off dozens of letters of indignation to the press on the issue of the Egyptian Question. He took to hanging around the Houses of Parliament, introducing himself to MPs such as Naoroji and the Irish Nationalist MP Frank Hugh O'Donnell. He also, following the publication of one of his letters in a national, started rubbing shoulders with the great and good of Fleet Street.

Ali was taken under the wing of veteran journalist Joshua Pearson, who introduced him to many prominent journalists, including George Augustus Sala of the *Illustrated London News*, who was himself mixed race

– his great grandmother being the celebrated Caribbean entrepreneur and former slave Doll Thomas – and Henry Labouchère.[17]

Ali was able to secure some 'penny-a-line' work from his journalism contacts. One notable commission was from a London daily about the same time that William Booth had published *In Darkest England*: his first assignment was to frequent the dosshouses of the Salvation Army and record the conditions there. He wrote:

> Upon leaving the Haymarket after performances, I hurried home and disguised myself as an employed 'Docker' and wandered into the Army Shelters in the East End of London … There I encountered the flotsam and jetsam of society; unfrocked clergy; disbarred lawyers; doctors who had been struck off for illegal practices; 'fallen gentleman'; tramps who wouldn't be guilty of doing a day's work were it handed to them on a silver platter – they would have 'pinched' the platter as a matter of course.[18]

Both the stage work and the journalism afforded Ali, despite the meagre pay, the opportunity to meet celebrities and even royalty, a position he clearly relished. In 1893, he met Oscar Wilde in the green room at the Theatre Royal, Haymarket, during rehearsals of Wilde's *A Woman of No Importance*; and he also crossed paths at the Savoy Theatre with the Prince of Wales, who was reportedly 'charmed' to meet a man whose father had died fighting for his country.[19]

Later that decade – although he does not elucidate exactly when in his autobiography – Ali took up an invitation to edit a new daily newspaper in Bombay. For whatever reason, this work did not transpire and Ali continued his travels from Bombay to Hong Kong and then eventually to the Caribbean, Panama and the US. Ill health and warmer climes are cited as the reasons for these extended journeys. It is not known how he funded these travels, which he termed his 'wanderings' in his autobiography. In Trinidad, encounters with intellectuals of colour – doctors, lawyers, academics – made a deep impression, and would later inform his proto-Pan-African world view.

On his return to England, records show that he settled in Hull, Yorkshire, in 1899, marrying local bookkeeper and part-time actress

Elizabeth Mary Brunyee in 1901, becoming a founder member of the local Shakespearean society.[20] He also became a freelance contributor for several local newspapers and the short-lived women's magazine the *Hull Lady*.[21] In Hull he produced *Othello* and *The Merchant of Venice* in 1902, playing the parts of Othello and the Prince of Morocco, to critical, local, acclaim. Touring in London took a heavy toll on his marriage and around 1903–04 he was divorced and trying to get acting work in towns all over the UK, before Liège.

Success continued to elude him, even though his own production of *A Daughter of Judah* at the Empire Theatre in Glasgow in 1906 garnered a spate of positive reviews. The *Daily Telegraph* wrote: 'Dusé Mohamed is an actor of great merit.'

After Liège and what can only be described as 'a career of wandering', Ali set up shop as a literary agent in Covent Garden, looking to settle down. His chief tasks were revising manuscripts and plays to make them fit for production. One such play was *The Lily of Bermuda*, the work of a fellow actor of colour, Bermudian Ernest Trimingham, which debuted in the Theatre Royal Manchester in November 1909.

It was appropriate that Ali's swansong for the theatre, *The Lily of Bermuda*'s final act, featured a mysterious flower's hallucinogenic scent that, once bystanders inhaled it, upended the traditional roles of that time, so the character of Joe Tucker, a Black waiter, is served champagne by his master, a foppish lord, and also ends up in a sexual liaison with the duchess, his mistress, who wants to marry him even after the flower's effects have faded. Perhaps this was wishful thinking on the part of Ali and Trimingham: portraying a more equitable society, albeit one under the influence of psychotropic substances.

A New Age

By late 1909 the glamour of greasepaint had truly faded and a 43-year-old Ali began to concentrate on campaigning journalism. He started to receive regular commissions from the well-respected literary and political journal *The New Age*, which was edited by Alfred Richard Orage and had George Bernard Shaw as its patron.

He was now living in London permanently at 55 Victoria Mansions, South Lambeth Road, and had married again, to Beatrice (an English woman whose maiden name was Pardoe Nash). His work at *The New Age* coincided with him becoming an active and supportive member of the African and Asian community in London.

The population of non-white citizens in the UK was largely unknown at that time, with the national census not recording ethnicity, although estimates place it as slightly more than 10,000 in an overall population of 45 million.[22] London, Liverpool, Manchester, Glasgow and Cardiff were home to Britain's oldest Black communities, in some cases dating back several centuries. In the port cities the development of a largely working-class Black presence was tied to the British shipping industry. Small pockets of university students and professionals from Africa and the Caribbean also formed in places such as Oxford, Cambridge, Newcastle and Edinburgh from the late nineteenth century.[23]

Ali's residence was remembered by the Nigerian lawyer al-Hajj L.B. Agusto, who rented a room, as an international hub for men of Asian and African descent. Agusto recalled meeting the Afro-American tenor Roland Hayes there – Ali had arranged the musician's passage and first presentation in the UK.[24]

He also became a patron to many young Egyptians who had recently arrived in London and was chosen as the Egyptian representative in the leading Muslim community organisation in London, the Central Islamic Society. Over time his membership of clubs and societies expanded to include the Anglo-Ottoman Society, the League of Justice of the Afro-Asian Nations, the Union for Students of Afro-Asian Descent, and numerous others. What is clear is that by his early 40s, he was enjoying helping bewildered African and Asian arrivals in the capital, offering hospitality, lodgings, education and ultimately friendship. Ali, who had never been particularly devout, was also becoming more interested in religion, and would occasionally visit the only mosque in the country at that time, the Shah Jahan mosque, in Woking, Surrey (established in 1889).

This progressive environment that Ali nurtured in many ways replicated Edwards' SRBM decades earlier. In his London home and in the various societies and clubs he championed, intellectuals from across the Empire could congregate and debate equal rights for the colonies. The times were propitious for such discussion: the People's Budget was making its way through parliament, in which those in power were contemplating a sweeping redistribution of wealth; it was only natural that equality of opportunity, especially for Britain's colonial subjects, should follow.

Ali's first article for *The New Age* was 'White Women and Coloured Men. The Other Side of the Picture', which was published on 21 January 1909. The article was a response to a racist diatribe by C. Hamilton Guinness that had appeared in the magazine *London Opinion*. During the late nineteenth century, there had been an influx of African and Asian students to London universities, Oxbridge and the Inns of Court.

Alarmed at the prospect of miscegenation, Guinness had argued against marriage or even social contact between white women and African and Asian men, demanding the police assume powers to intervene. Words like 'heathen' and 'half-civilised' were used abundantly in his prose. Ali wrote a scornful riposte for *The New Age*, arguing: 'The first civilised nations of the West obtained their knowledge and civilising influences from Egypt. The monuments and temples of the East attest by their antiquity a civilisation that obtained among "coloured persons" when the "white folk" of the West were untaught and unclothed savages.'[25]

The article was well received and Orage commissioned a further five articles from Ali; 'Western Civilization through Eastern Spectacles' in 1909, mostly skewering British political, religious and social life from an Egyptian perspective.[26] Further articles were commissioned in 1910 and 1911, covering Egyptian nationalism and the need to curb racial prejudice and oppression in all its forms. As a *New Age* contributor, Ali is likely to have met intellectuals such as Cecil Chesterton, H.G. Wells, the poet Ezra Pound and Katherine Mansfield.[27]

Illustrating his own progressive thinking, Ali became a frequent contributor to the radical feminist magazine *The Freewoman* (1911–12), edited by the suffragettes Dora Marsden and Mary Gawthorpe. Within its pages, the magazine would openly discuss sexuality, morality and marriage, and urge tolerance for homosexuality. Ali's articles vented against the religious establishment in Egypt for not improving the conditions of women in Islamic societies.

Fame had evaded Ali up until this point but a stab at notoriety came when the former US president Theodore Roosevelt made a speech at the Mansion House in London on 31 May 1910, following a tour of Uganda, Sudan and Egypt, in which he denounced Egyptian nationalism in favour of British rule. His speech praised the British, stating: 'You have given Egypt the best government it has had for 2,000 years – probably a better government than it has ever had before … a rule free from corruption and brutality.' Furthermore, he called Egyptians 'uncivilised' and 'fanatical'.[28]

An enraged Ali hurried to the offices of *The New Age*, his 'blood boiling over',[29] and demanded that Orage allow him to publish a strongly worded riposte. A piece appeared in the paper 'The Situation in Egypt' on 16 June 1910;[30] Ali railed against the 'rash meddlers', who were 'branding these well-intentioned patriots [nationalists] with murderous proclivities and anarchial tendencies'.[31] The article triggered a spat in the paper between Ali and Marmaduke Pickthall, a Middle Eastern scholar who had published an English translation of the Quran and would later convert to Islam, and who didn't care for Ali's high opinion of the nationalist Urabi Pasha.[32]

Roosevelt's speech and the ensuing brouhaha played out on his journal's pages led Orage to believe there was a need for more literature on the subject, particularly from an Egyptian perspective. He suggested a book to Ali and, using his literary connections, secured an advance of £30 from the publisher Stanley Paul for Ali to hastily write 100,000 words in three months.

In the Land of the Pharaohs, a history of modern Egypt, was published in 1911 in London and New York to initially widespread acclaim. Hailed as an 'authentic Egyptian and nationalist authority' on modern Egyptian affairs and an in-depth study of the grievances of British occupation, it was reviewed favourably. *The Scotsman* proselytised: '… the author has had better opportunity than most European writers have of becoming acquainted with the real meaning of the [nationalist] movement, the steps of which he chronicles.'[33]

However, when it was discovered that an undoubtedly pressurised and naïve Ali had plagiarised the works of the renowned Arabist Wilfred Scawen Blunt, as well as Theodore Rothstein and the Earl of Cromer, the criticisms rolled in. 'His song lacks originality: most of the verses are Mr Blunt's; the others are incomplete and unsatisfactory,' damned a review in the *World* on 14 April 1911.[34]

Ali was forced to publish a qualification, recognising those authors as sources of his work, otherwise Rothstein would have demanded that the book be withdrawn from sale.

Blunt, who had entertained Ali at his country house, Newbuildings Place in Sussex, on 19 April 1911, also cast shade on Ali's origins. He found it extremely puzzling that Ali was unable to recite the *shahada* (Muslim declaration of faith). 'He is an odd creature,' Blunt wrote in his diary, 'an Egyptian mulatto, he says, but knowing no word of Arabic; A Mohammedan, but unable to recite the formula of faith.'[35]

The historian Ian Duffield also noted that Ali's backstory, in particular his father's links to Urabi Pasha, are plagiarised from Blunt's 1907 *Secret History of the English Occupation of Egypt*.

These criticisms and doubts about his origins must have hurt Ali deeply, but as Duffield observed, 'Ali consistently and to his dying day claimed an Egypto-Sudanese parenthood, and stuck to his story, even when it caused him great inconvenience (such as when the British authorities registered him as an enemy alien during the First World War).'[36]

Ali found himself ostracised by *The New Age*. Plagiarism was viewed as the last taboo by the journal, and the last of his articles appeared shortly after the scandal broke. This must have been a difficult time for him, as Duffield noted: 'The promise of fame and influence, like so many of Dusé Mohamed Ali's dreams, must have seemed about to collapse.'[37]

Ali's background and the fact that he had allegedly survived the bombardment of Alexandria did garner him some sympathy from his critics. The book's conclusion, which warned that the scorn with which the British treated its subjects would further ostracise them, was praised for its vision. This and one of his final articles for *The New Age* 'Quo Vadis', published on 23 February 1911, was praised for its in-depth analysis of the world race situation – it was evident that those embryonic Pan-African leanings Ali experienced on his 'wanderings' were now becoming fully fledged.[38]

The plagiarism scandal aside, *In the Land of the Pharaohs* was well received in America, and Ali's attacks on Theodore Roosevelt and his arguments linking imperialism with unjust racial policy in the US found much favour. An autographed copy was presented to Arturo Schomburg, co-founder of the Negro Society for Historical Research in New York. This marked the beginnings of a relationship with Schomburg's circle, which included the American journalist John Edward Bruce. The book's longevity is such that it remains part of the canon of Pan-African literature and cemented Ali's position as a defender of Black rights.

'A word to you our brothers'

The strongest indication of Ali's next career move was given in an article he wrote for *TP's Weekly* magazine, 'The Coloured Man in Art and Letters', June 1911, where he references prominent writers of colour – Samuel Jules Celestine Edwards, Edward Wilmot Blyden, Booker T. Washington and W.E.B. Du Bois and the high quality of their work.[39]

It was evident that Ali was giving serious thought to producing his own journal, following in the footsteps of Edwards, whom he admired greatly and whose early death meant that his work had been cut back in its prime.

In the Land of the Pharaohs guaranteed Ali a place at the Universal Races Congress, which met between 26 and 29 July 1911 at the University of London. It attracted representatives from more than fifty countries, among them politicians, academics and reformers of international note. Attendees to the conference, including Blyden, future activist M.K. Gandhi, suffragette Jane Addams and the author Alain Locke, heard papers presented by Du Bois on 'The Negro Race and the USA', and Nigerian Baptist minister Mojolo Agbebi on the 'West African Problem'.

Ali had been hired to organise press and publicity, and entertainment for the delegates. Unable to secure the musician Samuel Coleridge-Taylor as originally planned, he presented the attendees with a performance of the third act of *Othello* and, with typical bombast, placed himself in the title role.

At the conference a 'racial unity paper' was mooted and a few months later the Sierra Leonean businessman John Eldridge Taylor approached Ali with the aim of setting up such a journal. Taylor, who had extensive

West African business projects in the spheres of fishery and produce, initially envisaged a West African trade journal. Ali confessed he knew little about trade, but the substantial space given over to commercial interests in the launch issue shows there may have been some compromise.[40]

Once he had secured Taylor's financial backing, Ali set about establishing his fledgling project. He obtained a list of attendees from the congress and from this was able to secure 200 subscriptions, from Britain and abroad, guaranteeing the paper an international readership. By September 1912, three months after the launch, the subscription list had reached 5,000. In that same issue Ali stated '… we mean to reach 25,000'. It is unlikely that this was achieved but mass circulation wasn't the primary aim; Ali wanted the journal to be a respected, high-brow publication like *The New Age*.[41]

To this end he commissioned the eminent art nouveau artist Walter Crane to create a strikingly beautiful cover image of Concordia, the Roman goddess of peace and harmony, linking hands across the globe with two women of Asian and African descent.

The first volume of the *African Times and Orient Review* (*ATOR*), launched amid much fanfare on 1 July 1912, boasted the strapline: 'A monthly journal devoted to the interests of the coloured races of the world', and featured thirty-five pages of editorial with a cover price of 4*d* monthly (4*s* per annum). On page two, in an address to his new readership, a smiling Ali is pictured above the narrow, cramped building of 158 Fleet Street where the paper was produced. He proclaims under the headline 'A Word to You Our Brothers': 'As for you of the Black race, the Brown race and the Yellow race, this is your very own journal. The more humble you are, the more need you have of us and the more readily we extend our sympathy and advice.'

The *Review* boasted a strong overseas network of distributors, particularly in West Africa, where it was well represented in Sierra Leone and Nigeria. Major US cities also featured, including New York City, Pittsburgh and Los Angeles. With agencies in Egypt, India, Malaysia, Japan, Jamaica, Sri Lanka, Guyana, Canada, Panama and Australia and New Zealand, the journal could claim to be truly global. Twenty-three steamship lines also took copies of the *Review* for distribution in their saloons.

The launch issue was a high-quality glossy, with articles as varied as a condemnation of the public flogging in Zaria, Nigeria, of two clerks, who had refused to salute the local British Resident; a focus on increasing crime in Egypt; and a report on the treatment of Sikh labourers by the Canadian government, which had refused entry to their wives and children. It boasted a similar international scope to Edwards' *Fraternity*. Prominence is also given to a three-page report on the first Universal Races Congress.

Among the lighter content, there was a double-page spread entitled 'A Monthly Round-up in London Town', with an article, 'White-washing Othello', that accused the capital's theatreland of hiring non-Black actors for the part. Poetry also featured prominently, with a page-four spot for *If I Were King* by John Vanderbilt. During its years of publication, the *Review* gave regular slots to poets, such as the African lawyer Kobina Sekyi and Japanese war correspondent Gonnoske Komai. Ali's wife, Beatrice, made occasional contributions and Ali penned verse under the pseudonym 'Delta'.[42]

Book reviews also featured, including *Alone in West Africa*, by Mary Gaunt, and *Light for John Bull on The Morocco Question With a Note on Tripoli*, by Charles Rosher. Rosher, an Englishman, was the author of several books on West African affairs and was the only other permanent full-time staff member of the *Review* listed along with Ali. As well as articles and book reviews, he contributed several humorous cartoons and illustrations to the magazine.

Like Edwards before him, Ali placed great weight on promoting positive stories of people of colour: a regular feature was biographies of people who had excelled in their chosen fields. The first issue featured a profile of H. Hunt, a Guyanese inventor who had constructed a collapsible pocket table, while a later edition carried the success story of Adeyemo and Olayimika Alakija, Nigerian brothers who had been called to the bar.

In the first issue, Ali gave liberal space to intellectual defenders of the publication, to whom he had written for quotes. Orage wrote supportively: 'Such a review as you appear to have in mind would, I think, be of considerable interest on condition that it is written exclusively by coloured people, maintains a high standard ... and aims at illustrating as much as expounding the genius of your race.'[43] Journalist and lawyer J.E. Casely Hayford also praised the journal, arguing that it was as important as the 1900 Pan-African meeting convened by Sylvester Williams twelve years before.

A prescient hire was the 25-year-old Marcus Garvey, who was taken on as a messenger boy and handyman between 1912 and 1913. The Jamaican was spending time in London before travelling to Europe and had heard about the *Review* while working on the east London docks with African seamen. After relentlessly badgering Ali for writing work, Garvey contributed a historical essay to the paper in October 1913, 'The British West Indies in the Mirror of Civilisation. History Making by Colonial Negroes', an account of colonial greed in the Caribbean. The article received praise from the author William H. Ferris, who acknowledged it as 'a powerful and telling summing up of the History of the British West Indies'.[44]

Ali must have been pleased with Garvey's work as he gave his young employee a fine reference for the British Museum. The resulting one-month reader's pass gave Garvey access to the works of Edward Blyden and *Up from Slavery* by Booker T. Washington. Garvey is said to have remarked on the latter autobiography 'and then my doom – if I may so call it – of being a race leader dawned on me'. This was a formative time for Garvey – it is widely acknowledged that Ali's ideas and personality had a profound influence on the Jamaican activist, and Ali imparted much knowledge on African history, literature, geography, mineral resources and labour conditions to his young charge.[45]

The launch issue of the *Review* promised much, with a range of international articles that received little to no coverage in the domestic press. However, the second issue almost failed to appear, after Taylor omitted to pay the printers. Ali had to rely on a cohort of influential West Africans in London, including the barristers Frans Dove and Hayford, for funds to keep the project afloat. A decision was taken to outmanoeuvre Taylor and the *African Times and Orient Review* was registered as a limited liability company. In a contract dated 21 August 1912 between Ali and Dove, Ali was awarded £500 in shares and £500 in cash for services, and listed as manager, editor and director.[46]

The years 1912–14 established the *Review* as a force to be reckoned with and these years (with Marcus Garvey on board) were very much the paper's heyday: in August 1912, Ali was back to provoking Theodore Roosevelt in an article 'Roosevelt's Remarkable Reticence', asking the presidential candidate what he was going to do to alleviate the economic and social conditions of the 10 million Black people in America, while Booker T. Washington's spread on the growth and history of the Tuskegee Institute in the same issue was given prominence. Articles on the riots in Cuba and Anglo-Russian meddling in Persia also illustrated the sheer global scope of the publication, which regularly appraised the political situation in India and that of the Black republics Liberia and Haiti. Following in Impey and Edwards' footsteps, Ali would regularly publish articles on Jim Crow America. 'America and its Race Problem' was featured on page seven of the 24 March 1914 edition and the *Review* kept a tally of the number of lynchings that had occurred in the US, state by state.

Hayford was a co-founder of the Gold Coast Aborigines' Rights Protection Society and would expound on African land rights in the paper. His first article 'Gold Coast Land Tenure and the Forest Bill' in August 1912, was followed by several others, all describing in detail European exploitation of African lands and resources.

The *Review* was a staunch ally of the Ottoman Empire, showing concern when it was threatened during the Balkan Wars of 1912–13 and at its break-up following the First World War (although it could not show support for Turkey during the war for fear of being accused of sedition). Muslim perspectives featured strongly throughout the journal. In 'Cross versus Crescent' Khwaja Kamal ud-Din wrote about an Indian Muslim's views on the Balkan Wars in the bimonthly December–January 1913 issue and the need for British intervention.[47] While Pickthall, Ali's old *New Age* combatant, wrote about 'The Fate of Turkey' after the war in January 1920.[48]

As war drums began to beat ever more strongly, the *Review* played an important and necessary role, reflecting the concerns of Britain's non-white population over the coming global conflagration. In August 1914, a long report on the assassination of Archduke Franz Ferdinand was featured. In a slimmed-down issue of April 1917 Ali launched the Indian Muslim Soldiers' Widows and Orphans' War Fund; patrons included Lloyd George, Sir Edward Grey and Lord Curzon, demonstrating Ali's considerable influence among the political elite. The fund raised £1,500 and was sent to widows and children of Muslim soldiers who had fallen on the battlefields of Flanders. An article in January 1917 'India and the War Contribution' outlined India's assistance in terms of troops and war chest to the British effort.[49]

In an editorial in the same issue Ali urged readers that 'we must do our part'. He continued: 'We are quite aware of the fact that the best blood of the sons of Africa has been shed in the cause for freedom ... If we help to win this freedom it very naturally follows that we are partakers therein ... We must give our rulers no legitimate excuse for withholding that to which we are justly entitled.'[50]

In January 1918, Ghanaian journalist and long-term London resident W.F. Hutchinson wrote in the 'Coloured Peoples' Part in the War', 'At the request of the editor ... I have undertaken to tell the story of the part taken by coloured people in the great struggle which is now being waged in Western and Eastern Europe, in the Balkans, Egypt and Mesopotamia, as well as in the campaigns which have been fought out in West Africa and that which is now drawing to a close in East Africa.'[51] Ali was adamant that this ultimate sacrifice must not fade from memory. He had previously petitioned the War Office in the autumn of 1917 to send Hutchinson to the front as a war correspondent.

He wrote to his friend Aubrey Herbert MP: 'As the coloured people of the world are taking a considerable part in the present war, both as combatants and industrially, there is a great desire on their part to know what their compatriots who have been recruited for service have been doing.'[52] The letter was shunted around the War Office departments, where Ali was callously referred to as 'the n——r editor'. As the matter was considered, a correspondence between James Baird and O.S. Ashcroft, dated Wellington House, 6 October 1917, stated: 'It may serve to encourage the coloured press in the US and the allied N——rs generally.'[53]

The contempt with which Ali's request was treated illustrated the blatant racist attitudes at the time. Ali's request was turned down on the grounds that 'accommodation for visitors to the front is already to the limit'.

The quality publication attracted a wide range of intellectuals, including Annie Besant, George Bernard Shaw and H.G. Wells. Prominent nationalist, anti-colonial leaders, including Egypt's Mohamed Farid Bey and Nigeria's Herbert Macaulay, also wrote for the paper, and Ali threw its considerable weight behind Saad Zaghloul's Wafd party, which went on to secure Egyptian independence from Britain in 1922.

The advent of the First World War brought with it a tide of suspicion – foreign nationals were forced to register at a police station as rumours of secret agents abounded. Ali had to present a photograph of his birth certificate at Brixton police station, to prove his Egyptian-Sudanese parenthood. Duffield states: 'he did, during the Great War apparently procure a photographic copy of his birth certificate from Alexandria ... but its very authenticity may be wondered at. It was obtained for Dusé through an Egyptian nationalist friend Ahmad Zaki Abushady.'[54] Despite residence in England since 1884, Ali was suspected to be an 'Ottoman alien'.[55]

Still the authorities doubted his origins and kept him under surveillance, marking Ali 'as a rather doubtful character whose paper was suspect ... and in touch with undesirable elements in India and Egypt'.[56] He was forbidden to travel to West Africa during this time. An MI5 report on Ali, dated 7 February 1915, accused him 'of assisting the Turkish officers with Senusi Arabs against the Italians ... and to have been active in 1913 in providing Arabs in Tripoli with arms'.[57] Around this time, Ali would note the constant presence of suited individuals stationed outside the offices of 158 Fleet Street.[58]

In a further blow, the British government banned the journal in India and British colonies in Africa towards the end of the First World War, citing its seditious nature.

'Exceptional methods'

Although Ali must have enjoyed being a colonial disrupter, he found, like Edwards before him, that financing a newspaper was to prove a challenge. At the end of 1912, the printers Page & Thomas took Ali's publishing company to court for an unpaid bill of £168, prompting its collapse as early as January 1914. The company was operating on little or no capital and lack of investment was a major reason for its demise. Ali alluded to rumours of his printers being pressured to ask for monies in advance by 'a soap manufacturer' with business interests in West Africa. Said soap manufacturer, according to Ali, had been negotiating exploitative prices for palm kernels and palm oil, and his activities had been lampooned by the *Review*. It is highly likely that the soap manufacturer Ali referred to was Sir William Lever.[59]

This feud apart, Ali was able to prop up the paper in various incarnations after the collapse of the publishing company, although it never really recovered from that financial blow, surviving in a haphazard manner. For eighteen months from July 1912 to December 1913, the paper came out as a monthly. Reflecting the court case and ongoing dispute with the printers, it emerged as a bi-monthly in early 1913. After the bi-monthly February–March 1913 edition, it was produced monthly from April 1913 (although there are gaps). On 24 March 1914, Ali reincarnated the *Review* as a weekly. The weekly survived to 19 August 1914. From January 1917 to October 1918, the *Review* appeared again as a monthly, although there are no issues for March to June 1918. The *Review*'s last gasp was from January 1920 to December 1920 as a monthly (but with no issues for October and November) under the modified title *African and Orient Review*.

In an editorial 'Yesterday, To-day and To-morrow', published on 30 June 1914, Ali laid bare the full scale of the *Review*'s financial trouble. He wrote: 'We have experienced trying and stirring times during the past two years. There were times when we felt we must give up the struggle so desperate was our position and so insistent were our creditors.'

Printers and the commitments of a weekly print run are mentioned, and the fact that on publication day there was no money in the bank and none in the office to pay debts. He continued: 'The Editor could not face the printer with excuses ... The Editor walked the inhospitable streets of London in despair ... He returned to the office at 6 o'clock when the staff had returned to their homes. He opened the letterbox and found two letters.'

One of the letters, Ali wrote, was from an oriental prince, the other from a subscriber, both from the same country, although he omits to say where. The subscriber complained about the non-arrival of his paper. Ali read this first, his mood dimming even more. He tentatively opened the second letter, from the prince, and was overjoyed when a cheque for £55 fell on the floor. 'The tears of joy rose unbidden to the eyes of the Editor,' he wrote.

To his critics he argued that, 'The average businessman will say, it is not possible to conduct a newspaper without adequate capital. Of course, the average businessman will be right, but you see this is not the average periodical. We are exceptional and as a consequence we adopt exceptional methods.'[60]

These 'exceptional methods' were to prove the *Review*'s undoing; Ali simply could not run an enterprise without adequate capital or regular advertising. How the *Review* was able to limp on after 1913 is cloaked in mystery. Duffield argued that one source of support may have been T.A. Doherty of Lagos, who was studying law in London at the time: 'It is said that he helped Dusé in recurring financial difficulties, giving him money to pay staff on several occasions.'[61] But this assertion is refuted by Doherty himself who, as a student, had little means to support himself let alone Ali's paper.

With resources becoming slender, Ali wrote the majority of the copy, particularly arts reviews, under various pseudonyms – as well as the aforementioned 'Delta', 'The Savage Satellite' was also a favourite.

The paper increasingly relied on subscriptions and costs rose from 4s 6d to 6s per annum in the first year. The annual subscription for post-war issues began at 8s 6d, while the final issue in 1920 raised this to 10s 6d, reflecting further desperation. As well as encouraging chain subscriptions, urging subscribers to sign up colleagues and friends etc, other circulation stunts were tried, some of which would have been frowned on by Orage's *New Age*. For example, a beauty competition was announced in the May 1920 issue solely for women of colour: the celebration of Black beauty was a radical concept at the time, so maybe the frivolity can be excused as it had laudable aims.

Earlier incarnations of the *Review* revealed regular advertising from Uganda Railways, the printers Page & Thomas, the African Steam Ship Company, Quilliam Ltd (a factory in Liverpool that supplied bags for ores and mineral products) and Volo River Coconut & Produce, shippers of cotton goods. As the war dragged on, however, advertising grew less and less reliable, and with the British government curtailing the journal's reach in India and the British colonies in Africa, there was less reason for advertisers to pay for space if a global journal was not truly global.

In January 1918, in an editorial entitled 'Our New Form of Journal', Ali elaborated that he was printing the journal in black and white, with lines of text closer together because of production costs. This was a tragic state of affairs: this once mighty journal with laudable aims was now shrinking, quite literally, in front of its editor's eyes. For Ali, who had poured his heart and soul into the enterprise, the situation must have been heart-breaking.

In December 1920, in the journal's last issue, he wrote: 'The Review has always been costly, and ever since its inception in 1912 it has been produced at a considerable loss, which the Editor has personally borne on behalf of the cause the Review represents.'

Ali was now, under the aegis of Hayford, becoming more interested in trade and commerce, realising that true political independence for African and Asian nations and their peoples was linked to economic and financial independence. West Africa was rich in mineral resources, but eight years at the *Review* had taught him that this was being exploited by European companies.

Six months before the *Review*'s closure, at the age of 53, Ali travelled to Lagos and the Gold Coast to meet various businessmen. According to one eyewitness, he received a true hero's welcome, 'The whole Muhammedean community thronged to the wharves to welcome Mr Dusé Mohamed Ali ... one of the zealous defenders of coloured rights throughout the world.' It was even declared by the Lagosians that 22 July be called 'Dusé Mohamed Day'.[62]

Ali travelled to the United States a few months later (it is not clear if he intended to permanently shut the *Review* at this stage or if it was just in abeyance). What is also not clear is his date of arriving in America; he returned to the UK and edited the December 1920 issue. Duffield states he was present at the general meeting of the African Progress Union in London on 20 July 1921, so he must have travelled there after this date.[63]

The US of the early 1920s was a speculators' paradise and Ali wanted to find a market for West African cocoa. Duffield wrote: 'Once there, he experienced a business failure of such severity that he had no choice but to close his London office and remain in the United States indefinitely. He never returned to Britain.[64]

Between 1921 and 1931, Ali was back to living a peripatetic lifestyle. He separated from Beatrice and launched himself into a variety of projects in the States: he reconnected with Garvey through John Edward Bruce and started writing a regular column for *The Negro World*.

Ali was impressed with his former student's organisational ability and zeal, and particularly with his Universal Negro Improvement Association (UNIA). He was not present when Garvey was convicted of fraud in 1923 and imprisoned in 1925. However, he wrote an obituary for *The Comet* following Garvey's death in 1940, praising his work and dedication: 'Perhaps no African living or dead has made such an impression on the world at large and quickened the desire for racial self-reliance and self-determination in the breasts of Africans the world over than the great leader.'[65]

Ali's other activities around this time included lecturing on African history and culture, and he visited New York, Boston, Washington, Detroit, Chicago, St Louis and Tuskegee. He also met his (possibly) third wife, Gertrude La Page, a professional singer and a committed Rosicrucian, and the daughter of a well-known hotel proprietress.

In 1933 Ali and La Page relocated to Lagos, Nigeria. Ali was again chasing the cocoa dream but the business climate in the 1930s, following the world slump, was increasingly unstable. He successfully sought work on the *Nigerian Daily Times*, writing a frothing weekly column entitled 'About it and About'; while his old friend Doherty got Ali work editing the Lagos *Nigerian Daily Telegraph*, where his Fleet Street expertise was greatly valued. While working on these papers, the idea of *The Comet* came to him: 'A real honest to goodness weekly publication of informative character was badly needed in Nigeria.'[66]

Ali founded *The Comet* in 1933, possibly with monies from La Page, or from tapping Garveyite networks for funds. The weekly, with a circulation of 4,000, was hugely successful and carried a mix of politics and features reminiscent of the best days of the *Review*. Ali also dabbled in fiction: he serialised his novel *Ere Roosevelt Came* in the paper and wrote a historical novel, *Daughter of the Pharaohs*, as well as short stories. La Page, who had set up a study centre in Lagos for Rosicrucian students, also wrote for the paper. With his fez and large theatrical floppy bow tie, Ali was a recognisable figure in African literary circles. In his 60s, it seemed that Ali had finally found peace, a certain degree of financial stability and domestic contentment.

In 1937 La Page left Ali and Africa to tend to her ailing mother. She never returned – the US Federal Census of 1940 states her place of residence as Oceanside San Diego, California, her status divorced.

In 1944, at the age of 78, Ali sold *The Comet* to Nnamdi Azikiwe's Zik's Press Limited (Azikiwe went on to serve as the first president of Nigeria from 1963 to 1966), and the paper became a lasting feature of the Nigerian press landscape. A year later, on 25 June 1945, Ali died. His obituary in *The Comet* two days later was titled 'We lose a Prince of the Pen'.

Prince of the Pen

The man who called himself Dusé Mohamed Ali was a stylistic chameleon, a journalistic huckster, an actor for whom the world *really* was a stage. His writing could be effervescent in its brilliance, as in his last *New Age* piece 'Quo Vadis', or nonsensical, as in his *Comet* columns 'About it and About'. What is evident is that this much-maligned figure left a remarkable legacy – the *Review*'s existence may have been relatively brief, and occasionally stuttering, but it burned extremely brightly, the arguments it wrought sustaining journalists through the interwar years. As late as 2007, history dismissed Ali as a 'penny a line' journalist but this summation was cruel and unfair. Ali's methods were unconventional, his financial situation awry, but he was a man who had achieved much in a hostile era.[67]

Ali's combination of chutzpah, sheer bloody-mindedness and raw talent had propelled him to the centre of literary London and *The New Age*, an intellectual and literary colossus of its time. As well as being a crusading journalist, he had admirers in parliament of all political hues. This was a substantial feat for a man of colour from a non-aristocratic background in Edwardian England.

The *Review* was international, progressive and of consistently high quality. Between 1912 and 1920, the offices of 158 Fleet Street were a meeting place of nascent Pan-African and Pan-Asian movements, as those nations and their peoples engaged in a struggle of real significance for political, social and economic freedom.

Like spilled ink, Ali's mentoring of a young Marcus Garvey during the paper's heyday left an indelible mark. Garvey founded the hugely influential UNIA in 1914, established *The Negro World* in the US, and is acknowledged as one of the twentieth century's foremost Black leaders. Garvey's first wife, Amy Ashwood Garvey (who later worked with C.L.R. James, George Padmore and later Claudia Jones in the UK), was also hugely inspired by the fez-wearing scribe.

Ali was right to identify the First World War as a seismic event, gouging the timeline into 'a before' and 'an after'. Colonial troops returned from the conflict with a global outlook: if they could risk their lives on the battlefields for imperial powers, surely they could determine their own destinies? Moreover, the 1917 Bolshevik Revolution in Russia promised much: here was a nation that bestrode east and west, which had established a socialist state and was now committed to equality for all regardless of race or class.

However, few progressive newspapers survived to record this uptick in international consciousness among troops of colour. The demise of Ali's *Review*, along with the *African Telegraph* (1914–18) and Shyamji Krishna Varma's *The Indian Sociologist* (1905–14, London, Paris; 1920–22 Geneva), compounded with the post-war costs of print, left an extraordinary hole to fill with regard to the reporting of national race issues and colonial news.

In the ensuing decades, this void was addressed by the radical progressive left newspapers – in particular, an extraordinary collaboration at the *Workers' Dreadnought*, whose offices at 10 Wine Office Court were within spitting distance of Ali's defunct *Review*.

Here a relationship between a militant suffragette and an aspiring Jamaican poet, the first of a clutch of Black journalists inspired by Lenin's grand experiment, would ensure that the stories of Britain's non-white population never remained far from the spotlight.

VAGABOND SOUL

CLAUDE McKAY, journalist, poet and author (*Workers'
Dreadnought, 1919–21; The Negro World, 1919–22; The Liberator,
1921–22; The Crisis, 1922–24*)

There was no greater vantage point to see America burn than the rail-road. Working in the summer of 1919 as a dining car waiter, a majority Black profession on the Pennsylvania Railroad, a fearful Claude McKay had resorted to travelling with a revolver secreted in his regulation starched white jacket.

This febrile time, which became known as the US's Red Summer, witnessed a wave of racial violence that engulfed the country following the end of the 'Great War', a conflict so bloody and brutal it had claimed the lives of nearly 10 million soldiers and resulted in countless civilian casualties.[1] In a situation replicated across the western world, hundreds of thousands of job-seeking veterans had returned home, among them Black troops that had fought for the allied powers and hoped that they would be awarded with equal rights in return for their service. It was not to be. In the US, the competition for labour and jobs would unveil ugly prejudices and trigger a prolonged spell of rioting and lynching that would flare from Arizona in the west of the country to Connecticut in the east. Hundreds of people – the majority Black Americans – were killed and thousands injured in that summer's bloodletting. According to Du Bois' National Association for the Advancement of Colored People (NAACP), at least fifty-two Black people were lynched, with many victims burned to death. In almost all of the cases, white mobs instigated the violence.[2] The historian John Hope Franklin described that summer as 'the greatest period of interracial strife that the nation has ever witnessed'.[3]

For McKay, a 28-year-old Jamaican immigrant and aspiring poet, the violence shook him to his core. He said: 'It was the first time I had ever come face to face with such manifest, implacable hate of my race, and my feelings were indescribable ... I had heard of prejudice in America but never dreamed of it being so intensely bitter.'[4]

McKay had joined the railroad a little before April 1917 and, follow-ing America's entry into the First World War that month, the industry served an indispensable role, ferrying men and materials across the vast country. McKay bore startling witness to the horrors of lynching – previously chronicled by Edwards, Impey and Ali – during that Red Summer and the experience would prove undeniably formative, shaping his views as an anti-racist, labour correspondent for Sylvia Pankhurst's UK-based *Workers' Dreadnought* mere months later. The grounding he received at that newspaper sustained him as a liberal correspondent in the US, and provided him with fodder for the fiction and poetry that established him as one of the leading figures of the Harlem Renaissance and an inspiration for France's Négritude movement.

McKay summed up the mood of the Red Summer in his autobiog-raphy *A Long Way From Home*: 'Travelling from city to city and unable to gauge the attitude and temper of each one, we Negro railroad men were nervous,' he recalled. 'We did not separate from one another gaily to spend ourselves in speakeasies and gambling joints. We stuck together, some of us armed, going from railroad station to our quarters. We stayed in our quarters all through the dreary ominous nights, for we never knew what was going to happen.'[5]

McKay had led a largely itinerant lifestyle since arriving in the US in the summer of 1912 to study agriculture at Booker T. Washington's Tuskegee Institute. His tenure at Alabama's most famous Black industrial college was brief: the 'military, machinelike' existence repelled him and he left its hallowed halls for Kansas State College, before moving to Harlem.[6]

In contrast, his childhood in Jamaica had been largely idyllic. Born on 15 September 1890 into a prosperous farming family, McKay grew up in the district of Sunny Ville, Clarendon, an area crowned with green hills and blessed with rich soil and lush vegetation.[7] The youngest of eight children, McKay was a sensitive child, close to his mother Hannah and his school teacher elder brother Uriah Theodore (known as U'Theo). He would often speak of his mother's 'rich, warm love' in contrast to his father's coldness. 'A real black Scotchman'; this 'patriarch of the mountain community' was a senior deacon of the Mt Zion Baptist church.[8] It was the intellectually independent, agnostic U'Theo who introduced McKay to a love of literature. McKay lived with him and his wife as a child when his brother was teaching in Montego Bay, and devoured the contents of the schoolmaster's library, which included classics such as Dickens, and tomes by Thomas Huxley and Ernst Haeckel.

After returning to Clarendon briefly, McKay was awarded a trade scholarship in Kingston. He was 16 and had grown into 'a strikingly handsome, quick-witted youth of average height and slim, muscular physique', with 'a broad, expressive face' featuring 'arched eyebrows that never came down'.[9] Term was to begin in January 1907 at his trade school, but that month a devastating 6.2 magnitude earthquake struck the island. McKay recalled his room buckling as if some 'giant had crushed in the walls of the house'.[10] The city was largely destroyed and gutted by fire and, after the chaos, McKay had to swap the excitement of Kingston for St Ann parish, just north of Clarendon, and an apprenticeship with a skilled cabinetmaker.

He was largely disappointed at this quick exit from city life, but it was here he made the acquaintance of Walter Jekyll, an Englishman who became another formative literary influence. Jekyll was an accomplished scholar, who in all likelihood allowed his friend Robert Louis Stevenson to use his name for the fictional Dr Jekyll. He had emigrated to Jamaica's warm climate for health reasons, and became fascinated with its folklore, particularly the Annancy tales. Jekyll encouraged McKay's poetry, particularly his use of Jamaican patois, and gave his young protégé access to his huge library, introducing him to the social elites of Jamaica. McKay wrote years later that Jekyll 'opened up a new world to my view, introduced me to a greater, deeper literature – to Buddha, Schopenhauer and Goethe, Carlyle and Browning, Wilde, [Edward] Carpenter, Whitman,

Hugo, Verlaine, Baudelaire, Shaw and the different writers of the rationalist press – more than I had time to read.'[11]

McKay's biographer Wayne F. Cooper intimated that the unmarried Jekyll was gay. McKay was definitely bisexual and explored relationships with men later in life in both the US and Europe.

In late 1909, McKay gave up his apprenticeship to nurse his mother, who was suffering from heart disease. Her death in December of that year devastated him. Cooper wrote: 'His devotion to her had been complete, even excessive.'[12]

McKay returned to Kingston, where he enrolled briefly in the Jamaican constabulary. All the while Jekyll helped him develop his poetry and in 1912, McKay published *Songs of Jamaica* and *Constab Ballads* to critical acclaim in Jamaica, the former receiving an award from the Jamaican Institute of Arts and Sciences. McKay's *Christmas in de Air* appeared in the *Jamaican Times* on 16 December 1911. Referencing Dickens, the poem made a political statement about profit being placed before people's welfare, and could be seen as a clear indication of McKay's future political stance.

McKay still had not worked out how to make a living but after hearing of the virtues of Booker T. Washington's Tuskegee Institute in Alabama, he made the impulsive decision to use his award to travel to the US and study agronomy there in the summer of 1912. When he arrived in Charleston, South Carolina, before travelling on to Alabama, he was faced with a harsh reality: segregated washrooms, restaurants and water fountains and blatant racism. He wrote: 'I had heard of prejudice in America but never dreamed of it being so intensely bitter; for at home there is also prejudice of the English sort, subtle and dignified, rooted in class distinction – color and race being hardly taken into account.'[13]

Despite his admiration of Washington, McKay transferred to Kansas, where a lecturer introduced him to Du Bois' *The Souls of Black Folk*. In a series of essays, Du Bois reflected on how racism permeated every aspect of American life and discussed what could be done to advance equal rights. The book, McKay would later state, 'shook me like an earthquake'.[14] Although he excelled in his classes at Kansas, McKay found it difficult to stay here too. He wrote he had been 'gripped by the lust to wander and wonder. The spirit of the vagabond, the daemon of some poets, had got hold of me.'[15]

McKay moved to New York with the help of a few thousand pounds that Jekyll had sent him. The city invigorated him – the skyscrapers, those mountains of steel and glass wreathed in cloud, an 'eye-dazzling picture', embodied hope.[16] He was delighted to find a Black quarter in the city with a burgeoning West Indian population. He stated:

> Harlem was my first positive reaction to American life … After two years in the blue-sky-law desert of Kansas, it was like entering a paradise of my own people … I gave myself entirely up to getting deep down into … [the] rhythm of Harlem life which still remains one of the most pleasurable sensations of my blood.[17]

An optimistic McKay invested a huge part of Jekyll's money in a restaurant venture in the city. Buoyed, he sent for his childhood sweetheart, Eulalie Imelda Lewars, with whom he had been corresponding for two years. At this point in his life, he was still unsure of his sexuality but getting married seemed the right and respectable thing for someone of his middle-class Jamaican background to do. He married Eulalie on 30 July 1914; he was 23, his bride a few years younger. Within six months, both the marriage and restaurant venture had collapsed, and Eulalie returned to Clarendon, Jamaica, where she gave birth to their only child, Rhue Hope McKay.

Pride stopped McKay returning to Jamaica and he stayed on in the US, taking a variety of jobs: 'janitor, butler, waiter – anything that came handy … I was determined to find expression in writing … I took my menial tasks like a student who is working his way through a university … If I would not graduate as a bachelor of arts or science, I would graduate as a poet.'[18]

These so-called 'graduate studies' coincided fortuitously with what was known as the 'Innocent rebellion', a new wave of forward-thinking art and literature magazines, typified by journals such as *The New Republic*, *The Masses* and *The Seven Arts*. In October 1917, the stridently anti-war *Seven Arts* published two of McKay's poems, *Invocation* and *The Harlem Dancer*. For both these poems McKay used the pseudonym E.H. Edwards, a play on his mother's maiden name, as he was afraid his work as a waiter would be compromised if he was linked to such a radical magazine. Sadly, the *Seven Arts*' moment was evanescent; it folded after a year.

Emboldened by publishing success, McKay sent out further poems and was delighted to receive acknowledgement from the great Irish editor of *Pearson's Magazine*, Frank Harris. In his autobiography, *A Long Way From Home*, McKay documents his unconventional first meeting with Harris in his Greenwich Village apartment, where the editor regaled him with tales of H.G. Wells and Oscar Wilde while pouring continual goblets of wine with a shaky hand. *Pearson's Magazine* went on to publish six of McKay's poems in September 1918.

McKay had now joined the railroad (because of their critical part in the war effort, railroad workers were draft exempt) and in the solitude of his dining car quarters he wrote poetry inflamed by racial tensions. In *To the White Fiends* (1918), he challenged the bigots: 'Think ye I am not fiend and savage too/Think ye I could not arm me with a gun/And shoot down ten of you for every one/Of my black brothers murdered, burnt by you?'[19]

This anger finally manifested in an impassioned sonnet, *If We Must Die*, written during the Red Summer's Washington riots, and published in 1919 by the New York-based leftist publication *The Liberator*, which had been founded by Max Eastman (who had previously edited *The Masses*) and his sister Crystal.

The powerful verse, acknowledged by one contemporary as 'the Marseillaise of the American Negro'[20] concluded with the lines, 'Like men we'll face the murderous, cowardly pack/Pressed to the wall, dying, but fighting back'. It established McKay, who was living in Harlem at the time, as a serious literary talent and after it was reprinted in all the major US Black newspapers and magazines of the time, McKay was lauded as 'a poet of his people'.[21] He wrote that when he read it to the members of his dining crew, they reacted with intense emotion, with one of them breaking down and weeping.[22]

His base remained in Harlem, a room on 131st Street. Here he lived a bohemian lifestyle, frequenting the bars and cabarets of the district, exploring his sexuality, and experimenting with cocaine and 'Chinese tobacco'.[23]

The publication of *If We Must Die* sparked a lifelong collaboration between McKay and the Eastman siblings: the two would not just publish, promote and advise him editorially, they would also provide him with financial support.

Publication, however, brought unwelcome attention from the Justice Department's committee investigating African American radicalism and sedition, which viewed the verse as inflammatory. By now McKay had left his job on the railroad and started work in a factory in Manhattan, where he had joined the revolutionary Industrial Workers of the World (IWW), influenced by his friend Hubert Harrison, Harlem's great socialist soapbox orator.

McKay was fascinated by their lyrical dexterity of these troubadours of the street and Harrison was one of the best performers. McKay had also become a member of the newly formed African Black Brotherhood, a Black socialist collective based in Harlem. Although attracted to Marcus Garvey's UNIA, writing for its *Negro World*, he never joined the organisation. Inspired by the Russian revolution and the anti-colonial struggles in India and Ireland, McKay had become vocal in his support for Bolshevism, which he saw as a channel for Black liberation.

An exchange of letters between McKay and W.H. Ferris, literary editor of *The Negro World*, was taken by the authorities as evidence of seditious conduct. McKay had written:

> Every negro who lays claim to leadership should make a study of Bolshevism and explain its meaning to the coloured masses. It is the greatest and most scientific idea afloat in the world today that can easily be put into practice by the proletariat to better its material and spiritual life. Bolshevism ... has made Russia safe for the Jew ... It might make these United States safe for the Negro.[24]

A 'true cultural homeland'

It is largely thought that pressure from the Justice Department led to McKay's decision to leave the US in September 1919 and travel to the UK, although he later stated that the spur was an opportunity to take advantage of an all-expenses trip from literary admirers of his and his childhood desire to visit his 'true cultural homeland'.[25]

Old England, a poem he had written in 1912, summed up his fondness for the mother country: 'Just to view de homeland England, in de streets of London walk/An' to see de famous sights dem 'bouten which dere's so much talk.'[26]

But this ideal of 'literary England' was dashed when he arrived in 1919, and he was disturbed to find the long shadow of racial violence had followed him across the Atlantic. According to the historian Jacqueline Jenkinson, the UK riots of 1919 emerged from the scorched earth of war: 'At a time of stress, when xenophobia had become almost a way of life after over four years of constant German and anti-alien propagandas, those deemed "foreign" by virtue of dark skin pigmentation were identified as legitimate targets for post-war grievances.'[27]

The multicultural enclaves of Britain's seaports were home to Africans, West Indians, Indians, Chinese, Malaysians, Arabs and other nationalities who had staffed British ships during the First World War. These men had settled in these towns but post-war competition for jobs had led to blatant discrimination (unions would bar seamen of colour from staffing British merchant ships) and ugly rioting dockside, which had spilled over into attacks on boarding lodges and businesses occupied by non-white citizens. Economic conditions were dire – retail prices in 1920 were 176 per cent higher than they had been in 1914 and the cost of basics, such as food and clothing, had tripled. For the wageless, non-whites were a convenient scapegoat. Ali's *Review*, which was embroiled in financial difficulties and publishing intermittently, missed reporting on these riots and giving the community a much-needed voice.

In the summer of 1919, riots blighted the major cities of London, Liverpool, Cardiff, Manchester and Hull. In the midst of the violence, five people were killed, dozens injured and at least 250 arrested. Further clashes took place in 1920 and 1921. As well as competition for jobs, presumed wealth or better housing, white hostility to ethnically mixed relationships also triggered violence. A Cardiff city police report stated: 'There can be no doubt that the aggressors have been those belonging to the white race,' and stated a contributing factor as: 'The white population appear to be alarmed at the association of so many white women with the coloured races and imagine that they entice the white women to their houses. (As a matter of fact as far as Police can observe certain white women court the favour of the coloured races.)'[28]

Some of the worst violence was in Liverpool, which faced a prolonged period of rioting in June. Mobs reached up to 10,000-strong and more than 700 non-white people were forced to leave their homes and seek police protection in Bridewell, the central lock-up. Following a rash of fights between sailors of all nationalities, the pursuit of a Royal Navy sailor, Charles Wootton, by a white mob after he had escaped a raid on a nearby boarding house proved to be the most shocking incident. The local *Globe* newspaper reported that a young Black man was pushed into the sea and then a crowd of white dockworkers 'threw bricks at him until he sank for the last time'.[29]

The *Liverpool Echo* covered the incident in slightly more detail. 'It is reported that a detective climbed down a ship's rope and was about to pull the man out of the water when a stone thrown from the middle of the crowd struck Wootton on the head and he sank. His body was later recovered by means of grappling irons.'[30]

No one was arrested for this crime of murder.

The violence caused McKay to think that things were as bad in England as they were in the US. He had encountered a particular brand of English racism on arrival in the country: difficulties acquiring accommodation in London led to him living in a 'hideous little gutter street near the Angel'; pubs would often refuse him service; and he would regularly receive verbal and even physical abuse, stating he was 'nearly mauled in Limehouse'.[31]

McKay searched for a scene similar to that he had left in Harlem: in time he came across a club for non-white soldiers in London's Drury Lane. Here he met 'a few colored Americans, East Indians and Egyptians', who would tell him about racism in the British army during the war and on the streets of London during the Armistice. He enjoyed attending the spit and sawdust boxing matches staged nearby, and he also acquainted his new friends with US journals *The Crisis*, *The Messenger* and *The Negro World*.

Harrison, who was now editor of *The Negro World*, asked McKay to contribute a series on London life. McKay wrote about the soldiers' club but incurred the wrath of its matron after describing her 'patronising white maternal attitude towards her colored charges'.[32]

With Drury Lane out of bounds, the London literary scene provided another refuge. Armed with letters of introduction from Harris, who had arranged for McKay to meet George Bernard Shaw, McKay found a home at the International Socialist Club (ISC) in London. Here he met fellow left-wing intellectuals, including George Lansbury, editor of the left-wing *Daily Herald*; Shapurji Saklatvala, who would later become the Labour MP for Battersea North; A.J. Cook of the Miners' Federation; Jack Tanner, leader of the shop stewards' movement; Guy Aldred, editor of the anarchist organ the *Spur*; the artist Frank Budgen and his wife Francine. (Budgen would later paint McKay's portrait, describing his face as 'illuminated by real intelligence'.) Notably, he had a rather fortuitous encounter with Sylvia Pankhurst, editor of the *Workers' Dreadnought*.[33]

McKay found the ISC fascinating. In his words, it was 'full of excitement with its dogmatists and doctrinaires of radical left ideas: Socialists, Communists, anarchists, syndicalists, one-big-unionists and trade unionists, soap-boxers, poetasters, scribblers, editors of little radical sheets which flourish in London.'[34] McKay brought along some of his own West Indian and African friends to the club, including 'three soldiers from the Drury Lane club and a couple of boxers'. In due course, the boxers staged an exhibition at the ISC, much to the members' bemusement.[35]

McKay described Pankhurst as 'a plain little Queen Victoria-sized woman with plenty of long unruly bronze-like hair. There was no distinction about her clothes, and on the whole [,] she was very undistinguished. But her eyes were fiery, even a little fanatic, with a glint of shrewdness ... And in the labor movement she was always jabbing her hat pin into the hides of the smug and slack labor leaders ... And wherever imperialism got drunk and went wild among native peoples, the Pankhurst paper would be on the job.'[36]

Pankhurst already knew of McKay. She was good friends with the Eastmans and in September 1919, a month before they met in person, she had republished a series of his poems that had appeared in *The Liberator*, including *If We Must Die*, in the *Dreadnought* under the title 'A Negro Poet', emphasising that he was a dining car waiter when he wrote them.[37]

Pankhurst and McKay had much in common. McKay was an out-spoken advocate of women's rights and suffrage, a pacifist and an agnostic, and the two became firm friends. McKay wrote admiringly of her personality as being as 'picturesque and passionate as any radical in London'.[38] Thus the unlikely partnership of the 29-year-old fresh-faced Jamaican with the battle-hardened suffragette proved to be enduring. Towards the end of 1919, McKay joined Pankhurst's Workers' Socialist Federation (WSF), a radical party that Lenin had roasted as 'left-wing communists' and which had been vocal in its support of the 1916 Easter Rising.[39]

In an editorial published in the *Dreadnought* at the height of that summer's riots, 'Stabbing Negroes in the London Dock Area', Pankhurst fully established her weekly paper's anti-racist credentials. In the article she submitted 'a few questions for the consideration of those who have been negro hunting'. These included: 'Do you not know that capitalists, and especially British capitalists, have seized by force of arms, the countries inhabited by black people and are ruling those countries and the black inhabitants for their own profit …

'Do you think you would be better employed in getting conditions made right for yourself and your fellow workers than in stabbing a black man?'[40]

Through the WSF, McKay found himself in the 'nest of extreme radicalism in London'.[41] The party's headquarters were in Bow, where he lived for a time, and McKay was privy to the lives and working conditions of the English proletariat up close. Pankhurst was active in the local area – she had converted a local pub, The Gunmakers Arms, into The Mothers Arms, a maternity clinic and day nursery, and had opened a number of cost-price restaurants for working women.

Pankhurst was impressed with McKay and hired him as the *Dreadnought*'s labour correspondent. As McKay stated in his autobiography, his perspective as an authentic Black proletarian artist was invaluable, particularly when the nation was embroiled in racial strife. One of his first tasks was to cover the volatile situation on London's docks, interviewing sailors of all races to gauge the root of their discontent. He was also assigned the task of aggregating articles from the foreign press, with a particular eye for any pieces that criticised the British imperial project.[42] In this latter activity, McKay worked with a young Finn named Erkki Veltheim, whom the *Dreadnought*'s staff had nicknamed Comrade Vie.

During his time at the *Dreadnought*, McKay's output was prolific. He published numerous essays, articles, book reviews and some of his most militant poems in the eight-page newspaper, often under pseudonyms. He was particularly moved by the workers' plight in the East End, publishing seven poems under the moniker Hugh Hope that related to the subject, such as *Song of the New Soldier and Worker* (3 April 1920) and *Joy in the Woods* (10 April 1920).

In January 1920, McKay wrote his first cover essay for the paper 'Socialism and the Negro'. In it he debated the relative merits of Du Bois' NAACP over Washington's Tuskegee Institute, criticising the former's 'myopic vision'. He also covered the successes of Garvey's UNIA, to which he vowed allegiance despite its non-socialist credentials – the organisation had recently launched the Black Star Line, a Black-owned shipping line. He argued that nationalist movements, particularly among subject peoples, would lead to an embrace of Communism, stating that 'the British Empire is the greatest obstacle to International Socialism, and any of its subjugated parts succeeding in breaking away from it would be helping the cause of World Communism'.[43]

The *Dreadnought* provided a much-needed Black perspective at a time when people of colour were being demonised in the mainstream media. This was especially valuable, considering that both the *Review* and the *African Telegraph* were no longer operational. In April 1920, French troops retaliating against Germany's violation of the Versailles Treaty occupied the major cities on the east bank of the Rhine. Approximately 2 per cent of the quarter of a million French troops in the Rhineland were from West Africa, but the idea of Black troops occupying part of a white European country was viewed as repugnant by some.

Following a clash between French troops and German civilians, the left-wing *Daily Herald* ran a series of articles, reporting the hostilities in racial terms by the journalist E.D. Morel. Under the headline 'Black Scourge in Europe/Sexual Horror Let Loose by France on the Rhine', Morel alleged that Black troops, 'primitive African barbarians', 'have become a terror and a horror unimaginable to the countryside, raping women and girls'. During the tirade, he claimed: 'Apart from the barely restrainable bestiality of the black troops, syphilis is making terrible ravages where they are stationed.' Morel admitted he had no evidence or reliable reports for this but continued to state that 'sexually [the African race] are unrestrained and unrestrainable. *That is perfectly well known.*'[44]

His words incensed McKay, who dispatched a letter to the *Herald*. Lansbury refused to publish it (he later cited matters of space); but Pankhurst published it in the *Dreadnought* under the heading 'A Black Man Replies'.

'Why all this obscene, maniacal outburst about the sex vitality of black men in a proletarian paper?' asked McKay, unable to hide his dismay at such racism in a working-class journal. He challenged the assertion that Black troops were syphilitic, arguing that the disease was endemic among soldiers of all races. In his conclusion he drew a direct correlation between such articles and the racial violence that was plaguing British cities:

I feel that the ultimate result of your propaganda will be further strife and blood-spilling between whites and many members of my race, boycotted economically and socially … I have been told in Limehouse by white men, who ought to know, that this summer will be a recrudescence of the outbreaks that occurred last year. The negro-baiting Bourbons of the United States will thank you, and the proletarian underworld will certainly gloat over the scoop of the Christian-Socialist pacifist *Daily Herald*.[45]

Like most of his comrades at the newspaper, McKay took an active role in distributing the tuppence-priced newssheet at workers' rallies.[46] At a Sinn Féin rally in Trafalgar Square in the summer of 1920, McKay donned a green necktie to sell the paper, along with Pankhurst's pamphlet, *Rebel Ireland*, and Herman Gorter's *Ireland: the Achilles' Heel of England*, and was welcomed with hearty handshakes as 'Black Murphy' or 'Black Irish' by the Sinn Féin members. Unbeknownst to McKay his activities were watched acutely by British intelligence. Articles he had written in the *Dreadnought* – 'Under the Iron Heel', where he praised Sinn Féin diplomacy 'as more than a match for English chicanery',[47] and 'The Martyrdom of Ireland, Will Sinn Féin Go Red?', which had detailed the ransacking of the Irish town of Trim by the Black and Tans and pleaded with British labour leaders to 'take action' – had not escaped the radar of security services.[48]

Cooper stated that McKay attended the Communist Unity Conference held in London's Cannon Street Hotel on 31 July and 1 August 1920, which laid the foundations for the formation of the Communist Party of Great Britain. Here McKay met and reported on Robert Smillie, the charismatic leader of the miners' federation, and later went to the official trade union conference in Portsmouth, where he was greeted warmly by the delegates. McKay's almost reverential praise of Smillie was not welcomed by Pankhurst though, who scorned this courting of an official labour leader.[49]

McKay smarted at this criticism, particularly as Pankhurst had earlier suppressed an article he had written with Comrade Vie about a strike at a large lumber mill near the *Dreadnought* offices. McKay had learned that William Lansbury, the owner, had employed non-union workers and had stressed Lansbury's family connections with the editor of the social-ist *Daily Herald*. It was one of their few disagreements. Pankhurst had her reasons for killing the piece: years before, as a militant suffragette, she had avoided arrest because William Lansbury had smuggled her out of town hidden beneath wood stacks on the floor of his timber wagon. She also owed several debts to his relative George Lansbury, which included the costs of printing the *Dreadnought*. McKay concluded that 'after all … there are items which the capitalist press does not consider fit to print for capitalist reasons and items which the radical press does not consider fit to print for radical reasons'.[50]

In spite of this, the collaboration between Pankhurst and McKay grew stronger and she entrusted him with great responsibility on the paper. He wrote to his friend C.K. Ogden, editor of the *Cambridge Magazine*, complaining of overwork: 'I have been kept so frightfully busy by Sylvia Pankhurst since she came back [from abroad]. She has been experiencing all sorts of domestic and business difficulties, due to her own erratic nature, & all the routine work of getting out the paper falls to me as consequence.'[51]

Ogden introduced him to the 1917 Club, which was frequented by the Bloomsbury set, and was instrumental in getting *Spring in New Hampshire*, his third collection of poetry, published. However, McKay later rued the fact that he'd allowed Ogden to siphon off his more revolutionary verse, including *If We Must Die*, and opted for the softer title as opposed to McKay's preferred *Songs of Struggle*.

While Pankhurst was away in Russia in July 1920, attending the Second World Congress of the Third International and fraternising with Lenin (the Home Office had confiscated her passport, so inventive methods of travel involved stowing away on a freighter), McKay acted as the de facto managing editor of the *Dreadnought*.

During this time McKay published the narrative essay 'The Yellow Peril and the Dockers' under the pseudonym Leon Lopez. The essay paints a picture of a multicultural, diverse London, in which 'scores of seamen, white, brown and black, waiting wistfully for an undermanned ship' are disappointed at West India docks in London's East End. He outlines the precarious nature of the work and how the dockers' wives and children were clothed in rags and starving. He then ventures along the West India Dock Road to the large Chinese restaurants, where the white waitresses are paid better than at Lyons, which had stopped its workers forming a union. The essay highlights how the capitalist system exploits workers and pits those deemed 'alien' against their fellows; its themes echoed Edwards' final speech made years before at the Liverpool docks. In his final passage he states: 'The country's riches are not in the West End, in the palatial homes of the suburbs; they are stored in the East End, and the jobless should lead the attack on the bastilles, the bonded warehouses along the docks, to solve the question of unemployment.'[52]

McKay commissioned the cover story in the same issue 'Discontent on the Lower Deck', which was written by Royal Navy sailor Dave Springhall and published under the pseudonym S. 000 (Gunner), H.M.S. Hunter. It also illustrated the issues facing dockworkers – paltry wages, the rising costs of seamen's clothing – and called for a formation of 'a Red Navy to protect the interests of the working class, exclaiming passionately: 'Are you going to see your class go under in the fight with the capitalist brutes who made millions out of your sacrifices during the war?'[53]

These articles, published on 16 October 1920, were seen by the authorities as instigating class war. The inner sanctum of the WSF had long been a thorn in the side of the security services and with fear of Bolshevism spreading, any excuse to shut down 'the organ of the Communist party' was to be seized.

The *Dreadnought*'s offices were subsequently raided two days later on 18 October 1920. McKay was descending the stairs when Pankhurst's secretary warned him that the police were downstairs ransacking the main offices and questioning Pankhurst about her informant in the Royal Navy. He returned to his small office upstairs, retrieved the original article by 'Hunter', and, secreting it in his sock, managed to evade the scrutiny of the officers, eventually flushing the offending article down the toilet. Pankhurst was arrested shortly after for inciting treason among the Royal Navy by advocating that its workers should go on strike.

Vie was also arrested and the police discovered in his possession letters from Pankhurst to Lenin and other Bolshevik officials, ciphered notes to the Comintern, key information on British industrial centres and, most incriminatingly, 'a manual for the officers of the future British Red Army'. Vie was revealed as a Bolshevik courier who had entered Britain illegally. His arrest threw Pankhurst's organisation into jeopardy and accusations flew as to who had betrayed the young Finn. Vie was deported after six months' imprisonment for alien non-registration.

Pankhurst was prosecuted as the paper's editor under the 1914 Defence of the Realm Act for an 'act calculated and likely to cause sedition among his Majesty's Forces, in the Navy, and among the civilian population' – both the Leon Lopez article and the 'Discontent on the Lower Deck' were cited as evidence, along with a piece written by Vie (under the alias Rubinstein) 'How to Get a Labour Government' – and following a trial on 28 October 1920 and a later appeal in January 1921, she was imprisoned for six months in Holloway. She would continue to edit the *Dreadnought* upon her release, with the last issue published in June 1924.[54]

A 'crazy craving'

The *Dreadnought*'s offices were shuttered and McKay found himself without a home or livelihood. He wrote later that: 'I was seized with a crazy craving to get quickly out of that atmosphere and away from London.'[55]

He returned to the US, sailing for New York on the same day that Pankhurst began serving her sentence in Holloway prison early in 1921.[56] He returned to his old apartment on 131st Street Harlem and was invited to become a staff correspondent on *The Liberator*, where he was quickly promoted to co-editor.

McKay would later downplay his connection to Pankhurst and the *Dreadnought* as an 'opportunity to practise a little practical journalism [which] was not to be missed'.[57] But the notoriety he had gained working for Pankhurst had increased 'his reputation among whites in America and abroad'.[58] In fact, the Eastmans gave him the even greater responsibility of running *The Liberator*. McKay wrote: 'I responded with my hand and my head and my heart ... My experience with the *Dreadnought* in London was of great service to me now.'[59]

Events in Russia fascinated the paper's editors, who reported on Lenin's strategies, such as the New Economic Policy, to western readers. Here was a country that had embraced significant political change and the world was watching. Contributors included artists, writers and intellectuals of the left. McKay was entranced by the famous and eccentric individuals that graced the *Liberator*'s offices: the English sculptor and diarist Clare Sheridan, the journalist Dorothy Day and Baroness von Freytag-Loringhoven, a Greenwich Village model whom he described as 'gaudily accoutered in rainbow raiment, festooned with barbaric beads and spangles, and toting along her inevitable poodle in gilded harness'.[60]

The great silent film star Charlie Chaplin shared the *Liberator*'s politics and McKay recalled a memorable evening spent in Greenwich Village with Chaplin, Harrison and the Eastmans, when Harrison's date vigorously pursued the silent screen star around the small apartment. Although the bohemian atmospheres of Greenwich Village and Harlem were a natural home for McKay, occasionally he suffered harsh reminders as to his status as the only Black editor on a white journal; he recalled visiting New Jersey with the Eastmans and the siblings struggling to find a restaurant that would seat them all. Later he would refuse such invitations as he did not want to be 'a problem'.[61]

McKay wrote more than forty poems for *The Liberator* and dozens of articles and reviews. One of the most notable was a review of the Theatre Guild's presentation of Leonid Andreyev's *He Who Gets Slapped*, when McKay and a colleague were refused the allotted seats by an usher and made to sit in the back. He wrote: 'I had ... come as a drama critic ... a lover of the theatre, and a free soul ... But I was abruptly reminded that all these things did not matter ... the important fact, with which I was suddenly slapped in the face, was my color. I am a Negro ... I had come to see a tragic farce – and I found myself unwillingly the hero of one.'[62] Again it didn't matter what bohemian circles he traversed, in the end he was reminded harshly of the racist, segregationist policies of the US at the time.

Sadly for McKay, the comforts of *The Liberator* were short-lived. In October 1921, it was discovered that the journal's Belgian-born book-keeper E.F. Mylius, who had left *The Liberator* three years earlier, had embezzled $4,000 of the magazine's funds and speculated on the stock market. Mylius had form: he had been jailed in the UK in 1911 for publishing a report that George V was a bigamist. His actions imperilled the magazine and Eastman resigned, leaving the editorship to Michael Gold and McKay. There followed six months of acrimonious joint editorship, from January to June 1922, with Gold at one point challenging McKay to a boxing match.

The publication of *Harlem Shadows* in the spring of 1922, which included all the poems he had written for various journals, including *If We Must Die*, revealed his vibrant talent to a wide, appreciative audience, and ensured his stature among the leading figures of the Harlem Renaissance. A new generation of Black American poets and novelists followed eagerly in his footsteps, with the middle of the decade producing such diverse talents as Jean Toomer, Langston Hughes and Countee Cullen, among others.

Meanwhile, cracks were appearing in the Gold–McKay double act. Inspired by the Russian example, McKay redoubled his efforts on behalf of working-class Black people, writing several articles in the UNIA's *Negro World* and the NAACP's *The Crisis*. The revolutionary urges he had nurtured at Pankhurst's *Dreadnought* and at the ISC had not left him. In fact, they had grown stronger. He was increasingly frustrated with the failure of Eastman and others to give space to or consider 'the revolutionary implications of the racial struggle in America or abroad', elaborating that Eastman never tried to seriously discuss the Indian or Irish question, adding pertinently: 'I never once thought you grasped fully the class struggle significance of national and racial problems.'[63]

In July 1922, *The Liberator* announced McKay's departure 'to be free to write poetry and to see more of the world than is permitted to an office worker on a magazine'.[64]

McKay, no doubt inspired by Pankhurst, had long harboured a yearning to see for himself what he termed 'the grand experiment taking place in Russia'.[65] He hoped to arrive in November in time to attend the Fourth Congress of the Third Communist International. Although *Harlem Shadows* had been a critical success, he was in desperate need of finances for an extended trip. His friends rallied round and helped him raise cash: signed copies of *Harlem Shadows* went for five dollars and a farewell party was also held. To conserve funds McKay worked as a stoker on the Atlantic crossing. In London he attempted to secure a visa to Russia, but most of his ISC friends had already left, while the Communist Party of Great Britain (CPGB) refused to help because of his association with 'the troublesome' Pankhurst, instead referring him to the American Communists.

Stranded in Berlin, where he embraced the vibrant cabaret scene, he relied on a Pankhurst contact Edgar Whitehead, who was working for the Comintern, to help him get as far as Moscow. However, his presence there was resented by the American Communist delegation, who conspired to get him thrown out of the conference, even though he was there to report on matters for the Black press. He was refused official accommodation in the Lux Hotel and the only alternative he could find as the Russian winter was about to set in was a single room with an army cot in a 'dilapidated house in a sinister *pereulok*'. He rushed to buy blankets and thigh-length felt boots 'that Russian peasants wore'.[66]

A fortuitous encounter with the leading Japanese Communist Sen Katayama, who knew McKay from *The Liberator*, secured his pass in to conference. McKay found himself a celebrity among ordinary Russian people: the opening of the Fourth Congress coincided with the fifth anniversary of the Bolshevik revolution, and he recounted being tossed in the air along an entire street by jovial crowds who had never seen a Black man before.[67]

Although McKay's experiences of both the UK and US Communist movements had made him sceptical of the willingness or ability of white comrades to embrace Black people as equals, he was keen to address the conference. In Moscow, along with the Black Guyanese Communist Otto Huiswoud, McKay presented a thoughtful and nuanced speech on the position and potential of Black workers within the international labour movement, emphasising in particular the issues of racial segregation, exploitation and disenfranchisement in the US.

The two were the first Black people to discuss such issues before the Comintern, also speaking about the shameless exploitation of Black troops by both Britain and France in the First World War. McKay stated:

> My race on this occasion is honoured, not because it is different from the white race and the yellow race, but [because it] is especially a race of toilers, hewers of wood and drawers of water, that belongs to the most oppressed, exploited, and suppressed section of the working class of the world. The Third International stands for the emancipation of all the workers of the world, regardless of race or color, and this stand of the Third International is not merely on paper like the Fifteenth Amendment of the Constitution of the United States of America. It is a real thing.[68]

The Congress speech was later reported in the international press and McKay spoke at length with Leon Trotsky, Lenin's likely successor, about the issues raised.

At the end of the conference, McKay remained in Russia for another six months feted as a celebrity, visiting Red army and navy bases at Trotsky's behest, and writing articles, stories and poems for *Izvestia* and others. He also hastily shaped some of his speeches and articles into two volumes published in Russian: *Negroes in America* (1923); and *Trial by Lynching* (1925). Both books examined race relations in the US, but it took half a century for them to be published outside Russia.

In one of his final days in Russia, he stood 'for hours' on May Day on the viewing stand with Grigory Zinoviev and other Russian leaders in Petrograd's Uritsky Square under 'the flaming standards', the 'red banners of hope'. Honoured and regaled, he was invited by his Russian hosts to the People's Theatre and spent his final night at the palace of the late Grand Duke Vladimir Alexander. He wrote: 'I could not sleep. I sat down at the table … looking out on the Neva, with the gorgeous silver of the beautiful white night of Petrograd shining upon its face, and wrote until dawn. I was happy. Petrograd had pulled a poem out of me.'[69]

The years 1919 to 1922 marked four years for McKay as a member of the radical and literary left. In that time, he had used his status as a Black journalist to highlight the issues facing Black workers in the US and Europe: Cooper writes of McKay's ardent belief that 'Marxist revolution … specifically the kind demonstrated under Lenin's clear-sighted leadership seemed to offer the only resolution to the binding exploitation still experienced by the majority of black peoples the world over.'[70]

Assured of his status within the movement, McKay could have stayed in Russia or at least continued his work within Europe, yet it seems his treatment by the American delegation had made him increasingly wary of Communist motives.

He was also suffering his own crisis of identity. McKay had had the mantle of speaking for his whole race thrust upon him, with the words of *If We Must Die* proving a heavy burden to bear. His activities were being monitored by the FBI, which unbeknownst to him, had drawn up an eighteen-page document describing him as a 'well known radical' and scrutinising his relationship with the IWW, the African Blood Brotherhood and Pankhurst. The bureau claimed he was her 'confidential man'.[71]

Wary of being classed as a radical, McKay allowed himself to be gripped yet again by the vagabond spirit – to write poetry and see the world. To this end, he returned to Germany in May 1923, to Hamburg and then on to his old cabaret haunts in Berlin, where he became a familiar figure in his flamboyant, chequered suits. It was a heady time: hyperinflation had gripped the country, with the price of basics increasing beyond most people's reach; at the height of the crisis a glass of beer would cost 4 billion marks.[72] McKay found that monies his friends had cabled in marks months previously had devalued overnight. The situation had crushed former acquaintances too; he was surprised to find the former model Baroness von Freytag-Loringhoven reduced to selling newspapers on a Berlin street corner, her fortune gone. He relied heavily on the kindness and hospitality of old friends and the occasional stranger, and was able to get a bit of journalistic work, writing in *The Crisis* about his Russian experiences. In these important articles, published in December 1923 and January 1924, he emphasised that the struggles of Black people at home could be no longer divorced from the international landscape. He urged African Americans to take their grievances to the world stage and praised Marcus Garvey's organising spirit.

McKay found it impossible to survive in Germany and travelled to Paris in the autumn of 1923, where economic conditions were more favourable. However, he had begun to be plagued by fevers, headaches and unsightly pimples and was hospitalised in Paris, where he was diagnosed with syphilis. The treatment for the disease at the time, measured doses of arsenic and mercury, had dangerous side effects and he spent several gloomy months battling the disease.

After his discharge, he slotted easily into a bohemian, ex-pat lifestyle of Paris, working as an artist's model, while wealthy friends and acquaintances from *The Liberator* helped with medical bills, and with board and lodging.

The Seeds of Black Power

It is likely to have been at this point that McKay met Paulette and Jeanne Nardal.[73] The sisters, originally from Martinique, had attended the Sorbonne and were now living in Paris and running a literary salon in Clamart in Paris, from their home. Their avant garde salon played host to a cosmopolitan set of Black intellectuals who had found themselves in the City of Light. In this rarefied space, where attendees were treated to an eclectic mix of classical and modern tunes, such as Mozart, Bach and Duke Ellington (the Nardals came from a family of seven sisters who were all accomplished musicians), Caribbeans, Africans and African Americans met and exchanged ideas without interference.

McKay is said to have introduced the American writer Alain Locke to the salon.[74] While Locke in turn introduced younger writers associated with the Harlem Renaissance – Cullen, Hughes and Jean Toomer – to the Nardals. Young French writers such as Senegal's future president Léopold Sédar Senghor and Aimé Césaire from Martinique thus became acquainted with their work.

Along with Locke and Jeanne Nardal (who wrote under the pseudonym Yadhé), McKay featured in Paulette's short-lived but impactful periodical *La Revue Du Monde Noir* (*The Review of the Black World*). The publication, which ran for six months, featured, essays, poems and short stories, and promoted a wider Black consciousness.

The novelist Joseph Zobel would later award Paulette the title the 'Godmother of Négritude', as her work highlighted the importance of Black values, culture and art a decade before the movement's inception, and was instrumental in bringing its leading proponents together. (The term Négritude, a unifier of Black identity, was coined in a famous poem by Césaire, *Cahier d'un Retour au Pays Natal*, in 1939.)

McKay's very presence in the French capital had stimulated a movement.

Both Césaire and Senghor stated that McKay's later novels *Home to Harlem* and *Banjo*, which defined a rich Black transnational community and in particular his use of synchopatic rhythms and direct emotional style had huge influence on their literature and writing over the next decades. Senghor remarked: 'Claude McKay can be considered … as the veritable inventor of Négritude … not of the word … but the values of Négritude.'[75] Both these writers provided huge stimulus and influence to the later Black Power movement.

Although a muse to many, McKay was desperately poor. A good friend of the Eastmans, the journalist Louise Bryant, who had met McKay in Moscow and was now living in Paris, was of huge support. She paid his medical bills when he was hospitalised and was instrumental in clearing his debts. When McKay's weakened immune system laid him low with influenza, after he had posed in a particularly chilly artist's studio in December 1923, it was Bryant who gave him enough money to settle and write on the country's warmer Mediterranean coast.

Here he wrote some of his most important and memorable fiction – *Home to Harlem* (1928) in which a former soldier tries to rebuild his fractured life after the First World War, and *Banjo* (1929), a picaresque novel that was billed as a story without a plot and was based largely on his experiences in Marseilles in the summer of 1926.

The decaying Vieux Port of Marseilles fascinated McKay, with its intriguing cosmopolitan community. He wrote of a flotsam and jetsam of 'beachcombers, guides, procurers, prostitutes of both sexes and bistro bandits – all of motley-making Marseilles, swarming, scrambling and scraping sustenance from the bodies of ships and crews'.[76] He later worked as a docker there, among an international crew that hailed from Senegal, Morocco, the Caribbean and the US, and experienced a strong sense of community. Both *Home to Harlem* and *Banjo* were widely praised, the former winning the Harmon Gold Award for Literature in 1929. *Banjo*'s portrait of the old port of Marseilles and La Fosse (the Ditch) the red light district, which was destroyed in the Second World War, is often cited as a key reportage of the lost quarter of the city.

The novels, however, split the Black American literary community. McKay was accused of generalisations and stereotypes in his portrayal of Black life. Du Bois said that the novel nauseated him,[77] while Aubrey Bowser in the *New York Amsterdam News*, stated of *Banjo*: 'He knows he is slurring his own people to please white readers.'[78]

The harshest criticism was from Marcus Garvey who, in a full-page tirade, stated *Home to Harlem* was 'damnable libel' and '[shows] up the worst traits in our people … to hold us up to ridicule and contempt and universal prejudice'.[79]

Others argued that these critics had missed the point and praised the novel's authenticity. Langston Hughes insisted that *Home to Harlem* was the 'flower of the Negro Renaissance, even if it is no lovely lily'.[80]

The criticism stung the sensitive McKay. He launched vituperative attacks on those who deemed his work racist, decrying them as 'spineless and spiteful',[81] and the rift that opened up between him and the Black intellectuals who had criticised his novels would in many ways dent his future prospects.

An alienated McKay continued to travel. The sailors he had befriended urged him to see Morocco and he travelled there by way of Seville, spending seven months in the country and learning about the history and poetry of Antar, a medieval Black poet famed in the region.[82] The trip whetted his appetite and he planned a wider one to West Africa; however, his militant past had not escaped the attention of colonial authorities. The British refused him entry into Gibraltar and it is likely his entry to West Africa would have been blocked. McKay returned to Europe briefly and then settled in Tangier, Morocco. British intelligence continued to surveil him, hampering any further travels, and he lived a threadbare existence on the little he received from grants and friends. The side effects from the prolonged use of syphilis treatment had begun to have adverse effects on his health, and constant headaches and joint pains made securing employment difficult.

He published two books, *Gingertown* (1932), a collection of short stories, and *Banana Bottom* (1933), early in the decade. Both suffered from poor sales in the US, largely because of the Great Depression. Divorced from the world economic situation in North Africa, McKay grew increasingly embittered, blaming his critics and his own shortcomings for his work's inability to sell.

After twelve years abroad, he returned to an economically broken US in February 1934, his finances dire; and his prospects dim. The optimism of the Harlem Renaissance had been crushed by the prevailing economic reality, and the majority Black district had become associated with unemployment and dire poverty. The downturn had winnowed the budgets of Black journals such as *The Crisis* and *Opportunity* that McKay previously depended on for work, and he struggled to find employment of any kind.

Desperate, he lodged in Harlem's YMCA, later accepting work at Greycourt, a camp for the unemployed and destitute, where residents laboured for a dollar a day. Conditions were barrack-like and dire, and especially harsh for a man of McKay's talents and stature. Cooper wrote:

> It is difficult to imagine a white writer, even in the depths of the depression, with past accomplishments equal to McKay's and with similar ambitions, ability, and drive, who could not have found a publisher or, as a last resort, some kind of job on which he could have lived. Vast areas of employment and opportunity were effectively closed to McKay merely because he was a black male ...[83]

The Depression had given the American Communist party a new lease of life in Harlem, a place that proved a fertile recruiting ground. McKay viewed the party with increasing cynicism and the dictatorship that had emerged under Stalin as the antithesis of the heady days of the

Bolshevik revolution. In his later fiction he parodied the Communist party's attempts to win followers in the district. In his lost manuscript *Amiable with Big Teeth* (written around 1940–41 but discovered more than sixty years after his death), McKay brilliantly captures the machinations of the Communist party in his burlesque treatment of the Harlem intelligentsia following Italy's invasion of Abyssinia.[84]

In time McKay got work with the Federal Writers' Project (FWP) in New York and it was here that he composed much of his autobiography *A Long Way From Home* (1937). The title was derived from an African American spiritual, the opening line of which is 'Sometimes I feel like a motherless child, a long way from home' and was an accurate summation of McKay's life since he left Jamaica. The autobiography charts his travels to England, Germany, Russia, Spain and Morocco, as well as his social, political and artistic evolution. It established McKay as essentially a romantic, wandering soul, eschewing any political role, and was critically well received, despite suffering poor sales.

His reaffirmed stance as an independent poet in his autobiography left him open to sneers: Locke criticised him as 'a spiritual truant' who, by disassociating with any political party or racial movement, deserved the title 'unabashed Playboy of the Negro Renaissance', but this was grossly unfair. McKay had grown disillusioned with all the 'isms' (whether Communism, capitalism, racism, nationalism, imperialism, etc) and had always taken a spiritually independent path.[85]

McKay had not lost his touch for acuity honed at the *Dreadnought*. His highly perceptive analysis of French colonial actions in North Africa for *The New Leader* in 1939 predated writers such as Frantz Fanon in observing that colonialism imperilled both colonised and coloniser, with such reactionary policy proving a fertile breeding ground for Franco's fascist regime.[86]

At the FWP, along with other Black writers, he focused on the history of New York's Black community. His articles included several biographical sketches on notable Harlemites, such as the famous tux-wearing, top-hatted lesbian singer Gladys Bentley and Sufi Abdul Hamid, a flamboyant religious and labour leader who dressed in a bright cape, Russian long boots and turban, who had been dubbed 'Black Hitler in Harlem' by Jewish newspapers for his controversial Black employment campaign.

These sketches survive in the Schomburg Archive and are an important chronicle of life in that period. They formed the basis of McKay's non-fiction work *Harlem: Negro Metropolis* (1940), in which he portrayed the neighbourhood's distinct personality but also attempted to analyse the cycle of deprivation that these communities found themselves trapped in. He received good reviews among the Black press, who praised the book's authenticity. Zora Neale Hurston, writing in *Common Ground*, stated '[the author knows] what he is talking about. He knows what is really happening among the folks … What is more, he fixes a well-travelled eye on the situation and thus achieves proportion.'[87]

The book, however, failed to garner mainstream reviews and did not sell. This must have hit McKay hard as, in essence, it was his final roll of the dice to retrieve the fame and optimism he once had in abundance as a young editor of *The Liberator*. He was back to living in New York in a 'Greenwich Village artist's roost of the musty variety'.[88]

As time wore on, McKay struggled to publish any new poetry, or even gain employment, and he suffered from increasingly poor health, with poverty's shadow never far from the door. Deprived of grants and other writing opportunities, and sick of begging for handouts, he took on physically demanding work as a riveter at the Federal Shipyard in Newark, New Jersey, as part of the war effort. The work was too arduous; he suffered a debilitating stroke in 1943 that affected his vision and ability to walk, and it was around this time that he embraced one final 'ism', the Catholic Church.

He later moved to Chicago to take on work at the city's Friendship House, reconnecting with the writer Dorothy Day, from his *Liberator* days, and published several poems in her *Catholic Worker*, many eulogising his new found faith. Despite ill health he continually strove to get his poems published as a collection, but his name had fallen increasingly out of vogue, with more than a dozen publishers rejecting his work.[89]

In his later years he'd started to correspond with his daughter Hope, who had come to New York to study teaching; he would ask his friends and colleagues in that city to look after her. In April 1948, father and daughter were making plans to meet for the first time. A month later McKay died of heart failure in a Chicago hospital on 22 May 1948.

He would never get to meet his daughter.

'A song of mine'

It was a cruel, forgotten ending, then, for this Jamaican Rover, this so-called 'playboy of the Negro Renaissance', this lover of the bacchanal and the bohemian. But for this scribbler of sonnets, his final act, a lonely death, could not be more fitting.

In his 1922 poem *When I Have Passed Away*, McKay uncannily prophesied his fate: 'When I have passed away and am forgotten/And no one living can recall my face/When under alien sod my bones lie rotten/With not a tree or stone to mark the place;/Perchance some pensive youth, with passion burning/For olden verse that smacks of love and wine, The musty pages of old volumes turning,/May light upon a little song of mine.'[90]

He wrote to his friend Harold Jackman that he was pleased with what he called his 'vagabond soul', that he was an outlaw without allegiance to any nation.[91]

His writing, inspired by his nomadism, provided a rare Black perspective of the time, and traversed continents – the Americas, Europe and Africa – at a period when the course of history was riven by the seismic events of the First World War, and when the Soviet Union was vaunted as a beacon of hope in terms of equality for all. As such, McKay's work stands as an invaluable historical record, especially when much of this material is absent in the archives. His propensity for travel provided breadth – he not only witnessed America's Red Summer; he observed and chronicled the race riots of 1919–20 Britain and was one of the first Black people to address the Comintern in Moscow.

His fiction and sketches documenting Harlem of that period, the clubs and bars of Weimar Germany and the old port of Marseille offered unparalleled insights into these multicultural communities. His writing on race issues and colonialism rivalled Fanon in its perceptiveness and fostered a new generation of radical thinkers through Négritude, a movement that would further inspire Black Power.

In truth, his 'song' very much lived on.

McKay's path would be emulated by others. Twelve years after he made his first trip to the US, another Black writer from the Caribbean, this time from Trinidad, would follow in his footsteps. The journalist who called himself George Padmore would find Communism's appeal, with its promise of Black liberation, equally alluring. Like McKay, he would stand under the Soviet Union's 'red banners of hope', except this time in Moscow with Stalin. And like McKay, he would become increasingly disillusioned with the Communist cause.

However, in contrast to the Jamaican poet, Padmore would relish his status as a political force, harnessing the historic convulsions taking place around him as another global conflict loomed. A passionate and prolific scribe, Padmore consistently argued for an end to discriminatory practices and better rights for Britain's colonies, sparking a nascent anti-colonial movement that would eventually lead to the toppling of empires and a transformation of the global order.

4

OUR MAN IN AFRICA

GEORGE PADMORE, journalist and freedom fighter (*The Negro Worker*, 1931–33; the IASB publications, 1937–38; *The New Leader* and *Controversy*, 1936–46; London interwar correspondent for *The Crisis, The Chicago Defender* and *Pittsburgh Courier*)

In the autumn of 1931, the building known as No. 8 Rothesoodstrasse, in a decaying working-class port district of Hamburg, was a hive of frenetic activity. Here the man known as George Padmore was busy preparing the editorial for the Communist organ *The Negro Worker*, the newspaper for the International Trade Union Committee of Negro Workers (ITUCNW). This radical waterfront was home to the offices of the labour unions of seamen and harbour workers, and the skeletal shacks that lined the Elbe sheltered many secrets. The Great Depression, which was entering its third year, had decimated the shipping industry, and the workers on these docks had seen their wages and living standards plummet. It was in these very buildings that they would organise a fightback against management's unfair practices.

When Padmore first arrived at the dock, to take over from the African American Communist trade union organiser James W. Ford, a series of strikes had convulsed the area. The chaos irked him: he complained that the ITUCNW office was 'a total mess' after the premises had been raided by police searching for militant ringleaders.[1]

Still this 'seamy waterfront district under cover of a seamen's club' suited the nature of his important yet clandestine work. Padmore's *Negro Worker* was an attempt to unite workers across the Black Atlantic in a fight for better rights and conditions. Its arresting cover image of a Black man breaking free of bondage across a Pan-African map of the US, the Caribbean and Africa left readers in no doubt of its content, and its strident tone led to it being banned in St Vincent, Grenada, Trinidad and Nigeria in 1932.[2] At the Hamburg docks, bulk copies would be stacked on ships under the cover of darkness; while individual sailors would bind their single issues tightly into Bibles to avoid police scrutiny.

For Padmore – who had been born Malcolm Ivan Meredith Nurse in Arouca, Trinidad, on 28 June 1903, to a middle-class family – the years in Hamburg marked a point when his star was on the ascendant. His father, James Hubert Alfonso Nurse, was a well-respected headmaster and renowned botanist in Trinidad.[3] Nurse senior had headed the Arouca branch of the Pan-African Association and was a close colleague of Henry Sylvester Williams, who had organised the first Pan-African conference in London in 1900. Consequently, the young Nurse/Padmore was well versed in the politics and pride of the movement.

He adopted the *nom de guerre* George Padmore while a student in the US, worried that his increasing involvement in radical politics at Fisk University in Nashville, Tennessee, and at Howard University in Washington, DC, would adversely affect his family. At the latter university, he enrolled in the Communist Party USA in 1927 at the age of 24. Like McKay, years earlier, whose trajectory he'd followed assiduously, he recognised the CPUSA was the only political body fighting for racial equality and the party's revival of the American Negro Labour Congress (ANLC) held a distinct attraction for young Black people. He would go on to explain the use of his adopted name to his Trinidadian friend Dudley Cobham: 'You see, all revolutionaries are compelled to adopt false names to hide their identity from the Party.'[4]

Padmore initially came to the US in 1924 to study medicine at Fisk as a way of improving his social and economic prospects in Trinidad, and to provide for his young family. A brief stint as the shipping news correspondent on the *Trinidad Guardian* before coming to the States had made him keenly aware of the racial inequalities in the colonial society he left behind. His editor at the paper, Edward J. Partridge, was a divisive figure who often admonished the majority Black staff. Padmore later wrote that he was 'one of the most arrogant agents of British Imperialism I have ever encountered. I held him in utter contempt.'[5]

He had married his neighbour Julia Semper, the daughter of a senior police officer in Trinidad, on 10 September 1924 and she was pregnant with their daughter Blyden (named after the 'father of Pan-Africanism' Edward Blyden at Padmore's insistence), their first and only child, when he left for the US mere weeks later.[6] However, he did not enrol at Fisk until autumn 1925, opting to settle in Harlem at 124, West 135th Street, and study sociology at Columbia University. The progressive environment of 1920s Harlem, where Black cultural and political life was coming to the fore, stood in stark contrast to the straitened, racial hierarchical society of Trinidad he had left behind, and Padmore thrived in a place where Black ideals were valued and celebrated.

At Fisk, student strikes were sweeping the campus, objecting to the conservatism and the 'white philanthropic control present at a number of colleges'.[7] The president, Fayette Mackenzie, had restricted student activities and 'the Ku Klux Klan had expressed concern about agitators, communists and "new Negroes"'.[8] It was a volatile time to be a student in Tennessee. Padmore became active at Fisk, dropping medicine in pursuit of law and becoming a popular debater, representing the university at several conferences. He also continued to pursue journalism by writing for the *Fisk Herald*, the student newspaper. In the end, he did not take a Fisk degree and instead opted to study law at Howard University in Washington after briefly enrolling at New York University.

At Howard, he continued to agitate for students' rights. His tutor, Dr Ralph Bunche, noted the protest Padmore had organised with his friend Cyril Ollivierre (president of the campus Garvey club) against a visit to the university by the British ambassador Sir Esme Howard, whom he attacked not only as an imperialist (in 'fluent, ringing rhetoric'[9]) but also for securing the deportation of Marcus Garvey to his native Jamaica. Padmore also attempted to form a Pan-African students' organisation with the Nigerian student (and future president of Nigeria) Nnamdi Azikiwe. The two would stay in touch: Padmore later wrote for the newspaper group that Azikiwe established, which would go on to purchase Ali's *Comet*.

In his appearance and his work, Padmore was a perfectionist: a 'West Indian of the old school. Always everything in order,' his boyhood friend Cyril Lionel Robert James (known as C.L.R. James) later wrote.[10] The Pan-African activist Ras Makonnen would later summarise Padmore's appearance in his inimitable style: '[He was] spic and span like a senator, and his shoes shone so you could see your face in them; his trouser creases could shave you.'[11]

Padmore had a youthful ambition to change the world, and his impressive debating skills and journalistic talent were a boon to the Communist Party. He quickly rose through the ranks, organising a rent strike in Harlem and writing for left-wing newspapers such as *Labour Unity* and the *Negro Champion* (which became the weekly *Liberator* late in 1929).

His journalism often assumed rallying cries, highlighting imperialism's role in the exploitation of Black people and urging action. In June 1928, his words echoed those of Ali's and McKay's years earlier when he wrote in the *Negro Champion*, a paper where he would briefly be the assistant editor: 'We have seen our brothers massacred on foreign battlefields in defence of the very imperialist social order that today crushes them to earth ... Let us join the masses of the rising colonial peoples and militant class-conscious workers to struggle for the establishment of a free and equitable world order.'[12]

A True Political Animal

Politics became Padmore's sole energising focus and his involvement with the Communist Party became a sticking point with his wife, who had joined him in the US in 1926 (leaving their child with grandparents). According to his biographer James Hooker, 'They had often quarrelled about his political activities, with Julia Nurse acknowledging, "New York University was my undoing".'[13]

The stress led to separation; Padmore maintained contact with Julia and his in-laws for several years after the marriage broke down, and provided for his wife and daughter in his will. What is indisputable is that his political ambitions had now subsumed him: the Malcolm Nurse who had gone to the States to provide for his wife and child had ceased to exist; in his place was George Padmore, a man who was determined to make the world a better place. Much later, the novelist Peter Abrahams would describe Padmore as 'a true political animal', showing undue devotion to the cause.[14]

Opportunity arose during the Communist Party leadership campaign for William Z. Foster. Padmore impressed and he was sent along with Ford to the Second Congress of the League Against Imperialism (LAI) in Frankfurt in 1928. Here he met Garan Kouyaté of the French Sudan and Johnstone Kenyatta of Kenya; these encounters with men who had left their homes and families to assert themselves on the world stage were significant, according to the author Carol Posgrove, because it was here that Padmore 'glimpsed the potential power of the African diaspora'.[15] He also met James Maxton, head of the Independent Labour Party, who would become a friend and advocate of Padmore later in the decade when he was in London.

Hooker noted that Padmore was now in the 'sphere of international communist activity' and on the 'threshold of a great career'.[16] In December 1929, Foster gave Padmore two one-way tickets to Moscow so he could accompany him at conference to report on trade union activities among Black workers in the US. (One of these tickets was for Julia but she refused to go.) It is not known if Padmore was aware that he would not be granted re-entry to the States after his visit, but he was never able to return. The night before he was due to leave his pocket was picked, including the tickets, but he remained determined to go to Moscow, borrowing a coat and hat from Ollivierre and securing passage on a ship with $3 he had cadged from friends.

The fact that he arrived in Moscow as the citadels of capitalism were crumbling (the Wall Street Crash happened in the autumn of that year) was significant, as Communism was seen as providing a viable alternative to the old order. Black political organisers such as Ford, Harry Haywood and McKay had preceded him, but Padmore noted the stares he received at a May Day rally in Red Square that was attended by Stalin. 'He was given a place on a reviewing stand ... and noticed with amusement the puzzled glances cast his way by public observers.'[17] The exotic and tokenistic image of a Black man in Soviet Russia notwithstanding,

Padmore earned his seat at the table during a period of intense activity for the party. He attended his first meeting in Moscow on 8 January 1930 and impressed the delegates there, rising through the ranks to head the Negro Bureau of the Red International of Labour Unions and commanding a significant budget.[18]

Much of the organisation's focus was centred on building up trade union support in South Africa, and Padmore was charged with this initiative as well as organising 'the first international conference of Negro workers' to be held in Hamburg from 7 to 9 July 1930. Despite a number of resolutions being passed, including a demand for 'equal pay regardless of race, nationality and sex', the success of the Hamburg conference was limited.[19] The American delegation was delayed because of 'the Jim Crow practices on steamships' and Padmore noted, '[it was] conducted poorly with unsatisfactory representation'.[20]

Meanwhile, Padmore's writing showed no signs of slowing: in Moscow, he wrote six pamphlets for the ITUCNW, and also found time to contribute to the *Moscow Daily News* and lecture at the University of Toilers of the East (KUTV), where he met like-minded colleagues from across the colonial world, including South Africans Moses Kotane and Albert Nzula. His seminal work *The Life and Struggles of Negro Toilers* was published in 1931. This slim 126-page volume featured graphic case studies, in which he noted, like Edwards half a century earlier, the impoverished social and economic conditions of West Indian workers in the British colonies and how this was linked to the 'yoke of imperialism'. In the final chapter, he urged practical steps for workers to conduct a common class struggle. Unsurprisingly, the book was banned in the colonies, but a well-thumbed copy would find its way into the hands of a young Guyanese, George Thomas Griffiths, (who would in time change his name to Ras Makonnen; his and Padmore's paths would cross later in the decade).

Padmore's strident writing aside, his comrades noted that he was self-contained and uncommunicative during his time in Russia. The Jewish Communist Y Berger related: '[Padmore] was not very talkative and quite reserved. He avoided entering any open conflicts.'[21]

In early 1931, Padmore was in Vienna for a brief time (his biographer Hooker has it as 1930 but historians, including Leslie James, have disputed this). Hooker stated that Padmore was living in a small flat in the Second District with an Austrian comrade and her two children and was 'not happy with his circumstances'. It is possible that this comrade was a woman called Frieda Schiff but apart from letters she wrote on Padmore's behalf, little remains of her in the archive. Berger stated that Padmore was 'isolated' in Vienna as his German was 'extremely inadequate' at the time.[22]

Padmore's moment came when he was asked to replace Ford, who had been stationed in Hamburg and was in charge of distributing ITUCNW propaganda, including *The Negro Worker*. Determined to make his mark, Padmore set about producing a professional monthly bulletin, which was sold for 5c/2p.[23]

The organisational and networking skills that he had honed during the two years in Moscow came to the fore, and he scrupulously built on Ford's contacts, reaching out to prominent trade union leaders, including Arnold Ward of London's Negro Welfare Association; Sierra Leonian I.T.A. (Isaac Theophilus Akunna) Wallace-Johnson and Frank Macauley of Nigeria. By the end of 1932, he had established trade union committees in Cameroon, Guadeloupe, Haiti, Senegal, Liberia, St Lucia and Madagascar, and in less than fourteen months, he had quadrupled *The Negro Worker*'s circulation from approximately one thousand to four thousand. In Africa, he also encouraged the establishment of local presses and the nascent labour movement. James would later write of the ideology Padmore helped sustain: 'Tens of thousands of black workers in various parts of the world received their first political education from the paper [Padmore] edited ...'[24]

James exaggerated the paper's reach: the circulation of *The Negro Worker* never went above 4,000 colonially based supporters but this was still significant considering that it was banned in some territories. Maxton, now head of the Independent Labour Party, fought the ban on the House of Commons floor but was unsuccessful in getting it rescinded.[25]

One of the most prominent causes for Padmore's *Negro Worker* was the international campaign to free the Scottsboro boys. On 25 March 1931, authorities in Paint Rock, Alabama, arrested nine Black youths after receiving reports of an altercation on a train. Two white women, Ruby

Bates and Victoria Price, accused the youths, ranging in ages from 13 to 20, of rape. A couple of weeks later, after four rushed separate trials, eight of the defendants were found guilty and sentenced to death. The trial of the ninth defendant, 13-year-old Roy Wright, ended in mistrial as jurors could not agree on whether the death sentence was appropriate for someone so young.

The CPUSA came to the defence of the young men, calling for an end to their 'legal lynching' and publishing an article in *The Daily Worker* in the boys' defence.

The injustice of the trial became a global cause célèbre. Mass protests were sparked in major US cities following the verdicts and, after the execution dates were announced on 10 July 1931, the international labour community lent its considerable weight to the campaign to free the boys. Letters and telegrams from Europe and Moscow deluged the White House and the Alabama authorities. The historians James Miller, Susan Pennybacker and Eve Rosenhaft, in their analysis of the International Campaign to Free the Scottsboro Boys, have identified Padmore and German activist Wilhelm Münzenberg as the early campaign's most important international agents.[26]

Padmore consistently amplified the boys' plight. In April 1932 he wrote 'An Appeal – the Scottsboro Boys Shall Not be Murdered'; while the following month he published a letter from one of the Scottsboro defendants, 'Scottsboro Boys Appeal from Death Cells to Toilers of the World', which stated that the boys believed they had been 'framed up on rape charges'.

As the young men languished in death cells, the international campaign gathered pace. (They would eventually experience three stays of execution.) A speaking tour of Europe by Ada Wright, the mother of two of the boys, and Louis Engdahl, general secretary of the International Labor Defense, began in Hamburg in May 1932, with Padmore present at the first address.[27]

The tour captured the public imagination: here was a mother who had never been out of Tennessee, travelling thousands of miles to save her children from the electric chair. When Wright was arrested in Charleroi, Belgium, thousands of women marched with her in solidarity to the police station. Saklatvala, George Lansbury and Ward were prominent

British voices in the campaign, with the latter communicating with Padmore regularly.

The case and its repercussions eventually spanned four decades, outliving its early champions. Price and Bates, who feared charges of vagrancy and illegal sexual activity, were found to have concocted the allegations of rape. Four of the boys were released in 1937; one was paroled in 1943 and another in 1946, while two were released in 1944. A parole violation meant that Clarence Norris, the last of the Scottsboro Boys, was officially pardoned and freed in 1976. Throughout his life, Padmore ensured that this grave miscarriage of justice was never out of the public eye.

Occasionally there were missteps. Padmore could be caustic about those he considered not fully attuned to the needs of his race. In 1933, he denounced the founder of the League of Coloured Peoples (LCP), Harold Moody, as a 'typical "Uncle Tom", whose coat strings are so tied up with the Colonial Office that he is out to have every self-respecting Negro kow-towing before his arrogant white imperialist masters'.[28] The criticism of Moody for negotiating with white parliamentarians was unfair. Moody was a Christian and deplored the atheist sensibilities of Communism. His belief was 'to do something for the race', but unlike Padmore he believed in working within the confines of the system rather than against it.[29]

Padmore employed the same lacerating prose on Marcus Garvey, calling him a 'Negro bourgeois leader' and a demagogue. Garvey's embrace of capitalism embodied in the Black Star Line was anathema to Padmore. 'The Negro masses of the West Indies must not forget the bitter lesson of disillusionment they experienced at the hands of the arch misleader Garvey,' he wrote.[30]

Support for *The Negro Worker* dwindled because of Padmore's continuous harsh criticism of Garvey. William Brown, an agent in Liverpool, reported the 'steady loss of Jamaican support for their movement such that Brown could not even give the bulletin away'.[31]

Still Padmore's individual lustre remained undimmed and he was courted as a voice of a generation. He was sought out by the heiress Nancy Cunard, who was active in the civil rights movement in the United States, for her anthology *Negro*, which included contributions from Langston Hughes and Zora Neale Hurston. Following their first meeting at a Montparnasse café in autumn 1932, the two struck up a lifelong friendship. 'We sat over the meal talking, talking as if we knew each other already – which in a sense we did,' said Cunard.[32] The heiress, whose appearance was described by her friend Anthony Hobson as 'bizarrely evocative of the Twenties, with her tall thin figure, waistless dress, bandeau and long string of beads' and African ivory bracelets whose 'rhythmic clash' would punctuate conversation, became a staunch ally, raising money for the Scottsboro Boys campaign in the UK.[33]

'All the devils in hell'

Padmore's time on Hamburg's dockside was running out. On 30 January 1933, Adolf Hitler became chancellor of Germany. Hitler's Nazi Party persecuted many minority groups, as well as Jewish people, including Roma, Black people, homosexuals and Communists. The double jeopardy of being both Black and a Communist would eventually make Padmore's position untenable.

Padmore was also concerned that the Communist Party was not taking his anti-colonial work seriously.[34] The International Seamen and Harbour Workers' Union, an ally of the ITUCNW, refused to honour its commitment to set up unions in Africa. Padmore intuited a lack of awareness of the risks supporters of the movement were taking in Africa and the Caribbean in receiving censored materials such as *The Negro Worker*. So when the police aided and abetted by Nazi stormtroopers raided the offices of *The Negro Worker* a fortnight after Hitler came to power, Padmore was already disillusioned with the Communist cause.

At the same time as the offices were raided, Padmore was arrested at Schiff's apartment in Altona, Hamburg, in an early morning raid; the police confiscated his journalism notes and his typewriter. Padmore was taken into custody and interrogated for twelve days, although no account of his arrest exists. According to Cunard, in whom he later confided, it had been 'ghastly and extremely dangerous'.[35]

Confusion about his identity protected him. The British consulate informed the Foreign Office that Nurse was a potential troublemaker 'who appears to have been operating in Berlin as a journalist', unaware that Padmore was an alias of Nurse. In fact, the British believed that 'Nurse' could furnish them with information about the notorious Black revolutionary Padmore.[36]

Padmore left Hamburg on SS *Bury* for Grimsby on 22 February 1933. He was targeted by the British security services on his arrival, stating in a letter he wrote after his arrest: 'everything I owned was searched, even my a ...'[37]

Compared to some of his colleagues, Padmore's treatment was mild. He left Germany five days before the Reichstag fire, an arson attack on the German parliament building, which Hitler used as a pretext to pursue a ruthless vendetta against the Communist Party. Many of those who staffed the party's Hamburg offices were forced to flee. A close friend of Padmore's, Edgar André, a well-liked labour leader, was arrested just weeks after Padmore and brutally tortured. At his show trial, on 4 May 1936, he was sentenced to death despite insufficient evidence, and beheaded in Hamburg on 5 November 1936. Padmore dedicated his third book, *Africa and World Peace*, to André, inscribing it to 'my teacher who fell in the struggle'.[38] Others such as Münzenberg, a staunch critic of the Nazis, would meet a grisly end in Vichy France. His partially decomposed corpse was found in woods near Montagne in mysterious circumstances in October 1940. Although the police assumed that he had taken his own life, one theory was that he was murdered by Gestapo agents.

Padmore stayed just one day in England, before heading to Paris, arriving early in March 1933.[39] The trauma of the arrest and deportation notwithstanding, Europe's turmoil had invested him with a new sense of urgency and he fired off numerous letters, stating there had been 'temporary setbacks' but, 'We are marching forward and not all the devils in hell will stop us.'[40]

However, these 'devils' would continue to plague an embattled Padmore, who now found the Comintern was making his life difficult. He put out three more issues of *The Negro Worker* from Paris in 1933. The April–May issue led with the article 'Fascist Terror against Negroes in Germany', in which he warned prophetically that the Nazis were 'preaching race hatred and advocating lynch law'. His 'Au-Revoir' was published in the August–September issue, stating lack of funds as the reason for closing the journal.[41]

The truth was that Padmore's *Negro Worker* was a victim of Stalin's geopolitical play. With Nazism on the rise, the Soviet Union had turned towards France as a potential ally and Padmore was asked to soften his criticism of imperial powers, including Britain and the US. This was a devastating blow, and yet further evidence to Padmore of the Communist Party being insincere in its anti-colonial work. He wrote to Ollivierre: '[…] our so-called friends have let us down, but today Stalin has given up the idea of support to those who are still under the yoke, in order to win capitalist support'.[42]

Padmore reconnected with Garan Kouyaté, rooming with him in Paris, and began making plans for a *Negro World* unity congress. Kouyaté had been blacklisted by the Communist Party in October 1933 and Padmore's association with him speeded up his own expulsion: in January of the following year he was expelled from the party.

Padmore's exit triggered a sustained smear campaign against him in the American Communist press by his former comrades and mentors. In June 1934, a revived *Negro Worker*, which was now being published from Copenhagen, under the editorship of Charles Woodson, labelled Padmore 'an arch betrayer of the Negro liberation'.[43]

The attacks were vicious and took their toll. A wounded Padmore retreated to Cunard's summerhouse in Réanville, Normandy, in the summer of 1934 and began to write *How Britain Rules Africa*. Cunard, who typed the manuscript, recalled that the criticism made 'the deepest impression on him possible'.[44]

He wrote to Ollivierre, sharing his thoughts on a much-needed break from political life after devoting five years to the Communist cause in the hope of Black liberation: 'It is time that I take a little holiday from this turbulent political life (a la Marcus Garvey) & look up my dear Julie & my child.'[45]

In 1935 Padmore settled permanently in London, resuming his friendship with James. The move from France was never fully explained, but he had been shuttling back and forth between the two countries. It is possible that he was seeking a British publisher for his work (with James' help) or that London was a better base to develop his journalism. He attributed his itinerant lifestyle to the fact that people like him were used to changing countries more often than their shoes.

James was already established in the capital, albeit in shoebox digs off Grays Inn Road, where he convened a weekly group of like-minded Trotskyite intellectuals. He had moved to London from Nelson, Lancashire, where he'd lived with the cricketer Learie Constantine; Constantine had solicited James' help from Trinidad with his autobiography *Cricket and I*. James had experienced publishing success as a short story writer in Trinidad and his first non-fiction work, *The Life of Captain Cipriani: An Account of British Government in the West Indies*, was published by a small, independent northern press in 1932. An abridged version of that work, *The Case for West Indian Self Government*, was published by Leonard and Virginia Woolf's Hogarth press in 1933.

James recalled in his memoirs that he'd seen Padmore speak in Grays Inn Road in 1932, where he was vaunted as 'a great Communist'. The next time he saw Padmore was three years later in London when he knocked on the door of James' flat in Grays Inn Road. His friend's dishevelled appearance and the haunted look in his eyes told him 'something was up'. He intimated that Padmore looked like he had been roughed up: 'Where these tough men came from, I don't know. George was not shaken at all by them, but he was a little disturbed that day.'[46]

Padmore said to James when he arrived: 'I have left those people, you know.' James was only later to understand what a brave decision it had been for his friend to refuse to toe the party line. As Padmore later explained: 'I had stayed there because there was a means of doing work for the black emancipation and there was no other place that I could think of.'[47]

What is apparent is that Padmore was in great physical danger after severing his links from the Comintern. His friend Nzula had warned him just before his expulsion not to visit Moscow, stressing in a cable smuggled out through Latvia, 'George for God's sake, don't come.'[48] Nzula, a well-known alcoholic, would loudly voice his disenchantment with Stalinism when drunk and had been scolded before a disciplinary committee for his Trotskyite ideals. Days after cabling Padmore, Nzula died in mysterious circumstances on 14 January 1934. The official version was that he had been on a vodka binge, collapsed on a snowbank and died of pneumonia. According to James, Nzula met his demise after he was forcibly removed from a meeting by two secret service agents and never seen again.[49]

Life was not easy in London: Hooker has Padmore renting rooms on Vauxhall Bridge Road with Kenyatta and 'a number of other destitute West Indians',[50] before moving to Guilford Street just off Russell Square. Padmore was earning a little income from teaching, but the Sri Lankan statesman T.B. Subasinghe, his student at that time, recalled 'Padmore went through very difficult times in that period' and 'earned very small sums of money'.[51]

Padmore lost no time in connecting with Ladipo Solanke's West African Students' Union (WASU), one of two prominent Black organisations in the capital, the other being Moody's LCP. WASU had been established nearly a decade earlier with the help of Amy Ashwood Garvey, Garvey's first wife, who had been keen to establish a name for herself separate from her famous husband.[52] Her influence and later presence among the 1930s activist-journalists directly linked their work to that of Ali. Ashwood Garvey had been so inspired by Ali's campaigning journalism, she had even produced a clone of the *Review* in the US, the *West Indian Times and American Review*.[53]

The young people he met at WASU impressed Padmore. He stated: 'I now feel that despite all our difficulties and the terrible plight of our fatherland, there is a future for Africa. The youth of today are waking up.'[54]

His impetuous and caustic nature was again on show when he got involved in the bitter dispute between Moody and Solanke, who were in a race to establish a colonial student hostel in the capital. Solanke had conceived the idea of a hostel and approached the Colonial Office for support. However, in his absence, Hanns Vischer's Colonial Office had approached Moody about setting up a hostel, Aggrey House. Solanke was furious at this outmanoeuvre by 'British imperialists' and accused Moody of being 'a colonial stooge'.[55]

Padmore jumped feet first into the row, decrying the CO's attempt 'to set up a little Jim Crow hostel', calling for its boycott, and endorsing the WASU hostel Africa House.[56] After peace talks, both hostels were established in the capital, Africa House in 1933 and Aggrey House a year later. Solanke had not been wrong about Aggrey House, it was very much an attempt by the CO to surveil Black groups. Vischer commented much later on the hostel's ability to quell what was seen as turbulent, anti-colonial feeling among the Black population. He stated: 'I have often seen Kenyatta Johnson there ... meek and mild and very happy and I am sure that the influence of Aggrey House on him and other wild lads from Africa ... cannot be overestimated.'[57]

'Seething like an African pot'

The capital would soon become a place for exiles, as Europe's turbulent politics roiled the continent. Makonnen later recalled: 'We were operating in the midst of radicalism unmatched in Europe, but it was a gay period, a period of purposefulness ... Britain was really in a ferment – seething in fact like an African pot.'[58]

In February 1935, some 300,000 heavily armed Italian troops massed on the banks of the Mareb River on the Eritrean border with Abyssinia (Ethiopia);[59] a similar military build-up occurred on the country's Italian–Somalian border. Motivated by revenge – Italy had been humiliated in the first Italo-Abyssinia War (1889–96), where it had failed to conquer the country – the Italian fascist leader Benito Mussolini sold this act of aggression to the Italian people as 'a civilising mission', and a return to the glory days of the Roman Empire. Mussolini's actions were viewed by the rest of the world with alarm, with African, Caribbean and African American communities united in condemning Italy's aggressive actions.[60]

Padmore had started writing for the NAACP's *The Crisis*: one of the first articles he wrote in May 1935 was on the Ethiopian situation and the French foreign minister Pierre Laval essentially giving Mussolini 'a free hand to grab as much of Ethiopia as he can'.[61] Other papers he wrote for included *The Chicago Defender* and the Baltimore *Afro-American*. However, the pay he earned from this journalism was intermittent, infrequent and often not forthcoming. He complained to his old friend Ollivierre: 'What rogues the black bourgeoise.'[62]

Alarmed by news of an impending invasion, James and Ashwood Garvey set up the International African Friends of Ethiopia (IAFE) in July 1935 to increase awareness and support for the Ethiopian cause.

Key members included Ashwood Garvey's partner the musician Samuel Manning; the Guyanese doctor Peter Milliard; the Barbadian Chris Braithwaite, the founder of the Colonial Seamen's Association; Kenyatta; and later Padmore and Makonnen. At the IAFE's first public meeting on 28 July in Farringdon Hall, the group vowed 'to assist by all means in their power ... the political independence of Ethiopia'.[63]

The group would convene in the lively and warm atmosphere of Ashwood Garvey's International Afro Restaurant beneath her residence at 62 Oxford Street. Here writers, artists and students would gather to eat home-made Caribbean food and listen to Manning's records. Regulars included Una Marson and Oxford history student Eric Williams, who would become the first prime minister of Trinidad and Tobago. Ashwood Garvey's restaurant proved so popular that she opened the Florence Mills Social Parlour, a restaurant and nightclub near Carnaby Street. These two venues became the main organising hubs for the IAFE. Other prominent supporters included McKay's old editor Sylvia Pankhurst, who opened up her home in Woodford Green, Essex, to campaigners.[64] In fact, Mussolini's aggression had the effect of galvanising the Black diaspora, with the LCP and WASU, both avowedly anti-Communist, joining forces with the IAFE.

A month after its inception, the IAFE organised an open-air meeting in Trafalgar Square on 25 August 1935, the first of a number of such meetings held in cities up and down the country. To a large crowd, Ashwood Garvey declared: 'No race has been so noble in forgiving, but now the hour has struck for our complete emancipation,' adding, 'You have talked of "the White Man's Burden" ... now we are standing between you and your fascism.' Her reference to Kipling's infamous defence of Empire had a purpose: to align the fight against fascism with that of anti-colonial resistance. An impressed Makonnen, who was passing through London on his way to study in Denmark, joined the group on the spot.[65] It was Makonnen who convinced Padmore to join the IAFE; he explained in his memoir that Padmore had only relatively recently broken with the Communists, and still firmly held to his 'old anti-chief and anti-emperor position'.[66]

Makonnen and Padmore roomed together in Calthorpe Street, visited the British Museum and swotted up on Ethiopian history, using their knowledge to fulminate on the crisis as stepladder orators in Hyde Park.[67] Makonnen used the race course tipster Prince Monolulu (Peter McKay), a charismatic character who dressed in a feathered headdress and colourful clothes (he styled himself as an Abyssinian chief but in reality was from St Croix in the Danish West Indies) as a warm-up act, before Padmore and Makonnen spoke on the crisis. The two would also distribute Pankhurst's *New Times and Ethiopia News*. Makonnen would recall that 'after you'd been slugging it out for two or three hours at Hyde Park [you could go to Florence Mills] … and get a lovely meal, dance and enjoy yourself', summarising the rich social and political milieu in the capital at the time.[68]

The LCP journal *The Keys* and WASU's journal regularly highlighted the crisis, and the group's objections to Italy's subsequent invasion in October 1935 were widely reported in the mainstream press.

The use of heavy artillery, aerial bombardment and mustard gas overwhelmed the Ethiopian forces in the spring of 1936. Hundreds of thousands of civilians lost their lives in the war, appalling the Black world, while emperor Haile Selassie was forced to flee Ethiopia on 2 May 1936.

Elevated Profiles

Both James and Padmore found their prolific activism elevated their profiles, particularly among the British left. The two found a home for their journalism in Fenner Brockway's *New Leader*. In March 1936 James' play *Toussaint L'Ouverture: The Story of the Only Successful Slave Revolt in History* was staged for two nights in the Westminster Theatre in London's West End, with Paul Robeson in the title role. James would go on to further publishing success: *Minty Alley* was published by Secker and Warburg in 1936; while his study of the Bolshevik revolution and the decline of the Communist International, *World Revolution*, hit the shelves the next year, followed by the classic *The Black Jacobins* in 1938.

Padmore struggled to find a publisher for *How Britain Rules Africa*, which eventually came out in 1936. In it he made a connection between imperialist 'oppression and exploitation' and that of Nazism and fascism, writing that 'the fight against fascism cannot be separated from the right of all colonial peoples and subject races to Self-Determination'.[69] He stated in his conclusion: 'The future belongs to the oppressed. The future of Africa belongs to the Blacks, for they are the most oppressed of the Earth.' A reviewer for the *Economist* warned that the book 'may mark the turn of the tide' and that the establishment should not ignore it.[70]

Africa and World Peace followed in 1937, where Padmore asserted that capitalist competition for scarce resources was at the heart of all wars and, in a nod to his years in the Comintern, argued that only by bringing down capitalism through world revolution could all wars be ended. As the world churned around him, Padmore hoped this would signal the start of a revolution that would offer parity for all. He noted that the Spanish Civil War, which began in 1936, had mobilised the international Left to fight the fascist forces of Spain, Germany and Italy in a way that they hadn't for the Ethiopian cause.

The IAFE's campaign failed to achieve its stated aim of preventing Italy's war with Ethiopia, but it did illustrate what a consolidated Black pressure group could do. Through its publications, whether pamphlets, bulletins or manifestos; speeches; plays and soap-box oratory, and even while socialising in their Soho haunts, this group of determined individuals disseminated and constantly recycled the message that a liberated Africa, free of colonial repression, was truly possible.

Inspired, Padmore set up the International African Service Bureau (IASB) in 1937 from small offices at 94 Grays Inn Road (the office relocated to 12a Westbourne Grove, Notting Hill, around 1938). Under his remit the group's activism broadened to encompass anti-colonial struggles in India, Africa and China. As well as the IAFE's original executive, a number of prominent WASU members joined the group. Others in its orbit included the St Lucian economist W. Arthur Lewis, who edited *The Keys* in the interwar years.

An important addition to the Bureau was Wallace-Johnson, who had established himself as a political activist and journalist in the Gold Coast, but an article he wrote for the *African Morning Post* in 1936 condemning the Pope for blessing Mussolini's troops, 'Has the African a God?', was deemed seditious by the authorities. He was tried, convicted and fined £50. He travelled to London in May 1937 to appeal against the judgement and hooked up with his old friend Padmore, but his presence led to the IASB being monitored constantly by the British authorities.[71]

Wallace-Johnson edited two ill-fated newsletters for the group, *Africa and the World* (June–July 1937) and *The African Sentinel* (October–November 1937); both bulletins were proscribed by the colonial authorities and showed their unwillingness to accept even mild dissent. A frustrated and penniless Wallace-Johnson, who had taken to living in the IASB's London offices over the winter months, returned to Sierra Leone in April 1938 with 2,000 copies of the *Sentinel* on his person. They were promptly seized by customs agents and never distributed.

Undeterred, Padmore's IASB pressed forward, with James editing a new monthly journal *International African Opinion* (*IAO*). It launched in July 1938, with the motto across its front declaring 'Educate–co-operate–emancipate: Neutral in nothing affecting the African peoples'. The IASB stated its newest journal's intent to 'become the mouthpiece of black workers and peasants, and those intellectuals who see the necessity of making the cause of the masses their own'.[72]

One of the organisation's prominent campaigns centred on Trinidad's labour unrest, which started in the oilfields but spread to the sugar belt and towns. Padmore wrote in *Controversy*, the ILP monthly journal: 'Thousands of East Indian agricultural labourers on the great sugar plantations refused to work. Motor transport in many parts of the country had to stop for want of petrol; ships arriving in the harbour of Port of Spain were unable to discharge their cargoes. The entire economic life of the country was at a standstill.'[73]

Strikes later spread to Barbados, Jamaica and Guyana, and often descended into violence; a policeman was burnt alive and several strikers lost their lives. The IASB's campaign trod a well-worn path. Its Trinidad Defence Committee called a rally for Sunday, 9 August 1937 in Trafalgar Square and Padmore lobbied sympathetic Labour MPs to raise questions in the House of Commons.

The day before the Trafalgar Square rally, James and Padmore went to hear Marcus Garvey speak at Hyde Park Speakers' Corner. They often mercilessly heckled the elder statesman; the once potent political operator was now a spent force and would strain to keep his argument flowing among the constant interruptions. Garvey had arrived back in

London two years earlier and his stance on Ethiopia had been an out-
lier among his peers. He had stated that Haile Selassie, the Ethiopian
emperor, had 'surrounded himself with white advisers [and] taken
the first step to the destruction of the country'.[74] Following a visit to
Trinidad in the summer of 1937, he made another grave blunder, refusing to side with the striking workers. Instead, he is reported to have
said: 'Trinidad workers ... should not risk their employment for the
sake of these agitators in London who have nothing to lose,' effectively
blaming Padmore and the IASB for stirring the unrest.[75] Garvey's conservative comments revealed just how out of touch he was with the
social, economic and political situation in the Caribbean, and indeed the
prevailing mood in the UK.

Three years later, Padmore wrote a premature obituary for Garvey
in *The Chicago Defender*. According to Garvey's biographer Colin Grant,
this uncharacteristically kind eulogy spawned a series of largely bitter
outpourings from former associates who mistakenly thought Garvey had
passed away. Garvey, who was actually recovering from a stroke, 'faced
with clippings of his obituary [and] pictures of himself with deep black
borders ... [read the] shocking correspondence ... and collapsed in his
chair', according to his secretary Daisy Whyte. He would not recover
from a second massive stroke, dying two weeks later. James later regretted his treatment of the elder statesman, realising that despite ideological
differences the two shared much common ground.[76]

Hundreds of people attended that first IASB rally, where working
conditions on Trinidad were condemned as being no better than the days
of enslavement. Over the next eighteen months, several more demonstrations would be held in Trafalgar Square, Hyde Park and London's
Memorial Hall. Print culture was utilised extensively, with tens of articles printed in the left-wing press, often authored by Padmore.

Following violent clashes in Jamaica in summer 1938, the LCP, IASB
and the Negro Welfare Association held a meeting at Memorial Hall
in London, where they demanded the British state act immediately
'to improve the economic condition of the population'.[77] The meeting
applied the right amount of pressure and in autumn 1938 the British
government set up a Royal Commission to investigate social and economic conditions on the island. The commission's findings, the Moyne

Report, were delayed significantly by the outbreak of the Second World War and not published until 1945.

Trinidadian historian Selwyn Ryan identified the labour rebellion from below as a significant moment, stating that 'the year 1937 was perhaps the most decisive watershed in the colony's history … it made the survival of the old colonial system virtually impossible'.[78] In amplifying the intolerable conditions of the striking workers, Padmore had highlighted that the imperial order that engendered such a system was itself untenable.

Padmore's own fortunes had changed somewhat and he was now living with Dorothy Pizer, a working-class English woman whom he had met through left-wing circles. He was now the *Chicago Defender* London correspondent and wrote a regular column for *The Crisis*. Despite no official separation from Julia, Padmore was struggling as late as 1938 to get a visa to see her and his daughter.[79] In the end, the chaos of war drew him and Pizer closer together and she became known as his wife.[80]

In October 1938, following the success of *The Black Jacobins*, James left on a speaking tour of the US; for the next two decades, the country would become his permanent residence. His departure hastened the bureau's demise. With war imminent, Padmore thought about getting out of the country – Haiti was suggested as a base where he could continue his work – but in the end, lack of funds meant that he stayed put.

The IASB's final campaign was a joint one with Moody's LCP to overturn the colour bar in the armed forces. Moody's son had qualified for basic training as an officer in the British Army but was told he was not eligible for commission as an officer because, in spite of being born in England, he was not of 'pure European descent'.[81] On 19 October 1939, the Colonial Office issued a temporary reprieve, declaring that British subjects from the colonies would be eligible for emergency commissions. Moody would campaign continually for this situation to be permanent.

One-Man News Service

In 1941, Padmore and Pizer moved to 22 Cranleigh Street in Camden. This dark, cramped flat up two flights of narrow stairs became an entertainment and hospitality hub for visiting Pan-Africanists, artists and intellectuals. Here a healthy cross-pollination of ideas occurred, despite the Blitz quelling any agitational activity. As Pizer noted in August 1946, in a letter to her friend Ivar Holm, '[p]eople pass in all the time, they are coming from India, East Africa, West Africa, the West Indies, the States, from all over the place.'[82] Pizer was hailed as a great hostess. James stated: 'She would cook rice and peas, she would cook fufu. Anybody from abroad who ... came to see Padmore, she would cook for them. I would see her cooking and yet being able to take part in the work that was going on.'[83]

Against the odds, *The New Leader* kept publishing despite the heavy bombing campaign destroying the *Evening Standard* offices nearby. Padmore was a valued and constant contributor. One of his most famous pieces was 'The British Empire is Worst Racket Yet Invented by Man' in December 1939, which excoriated Chamberlain for his own family connections to Rhodesia and South Africa, two countries that not only disenfranchised their native populations but also practised blatant racial superiority against them.[84]

Other contributors to *The New Leader* included the philosopher Simone Weil, Trotsky and George Orwell. Its editor Brockway wrote of pieces being written above ground and then in the cellar when they heard planes and gunfire overhead. Padmore confided to his friend Ollivierre on 16 April 1941, following an attack in which more than a thousand people died: 'It was hell ... I never expected to see daylight. And when it broke – God be praised!'[85]

The South African novelist Peter Abrahams described Padmore as a one-man news service during the Second World War, typing out dispatches on a worn typewriter surrounded by papers and books. The typewriter could take thin paper and produce a dozen or so carbon copies, which Padmore mailed out to small magazines and journals in Africa, Asia and the Caribbean.

Abrahams described it as an incredible industry Padmore created to 'inform the whole colonial world from London'.[86] He stated: 'This was the way most of the independent little papers and magazines in the colonies received a non-European perspective on what was happening in the world ... He was the news gatherer, the copy-taster, the sub-editor, the editor, the printer.'[87]

During the war, Padmore visited the Ministry of Information almost daily as foreign correspondent for *The Chicago Defender* and *Pittsburgh Courier*, collecting colonial news for his researches and dispatches. His output was prolific. Leslie James stated that the total number of articles Padmore produced for African American newspapers between 1934 and 1949 totalled over a thousand.[88] Much of his writing during the war reported on the activities of African American troops, the colour bar in Europe (Constantine, who was working as a welfare officer for the Ministry of Labour, was a high-profile casualty; he was turned away from the Imperial Hotel in London in September 1943, the incident making the national news[89]), and from 1948 Prime Minister Daniël Malan's implementation of the apartheid system in South Africa. Padmore also wrote for the Trinidad labour newspapers the *Vanguard*, the *People* and the *Clarion*, and for the *African Morning Post* (Gold Coast), the *Ashanti Pioneer* and Azikiwe's *West African Pilot*.

Cunard, who was also working as a war correspondent, recalled meeting him in the warm, congenial atmosphere of The Horseshoe public house in London's Tottenham Court Road. He 'would appear with "stacks of paper under his arm, exhausted but valiant"'.[90] The winter of 1941 was bitterly cold and the blackout made getting around difficult. Still Cunard and Padmore met up amid the bomb damage wreaked by the Blitz. The two embarked on a new project, the pamphlet *White Man's Duty*, on how the war should hasten self-government for the colonies, considering their significant contribution to the war effort; it was a position that echoed Ali's during the previous global conflagration. The pamphlet took the form of dialogue between the two authors and stated clearly on its bold red-and-black cover 'What do you know about the Colonial Question? ... It is your duty to know [the facts]'. The pamphlet was popular, selling more than 20,000 copies according to Cunard.[91]

In August 1941, Franklin D. Roosevelt and Winston Churchill set out British and American goals for a post-war world (months before the US entered the war following the attack on Pearl Harbor). One of its key aims was: 'The right of all people to choose the form of government under which they will live and the determination to see sovereign rights and self-government restored to those who have been forcibly deprived of them.'[92] This gave hope to the colonies, especially when the deputy prime minister Clement Attlee interpreted the declaration to WASU: 'We fight this war not just for ourselves alone but for all peoples. I look for an ever-increasing measure of self-government in Africa and for an ever-rising standard of life for all the peoples of Africa.'[93]

When later Churchill stated in the House of Commons that the Joint Declaration did not refer to 'the development of constitutional government in India and in other parts of the British Empire', Padmore was apoplectic. His friend Azikiwe cabled Churchill: 'Are we fighting for the security of Europe to enjoy the Four Freedoms whilst West Africans continue to live under pre-war status?' He urged Padmore to interview the PM, but the British government refused to entertain him, with Churchill later stating: 'I have not become the King's First Minister in order to preside over the liquidation of the British Empire.'[94]

The incident echoed Westminster's dismissive treatment of Ali during the First World War.

Padmore was busy finalising his manuscript for *How Russia Transformed Her Colonial Empire* (1946), which credits Pizer as co-author. Like all Londoners, he had endured the war's hardships: the Blitz, rations, sheltering in the underground as bombs rained down.

The V2 attacks, which started in September 1944, sapped his strength. He wrote: 'I am so tired ... that I have very little energy to do more than is absolutely necessary these days ... I am anxious to see the proof sheets before Hitler starts sending over his V3. It's no joke.'[95]

Pan-African Hopes

Towards the war's close, Padmore became involved in the Pan-African Federation (PAF), an initiative spearheaded by Milliard (president) and Makonnen (general secretary) in Manchester, which the latter had made his home. PAF united several British-based Black groups under one banner, including the Negro Association (Manchester), the Coloured Workers' Association (London) and the Coloured Peoples Association (Edinburgh). Significantly, it also had the support of African organisations such as the Kikuyu Central Association (Kenya), represented by Kenyatta, and the African Youth League (Sierra Leone section) represented by Wallace-Johnson. WASU and the LCP were the notable absences from PAF; even though both groups had worked in tandem with Padmore on issues such as Ethiopia and the Moyne Report, Moody, in particular, was unable to shake off his wariness of what he called 'labour groups'.[96] WASU was also experiencing its own internal crisis.

In its draft manifesto, PAF was keen for Africa's needs not to be neglected. It stressed: 'Any new world forum must take account of 160 million Africans, many of whom had fought, contributed and in some cases given their lives in World War II.'[97]

A significant addition to the group was Kwame Nkrumah. He had known James as a student in the US and James had written a letter of introduction to Padmore, stating: 'This young man is coming to England; I know him very well, he is not very bright.'[98] (Years later he would qualify that statement to mean that Nkrumah was not well versed on revolutionary politics.) Following the introduction, Padmore met Nkrumah at Waterloo Station and the two bonded instantly, with Padmore thrusting a battered copy of *The Black Jacobins* into the future President of Ghana's hands.[99]

Padmore was the organising spirit of PAF and Nkrumah very much his right-hand man. Padmore organised a series of conferences following PAF's inception in order to build momentum for a larger Pan-African Conference, which was to be held that autumn. In June 1945, a Nigerian general strike, triggered by high inflation and wage stagnation, further coalesced anti-colonial opinion, with Asian organisations lending substantial support to the cause. The Second World War had served as a catalyst – the heritage of anti-colonial protest nurtured by Edwards, Ali and McKay was coming to the fore. In truth, it was an opportune moment to demand rights for the colonies and Padmore took full advantage.

The Pan-African Conference opened in Manchester's Chorlton Town Hall on 15 October 1945, and ran for six days. Padmore noted that it was 'the largest and most representative congress yet convened'.[100] More than 200 people attended, with eighty-seven delegates representing some fifty organisations. The summit proved to be a significant coup for Padmore, who had secured the presence of the great American civil rights leader Du Bois as chairman.

The attendees read like a roll call of political talent; many would later assume leading statehood roles in Africa and the West Indies. Along with Padmore's inner circle – Nkrumah, Kenyatta, Appiah – Hastings Banda of Nyasaland and Nigeria's Obafemi Awolowo were also present. Ashwood Garvey was part of a small female contingent. Important motions included the application of the Atlantic Charter to the colonies; the release of colonial political prisoners; the formation of a World Colonial Council, with representatives from the colonies to oversee the devolution of imperial control; and a universal end to the colour bar.

Ashwood Garvey declared at the conference's start: 'We are here to tell the world that black peoples, supported by the semicolonial people in America and millions of other people, are determined to emancipate themselves.'[101] The exchange of ideas among those who attended the conference, especially the young African intellectuals, would help foster the independence movement in their own countries.

The timer had been set, the final countdown on the imperial project had started, and for this Padmore deserves much credit.

The success of the conference somewhat energised a war-weary Padmore and he was now busy with his fifth book, *Africa: Britain's Third Empire* (1949), which studied nationalist and progressive movements on the continent. The book did well – the first edition selling out – and it was well received in liberal circles. However, its account of nationalist movements in western, eastern and southern Africa led to it being banned in the Gold Coast, Gambia, Kenya, Uganda and Tanganyika.[102]

Padmore also had trouble with US distribution, with Du Bois stating that it was almost impossible to get radical books published in the US because of the anti-Communist climate. This had an adverse effect on Padmore's journalism and his work for Afro-American newspapers dried up. A check of *The Crisis* shows a considerable decline in his published articles: between 1949 and 1955 only an article a year appeared, and after that period none at all. It negatively affected his income, with Hooker stating that the couple installed at Cranleigh Street were barely living above subsistence level.[103]

With the independence movement picking up steam in the Gold Coast, Padmore was frequently corresponding with Nkrumah. Their missives were monitored and occasionally intercepted by Special Branch. A letter to the British diplomat Henry Hopkinson from Major General Sir Edward Louis Spears describes Padmore as a 'poisonous individual, who is forever pouring corrosives into the ear of the Gold Coast public'.[104]

The US state department, as well as the British, were now watching Padmore closely. The Gold Coast was at the forefront of African colonies moving towards independence and the fact that Nkrumah's chosen counsel had a Communist past presented huge concern. When Nkrumah's Convention People's Party (CPP) swept the board in the Gold Coast general election in February 1951 and the jailed politician was invited to form a government, it was evident that the first stacked domino towards decolonisation had been tipped.

When Padmore visited the country in June 1951, Nkrumah hailed him in front of a crowd of thousands, stating that 'Padmore was one of the greatest advocates on the freedom of the African'.[105]

By the end of 1955, Padmore was working on his most famous work, *Pan-Africanism or Communism?* (1956), his seventh and final work.[106] He wrote to his friend Richard Wright, who unbeknownst to Padmore was betraying him to both the British and Americans,[107] about the anti-colonial effect rippling through African colonies. 'Brother, what changes are taking place before our eyes ... I never expected such moves ten years ago. The west is beaten.'[108]

Ghanaian independence day on 6 March 1957 was bittersweet for Padmore. He was reluctant to attend, but a message from Nkrumah, refusing to accept any excuse whatsoever, forced his hand.[109] In Accra, political leaders from around the world, including Richard Nixon, Martin Luther King Jr and Norman Manley, gathered to celebrate the country's independence. Dressed in kente cloth, a sombre and unwell Padmore was too frail to accompany Nkrumah in the car on independence night and James (who had returned from the US) took his place. Padmore was suffering from liver cirrhosis as a result of hepatitis, but little remains on record of the effects of this debilitating condition.

That evening, as members of Ghana's elite danced into the night, James noticed tears in Padmore's eyes. James later told his wife, Selma, that Padmore explained that the 'people who are dancing in here are the ones who opposed the independence. Outside are all the market women, and others, who funded the movement, who fought for the movement, who did all the work for the movement, but they are not in here dancing.'[110]

In November of that year Padmore officially accepted a job as Nkrumah's adviser. In his mid-50s, a government job and a regular salary must have appealed to the former firebrand. Pizer travelled with him to Accra on 5 December 1957 and the couple were gifted a spacious, two-storey house with an impressive garden.

Padmore's office was tasked with information gathering and publishing, and he did much of the legwork for the All-African People's Conference that took place in Accra on 5–13 December 1958. He was still a formidable organiser: a stellar list of speakers included Algeria's Frantz Fanon and Patrice Lumumba of the Congo.

All was not rosy, though: Pizer confided her loneliness in letters to her friend Ellen Wright and their 'marriage', which had survived the war and near destitution, buckled under the strain. Open resentments were expressed about West Indians being involved in the Ghanaian government. Disapproval was voiced in Nkrumah's circle 'on the grounds that a West Indian could hardly have anything to teach them about Africa'.[111]

Padmore was physically and mentally exhausted. In the summer of 1958, he was taken ill in Liberia at a meeting to discuss Pan-African unity and was flown back to London for emergency medical treatment. He was treated by his friend and former LCP stalwart Dr Cecil Belfield Clarke. Padmore's condition was serious – his distended stomach betrayed signs of severe liver deterioration. Despite treatment, Padmore haemorrhaged, slipping into a coma and dying on the night of 23 September 1959. Rumours that he was poisoned would circulate, and Pizer was forced to type a five-and-a-half page statement to correct any misunderstandings about his death.

His funeral was held at Golders Green crematorium five days later and attended by 200 people. Despite his will explicitly stating that he wished his ashes to be buried with his mother, Nkrumah had other plans. Pizer took his ashes to Ghana and they were interred at Christiansborg Castle on 4 October in a ceremony that was televised by NBC.

The site of a former colonial fortress built to defend the slave trade was a poignant image for the African diaspora. The American activist St Clair Drake, who attended the ceremony, recalled how Nkrumah 'looked out where the surf was beating in against the walls of the slave castle and said: "Who knows, but from this very spot, his ancestors were carried out across the ocean there, while the kinsmen stood weeping here as silent sentinel. We've brought his ashes home to rest."' Then Drake watched, as Nkrumah slammed the ashes into the wall, took out his handkerchief and wept.[112]

Afterwards, Pizer wrote: 'When I saw the urn in which George's ashes had been placed, I thought how strange that the remains of so tremendous a personality, so great a man, could be put into a small compass.'[113]

Pizer stayed on in Ghana as an adviser to Nkrumah. She planned but never completed a biography of her husband. She wrote to Cunard, 'He was so much part of an epoch and mixed with so many of the names that have made history ... But where is my material? He was always destroying papers and he did not talk about the past.'[114]

In December 1964, she died of a heart attack in Accra, Ghana.

Ghost in the Archive

George Padmore was an extraordinary man – a child of Empire whose footsteps traced some of the most consequential moments in the twentieth century. His personal encounters read like a veritable *Who's Who* of that time; his life story intersecting with the great, the good and the downright ugly of that period. Here was a man from a small district in Trinidad who riled the Ku Klux Klan as an idealistic young student in Jim Crow America; who witnessed the economic hardships of the Wall Street Crash; who dodged Stalin's purges; and outwitted the Nazis in 1930s Hamburg, subsequently sheltering from their bombs in a war-weary London; and whose prolific activism triggered the start of the decolonisation process in Africa and the Caribbean.

James described him as 'one of the greatest politicians of the twentieth century. He earned for himself the title of "Father of African emancipation"'.[115] The historian Marika Sherwood argued that 'Padmore has a much more rightful claim to the title of the Father of Pan-Africanism than W.E.B. Du Bois on whom the title was bestowed. His life was devoted to the true emancipation and unification of Africans and those of African descent.'[116]

Padmore did not live to see Empire's endgame, but he played a huge part in instigating it. The seeds of his activism would continue to percolate through the decades, sustaining the British Black Power movement much later in the century.

The Jamaican poet, playwright and editor Una Marson would also follow McKay's footsteps – although she would not visit the States. Her work on women's rights in London during the interwar years acted as a counterbalance to the writings of Padmore and the majority male actors of the IASB, while the cultural enterprise she helped instigate, the Caribbean Artists Movement, was another taproot from which Black British resistance and journalism flourished.

Unlike Padmore, Marson's journalism would propel her to the heart of the establishment; however, her activism from within would lead to serious personal and professional consequences.

Ida B. Wells, pictured in 1894, the date of her second UK tour with Celestine Edwards. (Oscar B. Willis/New York Public Library)

Celestine Edwards, pictured in 1894. (William Harry Horlington; part of a series advertised in *Fraternity*, October 1894)

LUX

A WEEKLY

Christian Evidence Newspaper.

EDITED BY S. J. CELESTINE EDWARDS.

Publishing Offices: 18, PATERNOSTER ROW,
LONDON, E.C.

CONTENTS:

Vol. I. No. 23.　JANUARY 7, 1893.　ONE PENNY.

Fry's

PURE CONCENTRATED COCOA.

Christian Evidence Society.

Offices: 13, Buckingham Street, Strand, W.C.

NEW WORK BY CELESTINE EDWARDS.

From Slavery to a Bishopric

BEING A

SKETCH of the LIFE, STRUGGLES, and SUCCESSES
of BISHOP HAWKINS.

CLOTH GILT, 2/6 NET.

To be obtained at 18, Paternoster Row, London, E.C.

Sole Agent for Advertisements—F. LONGMAN, St. Paul's Chambers, Ludgate Hill.

Covers of *Lux* and *Fraternity*.
(British Library Collection:
Lux: MFM.MFO819-22;
Fraternity: MFM.M624,
1893–97)

Fraternity

OFFICIAL ORGAN OF THE

Society for the Recognition of the Universal Brotherhood of Man.

Edited by CELESTINE EDWARDS.

Vol. I. (New Series). No. 1.　JULY, 1893.　ONE CENT, OR HALFPENNY.

UNITY OUR AIM.

For years one has been longing for the opportunity to plead the cause of the oppressed and helpless, and when we first came into contact with *Anti-Caste* years ago, we thought that there was at least a prospect of helping those who were then actually doing a work which our own experience (in all the countries in which the work of this Society will extend) convinced us was how much needed. For more than six years *Anti-Caste* has been doing a quiet work in England, slowly but surely permeating society, and winning the hearts of good men and true women to the cause of the struggling helpless races in America, India, Africa, and Australia, and wherever tribes, races, and nations have been oppressed by the accursed enemy of mankind—Caste. That work has been found to be growing to such magnitude that it has been found necessary to organise a Society, which shall direct its attention to the work of removing inequality and wrongs from races, whom we feel sure will, with greater opportunity and freedom, do as much credit to themselves as any nation in Europe. It has been a very difficult matter to start such a Society; there are so many noble organisations to attract the sympathy and attention of large-hearted men and women here in England, that many feel that it is useless for them to undertake to do more; yet we venture to suggest to any such friends that there is no question which is so full of absorbing interest to us as the brotherhood of man. Upon that great fact rests the physical, moral, mental, and religious emancipation and salvation of the whole human race. From whatever standpoint we look at the question, the human race—whatever be their creed, colour, or nationality—are from one common origin, with like feelings, ambitions, and desires; this oneness of the race, forces upon us the great fact that the woes of one, ought to call for the immediate relief of the others. Yes! and in some quarters our charity extends to birds and beasts, we are armed with societies for the protection of wild birds and the prevention of cruelty to animals. In this country if a man ill-uses a horse, tortures a cat, maltreats a cow, thousands cry shame upon him for his in-

humanity. But alas ! how different the same English-speaking people treat the Negro in the United States of America! How unkind the same people have been and are to the poor pariahs of India and the Kanakas in Australia! All this ill-treatment we conceive to have sprung from a feeling of superiority existing in the mind of the English race over his darker brethren, and this feeling is in process of time breeds caste, and caste ends in reckless cruelty, such as we know exists in the United States of America. The business of the Society will be to use every lawful and peaceful means in its power to educate men to regard, nay, recognise, all men to be members of one family; that neither creed, colour, nor nationality ought to be a barrier to any man or woman in the great battle of life; that when we go into their countries we should recognise that they were designed by the all-knowing Father of our common humanity to inhabit that particular country, and that their lives are as precious to them as ours are to us.

We regret to say that the Society is not sufficiently developed to publish a full account in the present number, but we hope that the next issue will contain all necessary information. We are pleased to report elsewhere that in Scotland Mrs. Isabella Fyvie Mayo is doing a most excellent work on behalf of the Brotherhood. At Manchester and Bristol we held two large and enthusiastic meetings during the present month, and daily we have been enrolling new friends to the cause.

The last issue of *Anti-Caste* reached up to seven thousand, which we hope will not only be maintained, but increase with the new title of the Society's organ. It is to be hoped that friends, both at home and abroad, will send us such news as will be of general interest to our readers.

This has been an awful month for the Negroes in America, as will be seen in another column, and it is to be hoped that those who love their neighbours as themselves will do all in their power to circulate the information contained in this issue. We must thank the Bristol and Liverpool press for the kind words they have uttered on behalf of our cause, and all those friends who have volunteered to spread this paper and enrol new members. ED. FRATERNITY.

The *African Times and Orient Review* offices, pictured in the paper in September 1913. (British Library Collection: MFM. M33156)

Cover of the *African Times and Orient Review*, for the special Christmas 1912 edition. (British Library Collection: MFM.M33156)

Portrait of Dusé Mohamed Ali, 1911. (Schomburg Center for Research in Black Culture, New York Public Library)

Claude McKay, pictured as a young man, *c.* 1912–20. (New York Public Library)

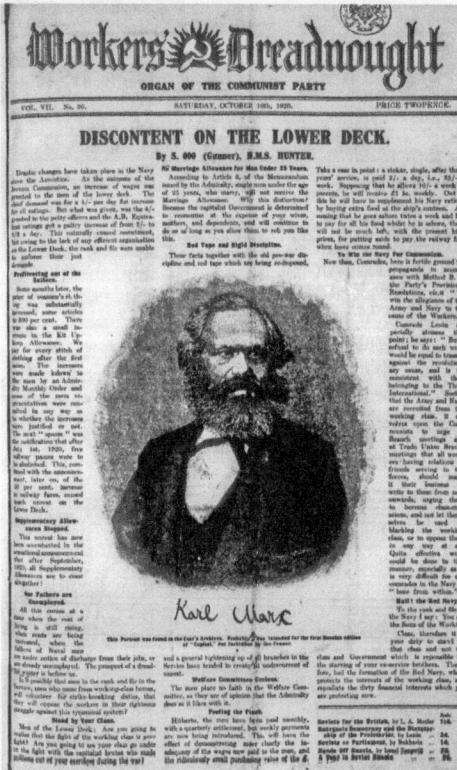

The cover of the *Workers' Dreadnought*, 16 October 1920, which Claude McKay edited; this edition featured the articles that later led to Sylvia Pankhurst's arrest. (British Newspaper Archive)

Claude McKay and the artist and model Baroness von Freytag-Loringhoven from his *Liberator* days, *c.* 1921–22. (Library of Congress)

Sylvia Pankhurst protesting British policy in India in Trafalgar Square, 1932. (Spaarnestad Photo/Nationaal Archief)

George Padmore pictured reading a newspaper, *c.* 1940s.

THE
NEGRO WORKER

No. 7   July 15, 1932   Vol. 2

Labour with a White Skin cannot Emancipate itself, where Labour with a Black Skin is Branded! - Marx.

Price 5 cents   Price 2 pence

Cover of *The Negro Worker*, 15 July 1932, and the last edition of *The Negro Worker*, August–September 1933, edited by George Padmore. (1932: Marxists Internet Archive; 1933: Marika Sherwood collection)

The Negro Worker

N° 8-9   August-September 1933   Vol. 4

TOUSSAINT L'OUVERTURE-THE BLACK NAPOLÉON

ICE 3d. (10c. U.S.A. and Canada)

INTERNATIONAL
AFRICAN OPINION

Motto:
EDUCATE—CO-OPERATE—EMANCIPATE
Neutral in nothing affecting the African Peoples

VOL. I. No. I.   JULY, 1938.

INTERNATIONAL AFRICAN OPINION is the monthly organ of the International African Service Bureau. Views expressed by contributors are not necessarily endorsed by either the Bureau or the Editorial Committee. No payment is made for MSS. submitted, and such contributions as are sent must include a self-addressed stamped envelope to ensure their return; the Editorial Committee will not undertake correspondence concerning MSS. otherwise sent.
Annual subscription is 3/6, while single copies are 3d. each.
All communications should be addressed to: Editorial Committee, International African Opinion, 12a, Westbourne Grove, London, W.2.

CONTENTS

International African Opinion, vol. 1, no. 1, July 1938, an International African Service Bureau publication, edited by C.L.R. James. (Marika Sherwood collection)

"THE KEYS"

The Official Organ of

The League of Coloured Peoples

Vol. 2. No. 1.   Price 6d.   July–September, 1934

Quo Vadis?   By courtesy of The "Topical" Press Agency Ltd.

Cover of *The Keys*, July–September 1934, edited by Una Marson. (British Newspaper Archive)

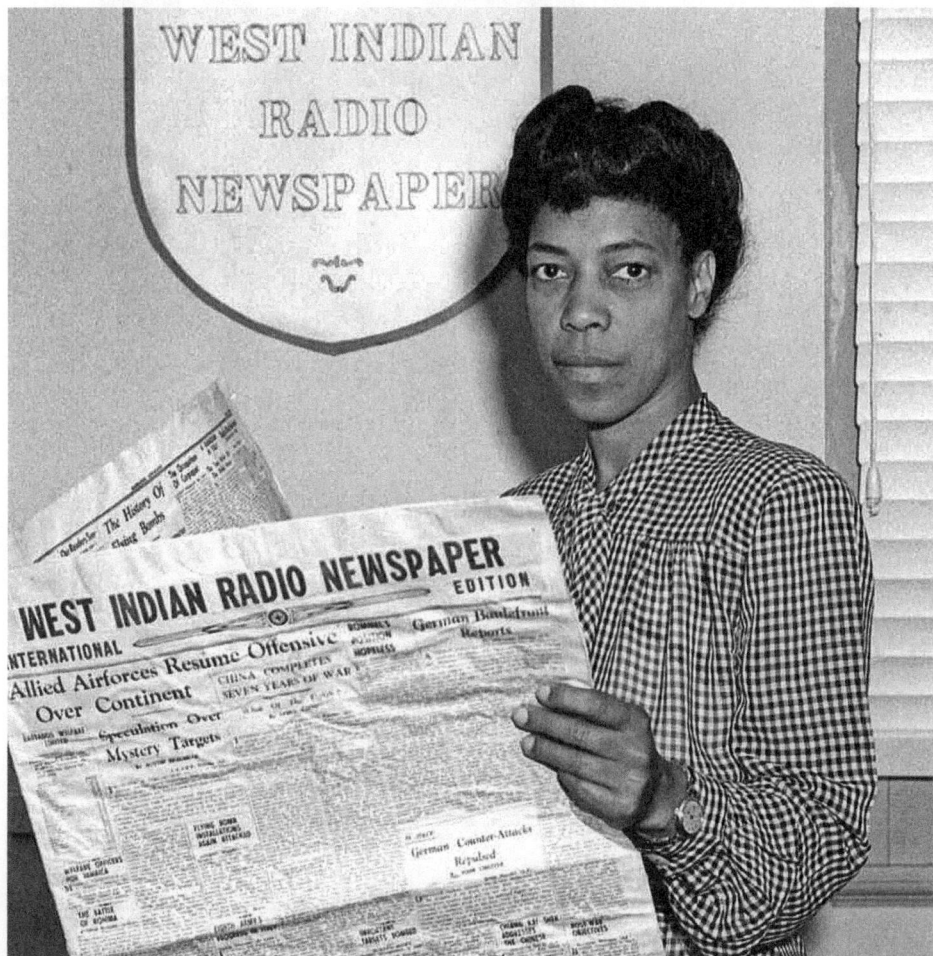

Una Marson reading a copy of the *West Indian Radio Newspaper* during the Second World War. (Wikimedia Commons)

STAGE and SOCIETY

MISS NINI THEILADE, who is regarded as one of Europe's most brilliant young dancers, leaving the S.S. *Franconia* on arrival in New York, where she is now fulfilling a number of engagements. She was born in Java

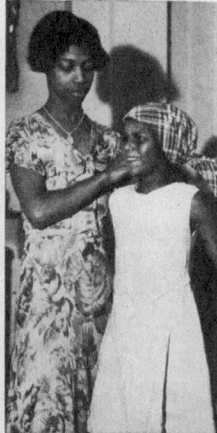

PREPARING FOR A REHEARSAL : Miss Una Marson, whose play, *At What a Price*—a study of life in Jamaica—is to be given at the Scala next week by a coloured cast of amateurs. She is seen adjusting the head-dress of a young player prior to one of the rehearsals

MME. ARPELS, who won first prize at a Society dress function staged at the Ambassadors, Paris. Her gown of black organdie is trimmed with flounces of the same material

GUELDA WALLER AND VERA MACONOCHIE, who broadcast old folk songs, songs from Shakespeare, and Mendelssohn duets in the London Regional programme last Saturday. These two artists are well known to listeners, and were among the first to be televised wearing costumes appropriate to the particular songs they were singing

THE COUNTESS OF CARRICK, who is chairman of the Winter Sports Dinner and Ball which is to be held at the Dorchester on January 18 in aid of the London Federation of Boys' Clubs

HARRY PILCER, partner of the late Gaby Deslys, has arrived back in London after an absence of twelve years. He will appear in the new French revue at the Prince of Wales Theatre, and is seen here coaching members of the chorus in their steps

BABIN AND VRONSKY who are to give a recital at the Wigmore Hall to-day (Saturday). Their programme consists of original works for two pianos

CHIC SALE, the well-known film comedian who specializes in "old man" parts. He is only thirty years of age

THE CHILDREN'S PARTY AT THE ICE CLUB, WESTMINSTER : Two of the 200 youthful guests who attended the party in fancy dress costume

The Sphere, 13 January 1934. Una Marson (top row, centre) pictured at rehearsals at the Scala for her play *At What a Price*. (British Newspaper Archive)

Claudia Jones and Abhimanyu Manchanda (Manu) pictured at the *West Indian Gazette* offices, *c.* 1961–62. (Henry O. Oduyoye/Estate of the late A. Manchanda)

Claudia Jones (second row, first from left) with fellow Smith Act defendants before a US Federal Court building, 1953. (New York Public Library)

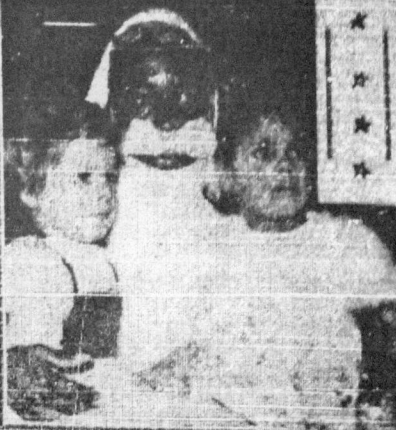

Cover of the *West Indian Gazette and Afro-Asian-Caribbean News*, December 1959. (©*West Indian Gazette*/Marika Sherwood Collection)

C.L.R. James and Darcus Howe pictured at James' 80th Birthday Lectures, Kingsway Princeton College, Camden, 1981. (Richard Denney/AfroLens)

Darcus Howe and Michael X in Black Eagle days, 9 December 1968. (Ron Gerelli/Getty Images)

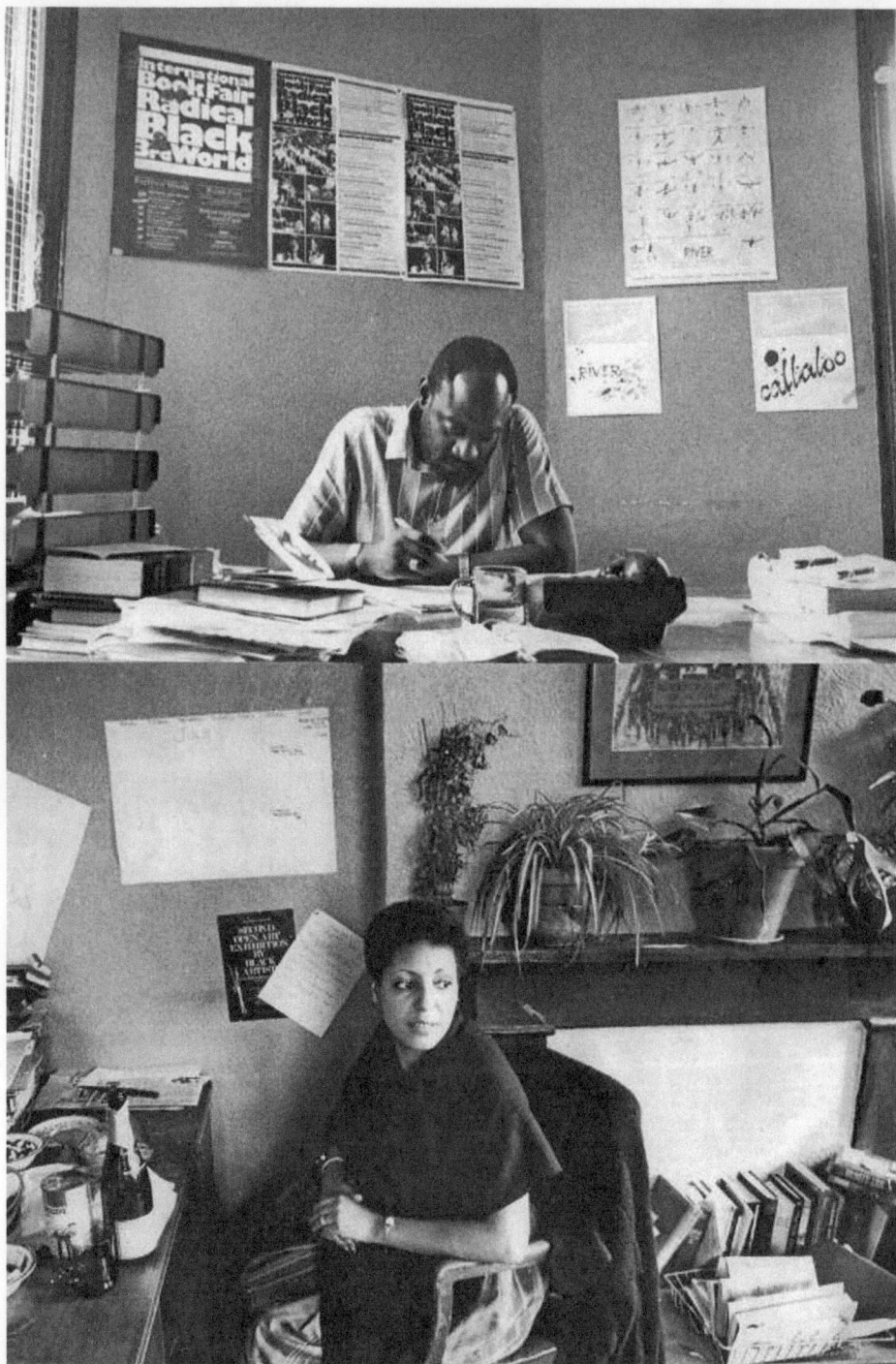

Darcus Howe and Leila Hassan Howe pictured at *Race Today* offices, *c.* 1980. (Leila Hassan Howe)

Darcus Howe pictured on the one-year anniversary of the New Cross Massacre in Deptford Town Hall, with the parents of the murdered children, 18 January 1982. (Julian Stapleton, courtesy of George Padmore Institute)

(Left and overleaf) *Freedom News*, 10 June 1972, and two *Race Today* covers from Darcus Howe's time as editor. (George Padmore Institute: NEW/17/12; *Race Today* collection)

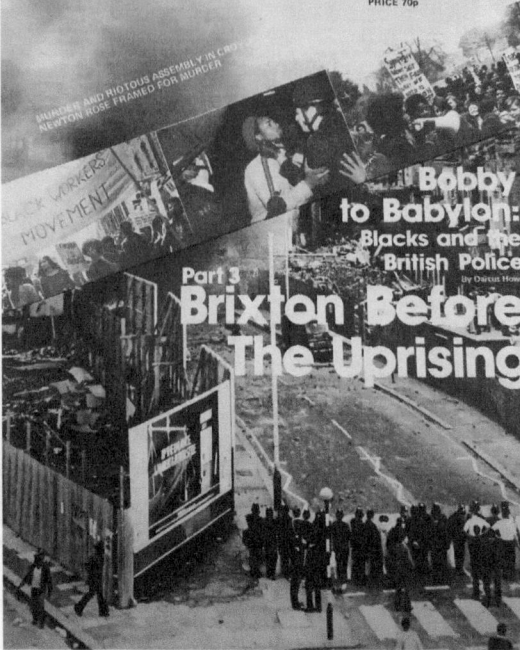

Race Today

VOICE OF THE BLACK COMMUNITY IN BRITAIN   FEBRUARY/MARCH 1982

PRICE 70p

MURDER AND RIOTOUS ASSEMBLY IN CRISIS
NEWTON ROSE FRAMED FOR MURDER

BLACK WORKERS
MOVEMENT

Bobby
to Babylon:
Blacks and the
British Police
by Darcus Howe

Part 3
Brixton Before
The Uprising

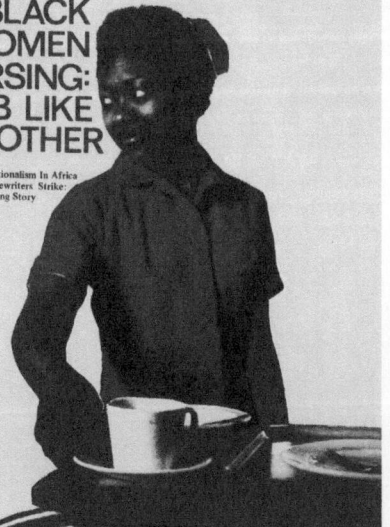

Race Today

AUGUST 1974 15p

BLACK
WOMEN
& NURSING:
A JOB LIKE
ANY OTHER

Class and Nationalism In Africa
Imperial Typewriters Strike:
The Continuing Story

5

TOWARDS THE STARS

UNA MARSON, feminist, poet, playwright, pioneering editor and broadcaster (the *Cosmopolitan*, 1928–31; *The Keys*, 1933–35; *Public Opinion*, 1937–38, *Jamaican Standard*, 1923–28 and *Daily Gleaner*, 1937–38)

'What made my face grow hot/The blood boil in my veins/And tears spring to my eyes.' So wrote Una Marson about being racially abused on a London street in the strongly worded poem *N——r*, which was published in the first issue of *The Keys*, the League of Coloured People's (LCP) journal.[1] Her visceral lyrics summoned the injustice and hurt heaped upon her by a gang of street urchins, and gave sharp vent to the mental and physical scars such racism inflicts.

Marson had arrived in London in July 1932, eschewing the footsteps of her poetic lodestar Claude McKay and choosing the 'Mother Country', rather than the US, as the land that would bring further literary opportunity. In Jamaica, she had already self-published two volumes of poetry, *Tropic Reveries* (1930) and *Heights and Depths* (1931), to critical acclaim. She was also an emerging playwright: *At What a Price*, a play she had written at just 26, was staged at Kingston's Ward Theatre on 11 June 1932, and received rave reviews in both the *Daily Gleaner* and the *Jamaican Times*. It was with the play's meagre profits that she bought a £50 return ticket for a three-month sojourn in the UK, hoping that the land of her beloved Wordsworth would recognise her talent.

Such naïve ambition was soon corrected: she was shocked to find that England, the mild, colour-blind nation she had encountered in novels, was truly fiction. During the interwar years, racial prejudice had become more pronounced, with the poor economic climate leading to suspicion and outright hostility towards the UK's colonial subjects. The population of colour had increased in the early twentieth century, with estimates placing it at around 20,000 between 1918 and 1945, a small but significant minority.[2]

The fallout from the 1929 Wall Street Crash had affected European export industries and the country was crippled by large-scale unemployment. Marson consequently struggled to find employment as a secretary; the perceived double disadvantage of being Black and a woman leading to multiple job rejections, with the prejudice she encountered adversely affecting her mental health.

When she arrived in the capital, Marson lodged with the indomitable Jamaican physician Harold Moody, the founder of the LCP, and his English wife Olive in their sprawling Victorian home at 164 Queen's Road, Peckham, which they had opened up to bewildered new arrivals from the colonies who were trying to navigate the metropole. Moody had himself suffered the indignities of being refused accommodation when he arrived in London in 1904 as a 22-year-old medical student, and he was determined that his fellow country people would not endure similar treatment.

The Moodys' Christian faith exerted a strong gravitational pull on the educated, middle-class daughter of a Jamaican Baptist minister, but the kindness and community she found there did little to alleviate the rejection she felt. The slim, fragile-looking Marson, her dainty features framed in a stylish flapper bob, was finding it increasingly difficult to withstand the blows. She wrote: 'I tried to register for work as a stenographer. One agent told me she didn't register Black women because they would have to work in offices with white women. Another agent tried to find me a position and he told me that though my references were excellent, firms did not want to employ a Black stenographer.'[3]

Her fellow lodger Sylvia Lowe witnessed one night how 'very emotional she was with frustration ... she was crying and working herself up and crying and crying, looking like a frightened child, helpless'.[4]

A few years later she would write in Jamaica's national newspaper the *Daily Gleaner* about the 'hurtful' racism she experienced in England:

'They point at you and stare at you and it is very embarrassing … In London everyone seems far off. You see groups of people and no one you know. It is very lonely.'[5] That same year Marson wrote to the *Daily Mirror* pointing out 'incident after incident' that she had experienced in England, concluding that 'spiritual and mental lynchings are just as bad as physical lynchings'.[6]

Una Maud Victoria Marson was born on 6 February 1905 in the rural village of Sharon, Jamaica, the youngest of nine children (three adopted), to the Rev. Solomon Isaac Marson and his wife Ada. Her status in the family meant she was forever known to villagers as 'Parson's Baby', even when she visited the district much later as a grown woman.[7] She grew up in the Sharon Mission House, which belonged to the Baptist church where her father ministered. Her father and sisters engendered a love of literature and poetry in the young Marson, the latter of which she termed 'the chief delight of our childhood days'.[8]

Marson's maternal grandmother, whose father was Irish, helped raise all the Marson children. According to Marson's biographer Delia Jarrett-Macauley, the fact that she did not look like her sisters, who were tall and olive-skinned like their mother, was a constant 'source of conflict and pain'.[9] As in many post-emancipation societies, a pigmentocracy existed in Jamaica and those who were fairer skinned were accorded more benefits in terms of status, education and employment.

Marson was awarded a scholarship at the age of 10 and attended Hampton High, a prestigious all-girls school in Jamaica, as a boarder, along with her sisters Edith and Ethel, and received an English public school education. Unfortunately, the death of her father in 1915, the same year she started school, impacted her studies. The children would lose their family home and eventually moved to Kingston to be near Ada's sisters.

After her schooling, Marson found work as a secretary for the Salvation Army and the newly established YMCA; here she found that the majority of Jamaicans still lived in absolute poverty, a situation that shocked and appalled her. Hundreds of thousands of her countrymen and women had migrated to Cuba and Panama in search of a better life, but many would find the relocation a temporary respite from their circumstances. At the Salvation Army, she saw the poor and the destitute returnees up close, their hollow cheeks and ragged clothes revealing the exhaustion of long journeys they had made from Santiago.

Marson's love of poetry endured and she began to give regular poetry readings at the headquarters of the Universal Negro Improvement Association (UNIA), founded by Marcus Garvey and Amy Ashwood Garvey, in Kingston's Edelweiss Park.[10] Garvey scholar Professor Rupert Lewis stated that in those early days the Garveys 'encouraged Marson's writings'.[11] Ashwood Garvey had established a women's division of the UNIA; this progressive organisation would regularly hold debates on feminism and exposure to such discussions undoubtedly moulded Marson's feminist and progressive views.

At the age of 20, Marson secured a position as assistant editor for the political journal the *Jamaica Critic*. However, she found the position limiting as she had to work within the constraints enforced by the conservative editor Dunbar Theophilus Wint. A few years later, in 1928, she managed to secure financial backing from a local businessman to set up her own magazine the *Cosmopolitan*, which, despite its cumbersome subtitle – *A Monthly Magazine for the Business Youth of Jamaica and the Official Organ of the Stenographers' Association* – established her feminist credentials. In her first editorial, Marson stated: 'This is the age of woman: What man has done woman may do.'[12]

The magazine published reports on women's pay and employment rights, and was the first of its kind to be started and edited by a Jamaican woman. Marson advocated for full women's suffrage in Jamaica and for women to have a wider choice when it came to education and employment opportunities.

The *Cosmopolitan* also gave ample space to the Jamaican arts scene, promoting poets, novelists, musicians and short story writers at a time when such coverage in Jamaica was virtually non-existent. When a blonde, blue-eyed contestant won the Miss Jamaica pageant in 1931, Marson wrote: 'There is a growing feeling that Miss Jamaica should be the type of girl who is more truly representative of the majority of Jamaicans.'[13] Although feminist issues were central to the journal, Marson also wrote about the stark inequalities in Jamaican society between the planter class and the ordinary agricultural worker, and praised Garvey for trying to help the Jamaican worker.

After the 1929 crash, the magazine struggled to stay afloat. Despite taking on a co-editor, Aimee Webster, who shared the financial burden of producing the magazine, it was nigh-on impossible for the *Cosmopolitan* to turn a profit, with both advertising and sales dwindling.

Marson was still juggling secretarial work along with her editorial responsibilities, and struggling to publish her first two collections of poetry. In an act of 'rascality', as Webster described it, Marson collected the final monies from advertisers to pay her personal bills and left Webster to cover the magazine's debts.[14] She was aware that her colleague was from a wealthy planter family and no doubt thought that Webster could well afford it, but it revealed a ruthless streak of ambition. Marson had outgrown the Jamaican literary scene and set her heart and hopes on London. The *Cosmopolitan* folded in April 1931 and Marson left soon after.

In London, Marson found solace in the LCP's roster of social events, which abated some of the loneliness and alienation she felt. Moody organised conferences and garden and tennis parties, often funded out of his own pocket, where young colonials could socialise. His professional position and relatively high income (Moody was on £3,000 p.a. in 1938[15]) provided a comfortable venue for people to meet. In comparison, many of the other Pan-African organisations in London in the 1930s, such as WASU, were small and financed on a shoestring. On occasion, Moody's leverage of the purse strings led to criticism that the League was 'a one-man show run by and for the Moody family'.[16] Makonnen was particularly scathing: 'You obstructionist, you are using the balm of aid and garden parties to seduce these young men. So instead of their leaving England after their studies ready to embrace the principles of the age of revolution in which we live, you are giving them ... the belief that their good friends in the Colonial Office will ameliorate things in good time.'[17]

Moody had established the League on 13 March 1931 at the Central YMCA in London, with several laudable aims that included 'to interest members in the Welfare of Coloured Peoples in all parts of the World' and 'to promote and protect the social, educational, economic and political interests of its members'.[18]

Sam Morris, who was the League's general secretary from 1945 to 1951, would later argue that it was 'the first real positive and conscious organised attempt at bringing together people of various ethnic groups within the UK'.[19]

The problem was that two years into its establishment, the organisation was flatlining. The deliberate, non-political agenda it had adopted drew little publicity. Its attempt to represent people from different national and ethnic backgrounds, not to mention economic and social classes, often proved cumbersome. Arguments over what constituted 'coloured' dominated the League and questions such as whether Indian members should be given more prominent roles as the independence movement in that country gained traction were the subject of much wrangling.

Moody would struggle to contain the heady politics of the 1930s, a combustible mix of nationalism and Marxism, that would seep into League debates. Those who attended League meetings in the Moodys' crowded drawing room and sipped tea served by Olive in delicate china crockery – Padmore, James and Saklatvala – would often bring their allegiances with them. Racial prejudice could not be discussed without criticising the imperial project and Moody was not comfortable with such overt political assertions. He was no anti-imperialist; rather his vision was of a democratic, colour-blind Empire. Morris wrote that it was not charisma that enabled Moody to exercise a tenuous hold over this disparate group of people, because he 'possessed little of that quality'. Instead his Edwardian sensibility made him 'one of those rare individuals who it was hard not to respect'.[20]

After a long, hard day with patients, Moody would retire to his office at night and bang out indignant letters on his typewriter, desperate to draw the Colonial Office's attention to instances of racial prejudice and the colour bar, particularly in the medical profession. Marson would often hear him typing late into the night. Racist language was a particular bugbear, whether on the BBC, in parliament or in the press, and letters were dispatched in bulk and with frequency. His activity was often met with derision, Colonial Office officials describing him as a 'busybody', 'a bit of a bore' and 'on the make'.[21]

Unable to find work a year after her arrival, Marson became more involved in League events, acting as its unpaid secretary and organising student activities, receptions, trips and concerts. Marson derived comfort and security from the League. Unlike WASU and the yet to be established

IAFE, it had a high proportion of women officers, including barrister Stella Thomas, Dulcina Armstrong (who later set up a League branch in Guyana), Dorothy Clarke (Bermuda) and Audrey Jeffers (Trinidad). Moody's wife Olive, as Moody duly acknowledged, provided much of the foundation, in terms of home and hospitality, from which the League could operate, and his daughter Christine would also become involved.

In June 1933, Moody put on a lavish reception at the Waldorf Hotel for the West Indies cricket team and Marson introduced the team in verse; she revelled in the limelight, enjoying the praise and attention she received. A month later she accompanied Moody to Hull, at the invitation of the Lord Mayor, for the week-long celebrations marking the centenary of the death of William Wilberforce.

A Decisive Gamble

That summer, Moody took a decisive gamble on a society newspaper to resuscitate the League's fortunes. The first issue of *The Keys* launched in July 1933, with the cover proudly boasting a picture of a palm-fringed beach. This initial twenty-eight-page quarterly publication derived its title and message of racial harmony from the parable popularised in a lecture given by the Ghanaian educator James Emman Kwegyir Aggrey: 'If you play only the white notes on a piano you get only sharps; if only the black keys you get flats; but if you play the two together you get harmony and beautiful music.'

In the paper's first issue, priced at 6*d*, Moody emphasised the *Keys'* mission: 'We are knocking on the door and will not be denied. *The Keys* will, we trust, be an open sesame to better racial understanding and goodwill.'[22] A promotional coup was scored when the inaugural issue of the paper, bound in blue leather and inscribed with gold lettering, was presented to the Prince of Wales, later Edward VIII.

Marson worked closely with the first editor of *The Keys*, the barrister David Tucker, to produce a well-designed, concise newspaper, with erudite news, features, reviews and even a humorous, brief section entitled 'Disclose'. Prominent space was awarded to League business, such as Moody's funding of children's trips to Epsom and upcoming functions. During Marson's time at the paper, it boasted a circulation of well over 2,000 subscribers worldwide and *The Keys* remains the only Black newspaper from that time that has been digitised in the British Newspaper Archive. It provides an indelible record of the treatment of the non-white population of the UK in the run-up to the Second World War.

Marson's editorial skills were such that she was promoted to acting editor for the paper's second issue and associate editor thereafter. The six years that she spent as a journalist at both the *Cosmopolitan* and the *Critic* would prove invaluable, particularly her skills in production, such as commissioning and copy editing. (She would be closely involved with the paper until her last issue as editor on 1 January 1935 and edited seven issues of the quarterly edition in total.)

In the first issue, the LCP's first weekend conference at High Leigh, Hoddesdon, received seven pages of coverage, with the newspaper stressing the international nature of the forty attendees, who came from as far afield as Ceylon, India, the Gold Coast, the US, and the Caribbean. The paper reported James' turn at the conference: the author of *The Life of Captain Cipriani* was introduced as 'a brilliant young man'. At the conference he argued for a universal West Indian consciousness as the Black man in the West Indies had 'been engulfed by western civilisation'. James reported on the West Indian cricket team's 1933 UK tour in the same issue.[23]

With Marson at the helm, *The Keys* offered a space to write about international and national issues regarding people of colour that had been largely ignored by the mainstream press. Its breadth was huge: in April 1934, James wrote an article promoting West Indies self-government, while Emmett J. Marshall's 'Cuba and the Colour Line' reflected on the lack of discrimination on that Caribbean island. Closer to home, Nancie Sharpe bemoaned the dire employment and economic conditions faced by the 5,000-strong population of colour, many of them sailors, in Cardiff.

The summer after Marson left as editor, *The Keys* would build on Sharpe's story, reporting on a subsidy that had been introduced during the Depression years, which stipulated the exclusive employment of British nationals on board all subsidised vessels. Despite many non-white seamen holding documentary proof of British nationality such as passports, birth certificates or military discharge papers, they were forced to register as aliens and denied employment. The volatile situation led to extensive rioting on the Cardiff docks. Brilliant investigative reporting by P. Cecil Lewis and African American economist George W. Brown resulted in the Home Office rescinding the alien orders. The paper that Marson had helped establish scored a significant coup.[24]

Marson used *The Keys* to consistently flag cases of discrimination in employment and training for nurses of colour, highlighting the case of a young Black nurse who was rejected for training by more than two dozen hospitals. Her expertise in the subject led to her addressing the British Commonwealth Institute, and she would later be instrumental in securing nursing posts for Princess Tsehai, the daughter of Haile Selassie, the exiled Emperor of Ethiopia, at Great Ormond Street Hospital, and the Nigerian Princess Adenrele Ademola, who worked at Guy's Hospital during the Second World War.

Under Marson's aegis, female poets, such as Margaret Seon and Sylvia Lowe, were championed in the publication. The latter wrote the powerful 'Disillusionment' in the October issue after seeing Trooping the Colour; the poem encapsulates 'the mockery' of pomp and state endured by citizens of the colonies who in reality find themselves rejected by the country they were told to hold dear.[25] Marson also promoted Black artists in general in the publication, commissioning reviews of Zora Neale Hurston's *Jonah's Gourd Vine* and Langston Hughes' *The Ways of White Folks*.

The infusion of talent and fresh blood Marson brought to *The Keys* was appreciated by Moody. Her first play, *At What a Price*, was staged at the YWCA Central Club Hall on 23 November 1933. Many of the members of the League took notable roles, including Moody and his daughters Christine and Joan. Later, it transferred to West End's Scala Theatre, where its performance was praised widely in the national press.[26] The play incurred substantial financial losses for the League, but Moody was buoyed by its success. He boasted: 'We have not made money, but we have made history as it is the first time that a play written and performed by coloured colonials has been staged in London.'[27]

In her final issue for *The Keys* in January 1935 (the paper would continue till 1939, re-emerging after that as the slimmer *Newsletter* during the war), Marson's editorial struck a solemn tone, quoting Booker T. Washington and urging Black people to unite for their own betterment: 'No race that has anything to contribute to the markets of the world is long in any degree ostracized.' In a renunciation of the Padmore and James grouping, she stated: 'Communism won't help us. We don't want to fight, we are pacifists.'[28]

The status Marson was awarded as editor of *The Keys* provided a passport to other sections of British society. In 1934, she gave a well-received speech at the Women's International League in London, and she organised and compered an evening's entertainment at the Indian Students' Hostel. *The Keys* reported 'the star turns' to be John Payne, who sang African American spirituals, and Guyanese musician Bruce Wendell on the pianoforte. Marson even employed her fellow lodger Lowe to give a humorous sketch and gave two recitations of her own. The whole programme was 'enthusiastically received' stated *The Keys*, which gave the concert generous coverage. Slowly and surely, Marson was making a name for herself.[29]

A key encounter came in July 1934 when she was charged with welcoming Nana Ofori Atta, a chief from the Gold Coast, and his delegation. At a garden party that the Moodys put on in his honour, the chief arrived wearing a 'suit of gold and purple velvet, leopard skin, sandals with gold clasp and a large golden cloth umbrella'; he charmed all, including Marson.[30] That summer she proudly showed Atta around the city, accompanying his party to Colonial Office meetings and media events. The Gold Coast delegation had a purpose: to amend colonial powers in the region, moderating the governor's power and giving Africans greater representation in their own country's legislature.

Marson found what she learned about colonial policy in the region both enlightening and disturbing. She began to develop a Pan-African consciousness, bolstering the gaps in her knowledge by reading African books and pamphlets, and fostering friendships with Solanke and Kenyatta. The latter had received an advance for his memoirs *Facing Mount Kenya*, which helped somewhat with his dire living circumstances. Fellow students described him as cutting a stylish figure through town, 'dressing flashily in loud checked trousers and a belted jacket [and] carrying a walking stick with an amber-coloured stone in its top' that he would use intermittently as a fly-whisk.[31]

Marson became interested in African style and clothes. Her housemate Lowe stated: 'She liked to look African. She put her hair as they did ... natural not plaited, and combed out ... She also had good African flair and was more interested in them [Africans] than in our own affairs ... she was a bit ahead of most people ...'[32] In Jamaica, Marson had written a poem 'Kinky Haired Blues', eschewing 'ironed hair' and 'bleaching skin'. It seems meeting Atta and others had finally given her the strength to practise what she preached.

Atta was a progressive and believed in education as a route to a better society, but did not think it should come at the expense of culture. He practised polygamy and had several children. During his time in London, his wives were at home and it was rumoured that Marson had a brief, albeit passionate, affair with the much older man.[33]

'Charming but not one of us'

The London that Marson was settling into was becoming a hotbed of Pan-African activity and, like other Black Londoners at the time, she often socialised at Ashwood Garvey's Florence Mills Social Parlour and visited WASU's Africa House, which largely thanks to Solanke's future wife, Opeolu Obisanya, was a comfortable 'home from home', with its rich West African food and culture. Makonnen recalled it as 'much more of a social outlet, for WASU house was a homely place where you could always get your groundnut chop and there would always be dances on a Saturday night'.[34] Still Marson found the 'loner' epithet that some at the League branded her with was hard to dodge. The Sierra Leonean doctor Dr Robert Wellesley Cole recalled her as 'extremely charming but not one of us'.[35]

An extraordinary public row that erupted between Marson and the famed US actor and singer Paul Robeson, who was living in London between 1927 and 1939 and traversing in much the same circles, seemed to confirm this. Kenyatta and a number of West African students in WASU had been given parts in Robeson's film *Sanders of the River*, which was filming in London. Robeson had been researching African cultures and it was his sincere intention to portray his character, an African chief, with authenticity and dignity. Sadly, the final rushes were edited, changing his character to one that was obsequious to his colonial masters. Robeson later declared he hated the picture.[36]

In the WASU journal and *The New Statesman and Nation*, he proposed establishing a West End theatre for Black plays, free from interference or colonial interpretation. Marson fired off a vituperative response to Robeson's article that was printed in the journal's letters pages, stating his 'cry for negro culture is putting the cart before the horse' and 'the first task of the negro who has achieved is to teach his people the value of unity'. She implied that Robeson placed his fame before the collective interests of his people.[37] It was an odd, divisive and petty statement to make, and did not earn Marson many fans. It was possible that she was envious of Robeson's status and his popularity among West African students, and also suspicious of his radical political leanings. (He had become closer to the Padmore/James grouping than the LCP.)[38]

The League awarded Marson companionship and purpose, but she increasingly struggled to fit in. In Jamaica, she had been involved in the British Commonwealth League (BCL), which was formed to promote women's groups. Those feminist values that she had nurtured during her time at the *Cosmopolitan*, and her knowledge and experience as a Black woman overseas, were now being sought by a number of women's organisations, and she received several invitations to speak from the Women's Freedom League, the Women's International Alliance and the Women's Peace Crusade, all of which praised her eloquence on what it meant to face multiple disadvantages.

In June 1934 she met the novelist and progressive journalist Winifred Holtby at a BCL conference in London. Marson was familiar with Holtby's satirical anti-colonial work *Mandoa, Mandoa!*, and the two connected on feminism, politics and literature, with Holtby inviting Marson to her Maida Vale flat to discuss her writing career. The staunch anti-fascist, anti-colonialist drew Marson into her orbit. In Jamaica's *Public Opinion* in 1937, Marson wrote: 'She encouraged me to write a book of my experiences in Europe. She felt it would be a real contribution to the solution of the problem of racial antagonism and make for better understanding between races.'[39]

The two would keep in touch, discussing intersectionality before it became a buzzword. Holtby regularly hosted literary soirees, and she and Marson spent one evening discussing 'the colour question, miscegenation, birth control and race prejudice inside out'.[40] Sadly, Holtby's early death in 1935 from kidney disease cruelly severed the friendship in its prime. Marson was deeply affected. In her 1937 collection *The Moth and the Star*, she eulogises Holtby: 'O valiant woman, author, speaker, friend/With sympathies as wide as they were true;/Thy heart was like a fount where all might bend/To drink, and find their faith in life anew.'[41]

The stage that the women's rights movement awarded Marson led to further opportunity and in April 1935, at the age of 30, she was invited to speak at the International Alliance of Women for Suffrage and Equal Citizenship Conference (IAWSEC) in Istanbul. The conference was a huge gathering of international feminism at a time when economic instability and the rise of the far right in Europe were eroding women's rights in the workplace. In the sumptuous confines of Yildiz Palace, more than thirty nations from all five continents were represented, and Marson was invigorated by the solidarity she witnessed among the hundreds of female delegates there.

Under President Mustafa Kemal Atatürk, the founding father of the Republic of Turkey, the nation had undergone a series of modernising reforms. Primary education was made free and compulsory, and thousands of new schools were opened. A year before Marson's arrival, women were granted universal suffrage. Marson took the opportunity to see this progress at first-hand, touring the city's cobbled streets and taking sweet tea with the country's new women MPs. The reforms she saw made her giddy with delight. In a later interview with Nancy Cunard, she declared it was the 'most exciting time of my life' and in an interview with *Cumhuriyet* newspaper, just after the conference, she praised Atatürk, stating: 'I have been following from afar how this great person transformed the spirit and condition of his nation ... How I wish that other races would also produce a personality like Atatürk to fight for their freedom.'[42]

On 19 April 1935, Marson took to the conference stage, looking 'smart and self-assured in her small felt hat and pearls', her hands clutching typed cards of her lecture notes, according to her biographer.[43] Her speech wowed the delegates: not only did she inform them about the social history of Jamaica, but she made an impassioned plea about the dire situation in America for Black people and 'the barbarism' of lynching. She also outlined the discrimination that people of colour experienced in Britain, bringing tears to the eyes of the audience when she described the effect of the colour bar on international university students.[44] To thunderous applause, she made her Pan-Africanism clear:

> I talk on behalf of all Negroes in the world not only Jamaicans ...
> Negroes are suffering under enormous difficulties in most countries in the world. We must count upon all countries where there are Negroes
> – for women always possess a better developed sense of justice – to obtain for them a life more pleasant and less severe ... I get the impression that representatives gathered here are big hearted and will defend and help my race. We are optimistic for a big future for our race.[45]

Marson's ability to telescope on racial politics at a women's conference made the national press in the UK and its coverage was reported proudly in *The Keys*. *The Manchester Guardian* stated that, 'a negro woman of African origin from the former slave world of Jamaica, brought a new note into the assembly and astonished them by the vigour of her intellect and by her feminist optimism'.[46]

Climaxing with a gilded reception in Ankara at Atatürk's palace, the conference was a high point for Marson; she was respected as both an intellectual and a Black woman, and the days spent sobbing into her pillow at Moody's house seemed far away. As was her way, when she experienced a shift in emotion, Marson committed her time at the conference to verse. In 'To the IAWSEC', which appears in *The Moth and the Star*, she stated: 'In Istanbul they took me to their heart/Where women of far lands met glad and free.'[47] She would later explain to the civil rights activist James Weldon Johnson that her poetry writing was an 'impulse' that 'comes on like a madness'.[48]

Just before she had attended the conference in Turkey, Marson had found a bedsit in Brunswick Square. Although she had left *The Keys* amicably, the bustling Moody household did not provide her with the solitude to write, and Marson was keen to fulfil the literary ambitions that had been fuelled by her friendship with Holtby.

Fate had other ideas. Her turn at the conference had impressed the League of Nations, which invited her to spend September at its headquarters in Geneva as a temporary collaborator, the first Black person to do so. She told Cunard excitedly: 'I was one of 30 people invited from 28 countries to do collaboration work. A negro has never been there before.'[49]

An Inauspicious Month

It was an inauspicious month. That autumn the League of Nations was trying to avoid all-out war in Abyssinia (Ethiopia). Marson was there as the League discussed sanctions against fascist Italy; such proclamations did little to avert the crisis and the organisation was shamed as toothless. Ethiopia (along with Liberia) had managed to maintain its sovereignty and independence during the 'Scramble for Africa' and remained free of European colonial interference. The significance of this African country being invaded by Italy was not lost on Marson.

Gravely upset and alarmed by the lack of agency of the Abyssinians, she offered her services to their delegation, who referred her to the Abyssinian ambassador in London, Dr Charles W. Martin (also known as Hakim Wärqenäh). This gentle, elderly doctor had an amazing backstory: he was discovered as an orphaned infant on the battlefield of Magdala by Anglo-Indian troops, and grew up in India, assuming the name of his guardian, Colonel Charles Martin.[50] He studied medicine in Scotland and later became an influential and progressive figure in the Ethiopian court, a major anti-slavery campaigner and a champion of education.

When Marson met him, he was well into his seventh decade, asthmatic and rattling around a grand alabaster, three-storey building in Kensington with very few staff to help him as the crisis in his country mounted. Marson took on the role of secretary, dealing with reams of correspondence, press reports, meetings and lectures. 'The entire correspondence of the Legation passed through the Minister's hands to me,' she recalled. 'He made pencil notes on the letters and sent them to me, I dealt with thousands of thousands of letters.'[51] Marson absorbed herself in the politics, history and culture of the country. In the words of her biographer: 'Abyssinia took over Una's life.'[52] This was not without consequence: Marson found herself subsumed with work, and this 'call-ing' took a toll on her health.

Her former paper *The Keys* published numerous articles alerting its readers to the crisis and in December 1935, James wrote a scathing piece in which he outlined the flaws inherent in the British policy of appeasement:

Africans and those of African descent, especially those who have been poisoned by a British imperialist education, needed a lesson. They have got it. Every succeeding day shows the real motives which move imperialism in its contact with Africa, shows the incredible savagery and duplicity of European imperialism in its quest for markets and raw materials. Let the lesson sink in deep.[53]

The *Keys'* editorial in July 1936 did not mince words, declaring 'The Rape of a Black Empire' had occurred.[54] W.E.B. Du Bois wrote that Italy had proceeded with the invasion: 'in spite of the League of Nations ... in spite of efforts at conciliation and adjustment' and its actions perpetrated a colonial system of 'economic exploitation based on the excuse of race prejudice'. Despite the League of Nations implicit condemnation of the war, it could not prevent it. Du Bois stated prophetically, 'if Italy takes her pound of flesh by force, does anyone suppose Germany will not make a similar attempt?'[55]

The David and Goliath nature of the conflict won the hearts of the British public. Plucky, gallant Abyssinia's outdated weaponry was no match for Italy's sophisticated military machine. Years later, Italy admitted the use of chemical weapons: it had indiscriminately sprayed civilians, fields and waterways with poison gas.

British war correspondents affectionately nicknamed the diminutive, elegant, caped Emperor Haile Selassie 'Little Charlie'.[56] He took an active part in the conflict, working closely with Commander Ras Kassa on the frontline and sustaining mustard gas burns to his hands and arms. A photograph shows the Emperor dressed all in white, crouched on the ground manning an anti-aircraft weapon, and the author Keith Bowers reported that when a squadron of Italian bombers appeared overhead, the Emperor 'gunned them down with terrific effect'.[57]

Marson was submerged by her workload at the embassy, desper-ately engaging in back channel diplomacy with Martin. With Italian troops encircling Addis Ababa, it was thought safer to get the Emperor to the UK where he could lobby the League of Nations. Enthusiastic and cheering crowds greeted the Emperor and his entourage when he arrived at Waterloo station from Southampton, on 3 June 1936. Marson and Martin, the latter having travelled with the Ethiopian delegation on the boat train, escorted the Emperor to his car.

The warm reception from the British public was not reciprocated by the government. When the Emperor turned up unannounced at the Houses of Parliament, the prime minister Stanley Baldwin dived under a table to avoid meeting him and sparking any conflict with Hitler. The only parliamentarian to greet the Emperor was former prime minister David Lloyd George, who condemned Baldwin and the Foreign Secretary Anthony Eden as 'cowards, poltroons and jellyfish'.[58]

With the diplomatic machinations of Downing Street wanting, the Emperor's only recourse was to address the League of Nations directly. Abyssinia's sovereignty had been explicitly violated, and Italy's use of chemical weapons had contravened the Geneva Protocol and the Hague Conventions. It was Selassie's sincere hope that the League would come to the small nation's aid. On 30 June he travelled to Geneva with a fourteen-strong entourage, including Marson as his personal secretary. Marson sat in the diplomatic gallery while Selassie made his address. As the quietly spoken Emperor began his plea for help in his native Amharic, the Italian press corps started to catcall and blow shrill whistles provided by the Italian foreign minister, Mussolini's son-in-law, drowning out his speech. The audience was horrified by such disrespectful behaviour, with the Romanian delegate labelling the noxious journalists, who were later ejected, 'savages'.[59]

Selassie's voice broke with emotion when he concluded his speech: 'Representatives of the world, I have come to Geneva to fulfil, with you, the most difficult of the duties of a head of state. What answer will I have to bring back to my people?'[60]

In the end only Russia and the US voted to condemn the invasion. The rest of the League was more preoccupied with the fate of the emerging Hitler–Mussolini alliance than that of a small African nation.

Cunard, who was reporting on the address, later described the Emperor's countenance at the Carleton Park Hotel:

The defeated Emperor ... a single and tragic figure in the garden of
June roses. And then Una Marson came in in a golden dress, a figure
of what is termed 'oriental splendour'. [Seeing her like this] made you
feel that all ... had not been extinguished for the last country in Africa
that is not ruled over by white men and somehow the wheel would
turn again, for Abyssinia to be liberated from the Fascist invader.
Inside that golden dress was a capable well-informed secretary.[61]

The futility of the situation and the suffering of the Abyssinian people
took a huge toll on an already fragile Marson and she became physically
sick with overwork. Her doctor warned she was on the edge of a nervous breakdown, and she decided to return to Kingston for a rest and
respite from turbulent world affairs.

As for Selassie, in the deepest of ironies, he and his family were
offered sanctuary in Fairfield House in the former Roman city of Bath.
Here he spent five years in exile, forced to sell his branded cutlery to
heat his residence. At no point did he forget the war in his homeland.
The house's nanny recalled someone putting a record on the radiogram,
which played what was happening in the war in Ethiopia. When the
sounds of bombs, gunfire and the cries and screams of his people echoed
around the room, the nanny glanced at the Emperor and witnessed tears
streaming down his face. She remembered them hitting the mustard gas
burns on his hands and arms, and splashing off them.[62]

Back to Jamaica

On arriving back in Kingston on 24 September 1936, where she was
met by her delighted sisters Ethel and Edith, an exhausted and enraged
Marson admitted in an interview with the *Jamaica Gleaner*: 'The position
of Ethiopia is very heartbreaking and the tribulations of the Ethiopians
have cracked me up.'[63] In another interview, she stated: 'Abyssinians
cannot fight poison gas and they have not got ammunition. I do not
know what will happen, nobody knows.'[64]

Marson was thoroughly disenchanted with the western world and its
chicanery, her close proximity to the leading players in the Abyssinian

conflict having crystallised this view. From her new home in Kingston, which she rented with her sister Ethel, she registered her anger at the situation in articles and poems for the *Gleaner*. Two of Martin's sons, Joe and Benjamin, who had shared the stage with Ashwood Garvey in Trafalgar Square at the inaugural IAFE meeting, died during 'three terrible days' of the Addis Ababa massacre.[65] When it later transpired that they had been captured by Italian forces and executed, Marson wrote in 'To Joe and Ben': 'I wept for you/As you two gallant sons/Went forth/From the brightness/Of an English summer/To die/On the mountain heights/Of Ethiopia.'[66]

In 1937, she had a regular column in *Public Opinion*, a weekly newspaper that was later affiliated to Norman Manley's People's National Party. A number of prominent women in the arts played an active role in the paper: the artist Edna Manley was editor, Marson and the social worker Amy Bailey were board members, and the artist and poet Gloria Escoffery was the books editor.

In *Public Opinion*, she wrote some of her most strident and radical journalism. Jamaica and the rest of the Caribbean had been hit hard by the Depression and between 1929 and 1931 prices of the leading exports had fallen sharply: the price of sugar dropped by 31 per cent, bananas by 24.5 per cent, coffee by 28.4 per cent and cocoa by 49.9 per cent. The dire state of the economy triggered chronic unemployment, low wages and abject social conditions.[67] An article in *The Keys* by R.O. Thomas entitled 'Revolt in the West Indies' states that with industries teetering on collapse 'several hundred thousand labourers and their dependants were faced with immediate starvation'.[68]

In 'Traitors All', Marson addressed this situation, expressing her anger at the League of Nations conference for the lack of a protective quota for the colonies: 'I felt like getting up at the conference and screaming out that such was the loyalty with which some Jamaicans had chewed and digested the Union Jack that Jamaica had not been able to enter at all into their system. Instead, I crept up to the platform after the session like a worm ...'[69]

She again emphasised Pan-Africanism, stressing that Jamaicans needed to connect with their wider heritage: 'We can never be free from inhibitions, complexes, indecision and lack of confidence until we accept ourselves for what we are.'[70]

During this time, she also produced some of her best art. In the poem 'Little Brown Girl', an unnamed white narrator questions 'the brown girl' in the 'white, white city'. The narrator expresses an ignorance about the Caribbean: 'You speak good English ... How is it that you speak/ English as though it belonged/To you?'

The further nescience of non-white peoples is conveyed when the narrator states: 'And from whence are you,/I guess Africa, or India,/In the West Indies/ But isn't that India/All the same?'[71]

The poem explores what it is like to be a person of colour in the context of white predominance (in this case the imperial metropole): the stares, the constant questions about background, the exclusion experienced and the need to justify the space one occupies. It's a finely attuned piece of work, exploring the impact of colonialism and the servile psychology it imparted in much the same way that Frantz Fanon's *Black Skin, White Masks* did decades later.

Marson revisited similar themes in her third play *Pocomania*,[72] which was performed at Kingston's Ward Theatre on 8 January 1938, and which the *Jamaican Times* referred to as 'landmark theatre'. This loosely autobiographical work examined how a middle-class Baptist minister's daughter, Stella, became enthralled by the African drums used in nearby Sister Kate's Jamaican religion. The play illustrated how a Black woman struggled to reclaim her African heritage in a repressive colonial society stained with the legacy of enslavement. Marson's use of Jamaican Creole (which she uses in some of her poetry) was also praised.

In 1938, economic conditions in Jamaica had come to a head and a series of violent strikes rippled through the colony, affecting every sector of society. Marson was tasked with covering the industrial action for the *Jamaica Standard*, an assignment that she undertook with relish, reporting on the strike from a female perspective and braving violent clashes to get an insider's take. Her editor William Makin praised her in his autobiography as one of 'Jamaica's finest' reporters.[73] Her friend W.M. Macmillan had published *Warning from the West Indies* in 1936 to alert the British public to the social deprivation in the region and the propensity for uprising, arguing that this was a situation for which the UK bore responsibility. The text was reissued in 1938 as the riots grew more serious and Marson helped distribute the book's powerful message on the island.[74]

Disturbed by the impoverished conditions of some workers, Marson launched the Jamaican Save the Children Association, Jamsave, which aimed to redistribute food, clothing and cash for those in need. The organisation was reliant on the generosity of local businesses, which Marson was particularly effective at lobbying. On the executive committee was Bailey, whom Marson had worked with at *Public Opinion* and Dr Oswald Anderson, the mayor of Kingston. Marson took on the role of secretary and reported on Jamsave from the offices of the *Standard*, where she would also sort through heavy postbags, fielding requests for help.

Her editor Makin suggested that Marson's insight on the Jamaican situation might be useful for the Moyne Commission, which was investigating the disturbances, and she returned to London to give evidence in September 1938. Her argument for a variant of child support was reported in *The Times*: Marson suggested a special tax on Jamaican bachelors that would be used 'to give children with no support from fathers the simple amenities in life'.[75]

Her trip to London was supposed to be a temporary fundraising opportunity for Jamsave but when Bailey turned up a few weeks later, she could see Marson was 'torn between a desire to "do the right thing", which meant returning home to build Jamsave, and a compulsion to fulfil her potential as an artist'.[76] The latter urge would win out and Marson would spend another seven years in England, a country she would struggle to call home.

London Calling

Marson continued to write for *Public Opinion* and the *Standard* while she was in the UK. Her financial situation was precarious, and she even considered working for Aggrey House as a social secretary. In 1938, she covered the visit to London by another blonde Miss Jamaica, Winnie Casserley, for the *Standard*. The visit took in the annual radio exhibition, Radiolympia, which that year focused on television and both Casserley and Marson were interviewed about the innovative small screen. Marson's broadcast impressed and, on the back of it, she was offered freelance work by the BBC producer Cecil Madden on *Picture Page*.

Earlier in the decade, Marson had encountered a vibrant Black London, with hostels, coffee shops and bars that buzzed with promise. Now, with war on the horizon, the population of Black London had thinned. Universities had evacuated and some people had enlisted or retreated overseas, while friends such as Kenyatta had relocated to the coast.

Padmore remained in the capital but, curiously, Marson is absent from his writing. Their paths are likely to have crossed. Padmore had visited the Moodys' home where Marson first lodged. They both knew Cunard and Kenyatta, although James, another mutual contact that Marson knew from the League, had left for the US. But even though they were moving in much the same circles (and even the same neighbourhoods) during the war, neither mentioned the other. Maybe this notable void was because Marson was now associated with the establishment. Her fear of left-wing groups had now left her somewhat isolated.

Work was sporadic, but Marson was an excellent networker and kept in touch with Madden, advising him on West Indian broadcasts. He received her counsel gratefully, writing that improvements to the service were 'with Una Marson's help as she is very intelligent' and praising her unrivalled local knowledge.[77]

The West Indies received few BBC broadcasts, compared to other British colonies. Now that the broadcaster was under the aegis of the Ministry of Information, it was necessary for programme content to remain neutral and the recent unrest in the Caribbean had shown there was much anti-colonial sentiment in the region.

The Guyanese musician and journalist Rudolph Dunbar was the Ministry of Information's West Indian press officer and had been lobbying it for a weekly feature in which the five hundred West Indian troops based in the UK could send messages home.[78]

Meanwhile, Marson continually reminded the BBC higher-ups (through Madden) that such a programme could act as a morale booster for West Indians at home and abroad. Her impressive journalistic career and contacts book also meant that she could bring in a substantive Caribbean audience. The pressure paid off and Marson was invited to front a series of programmes, illustrating the Caribbean's contribution to the war effort: *The Empire at War and the Colonies* went out on

1 April 1940 and *West Indians' Part in the War* later that month. Marson was a hit and she was also an able researcher, tracking down and interviewing West Indian cricketers and musicians, such as Ken 'Snakehips' Johnson, who was tragically killed in a bombing raid while performing at London's Café de Paris in March 1941.

In *Hello! West Indies* (a rare surviving broadcast produced in 1942–43 by the Ministry of Information), she hosts the programme dressed in a mid-length white lace dress and matching jacket, a floral corsage pinned to her lapel and her hair styled in fashionable victory rolls.[79] She looks stylish, slightly nervous and watchful. To a mixed crowd of army and navy personnel, who are drinking and dancing together to an Al Jennings score, Marson introduces with clipped tones the contribution of the West Indians to the war effort. The programme not only covers pilots, navigators, wireless and switchboard operators, air gunners and ground staff, but also the substantial numbers of West Indian women in the Wrens and Auxiliary Territorial Service. On face value, this film is propaganda, produced to encourage military recruitment in the Caribbean colonies as the war rumbled on, as well as promote a patriotic view of a wartime Empire pulling together regardless of race or creed. Yet it reveals several startling truths about the significant contribution of the West Indies to the war effort, a fact that today has been almost airbrushed out of history. In this way, Marson's work (much like Ali's use of the *Review* to consistently flag the contribution of India, Africa and other colonies to the First World War) is extremely valuable.

Marson was enjoying life at this point. She was living in an unkempt flat in Mill Lane, Hampstead, with Jamaican student Linda Edwards and, after the parties in the BBC studios, she would invite the West Indian servicemen (whom she nicknamed 'her chicks') back for dinner parties (rustled up from rations) and singalongs.[80] Serviceman Thomas Wright said: 'Una spent enormous amounts of time and a good deal of her own slender resources in helping West Indians … when they got into some sort of jam, which was often … all of us had a deep affection for her.'[81] It wasn't all chat and fun, though. The trade unionist and activist Maida Springer recalled: 'Una was very selective about the people she invited … these were men who had a vision of the future, and they were looking forward to the day when they were going to have a country, not a colonial dependency. So it was very good talk ... Very explosive talk! Had they been heard, they would have all been court martialled.'[82] Springer credits both Marson and Padmore for encouraging her later activism.

On 3 March 1941, graft, research and freelance work with Madden paid off, and Marson was appointed full-time programme assistant on the Empire Service on a starting salary of £480 plus allowances p.a., which was higher than the national average.[83] (In the background the BBC were 'debating employing coloured staff' and had extended the probationary period for Marson's post.)[84] Operating out of a tiny office in Bedford College, Regent's Park, which was later destroyed by a German bomb, she hosted and produced a set of programmes entitled *Calling the West Indies*, again publicising the African and Caribbean contribution to the war effort, as well as the activities of British feminists. Her work would bring her into contact with George Orwell, who was the radio producer for the Overseas Eastern Service, and in 1942 she contributed twice to his six-part radio magazine *Voice*.

A month after her appointment Marson claimed she was being 'bullied on stage' by Dunbar and his choir, who were 'trying to interfere with her role as compere'. Dunbar made clear in a letter that he felt Marson was meddling with his choir's musical material. The situation came to a head with both artists threatening to 'down tools'.[85] Madden acknowledged Dunbar was difficult but stated that Marson 'deliberately antagonises him to test her own strength'.[86] This ugly power struggle at the heart of the new programming schedule threatened to derail it completely. To compound matters, Joan Gilbert, Madden's production assistant, who had initially worked well with Marson when she was employed as a freelancer, accused her of being rude. She stated in avowedly racist terms: 'Since Una Marson joined the staff she seems to have got an exaggerated idea of her own position and her authority ... consequently at the slightest opposition she becomes extremely rude. Quite frankly, I wouldn't let anyone speak to me in the way Una does, and certainly not a coloured woman.'[87]

It is impossible to know what Marson felt about these rows – roles as a compère and as a producer demanded a close working relationship with support staff, and fissures had started to appear almost immediately.

Her biographer reported a strange incident where she accused a fellow co-worker of riffling through her bag when she was absent from the room.[88] With the attacks on her personality becoming more intense, she was becoming distrustful and paranoid.

Marson was an intensely private person, but her biographer states that she was having affairs. An unsuitable suitor was an Austrian named Rosenstein who lived nearby in Mill Lane. This romantic liaison, like others, fizzled out, but in 1941 she fell hard for Dudley Thompson, a fellow Jamaican and RAF officer who served in Europe as a flight lieutenant in Bomber Command.[89] The couple spent two intense years together, attending nightclubs and dinner dances, and Thompson was a regular at Marson's parties. Marson would send him neatly written poems on violet paper almost daily, but the affair ended abruptly, leaving Marson distraught.[90] A year later, Thompson married Genevieve Hannah Cezair, explaining that he lost touch with Marson, whom he thought 'had been very disappointed that we did not marry'.[91] He also mentioned his political leanings towards the end of the war; he became drawn to the Pan-African movement, spending more time with Kenyatta, Padmore and Nkrumah and attending the 1945 Pan-African Congress in Manchester.[92] Whether this facilitated the break from Marson is unclear. He distinguished Marson as a 'literary' artist from the mostly male Pan-Africanists but in his autobiography, his only, rather condescending, reference to her is that she was a secretary to Haile Selassie. What is evident is that the 38-year-old Marson was inconsolable following the breakdown of their relationship.[93]

The relationship with Thompson had mitigated some of the toxicity and prejudices that she experienced in her new post. John Grenfell Williams, director of African services, praised Marson's work, vaunting her 'admirable success' and 'incredible results' in 1942.

Nevertheless, tensions continued to mount, this time from external forces. Marson's representation of West Indian interests was being criticised by two opposing parties: Lady Davson of the West India Committee, which represented the white elite and their commercial interests, was not pleased with Marson's coverage, citing lack of racial representation; while a group of Caribbean radicals from Aggrey House was questioning Marson's suitability to represent the Caribbean, arguing that her supposed focus on Jamaica marginalised other territories. The vicious assaults stung a sensitive Marson, with fellow workers noting that she looked drawn. War was also wearing her down: fear punctuated the lives of London civilians and Marson was no exception. She wrote in the 1960s of the craters and battle-scarred buildings: 'Those of us who witnessed the devastation could not help feeling that within our own hearts there were scars of loss and sorrow that would live on with us long after the physical scars were repaired.'[94]

Grenfell Williams, her staunchest ally at the BBC, said in March 1942 that the Aggrey House group was 'out to get Miss Marson and anyone who protected her ... at all costs' and were collecting 'ammunition' in the form of the 'foulest' allegations. He stated that these accusations included questions about the suitability of a woman for such a position and slanderous accusations about her sexuality.[95]

On 1 October 1944, Marson launched the programme *Caribbean Voices*, although she was suffering from nervous exhaustion.[96] That spring she had taken four weeks' sick leave for what her doctor described as 'nervous debility, insomnia, indigestion and general lassitude'. *Caribbean Voices* was a wonderful concept, a twenty-minute on-air creative writing workshop that launched the careers of Nobel Prize winners Derek Walcott of St Lucia, Trinidadian V.S. Naipaul and many other Caribbean writers, including Sam Selvon and Andrew Salkey. Braithwaite would later state, 'it was the single most important literary catalyst for Caribbean creative and critical writing in English'.[97]

Marson was too ill to develop her programme, leaving the Irish producer Henry Swanzy to nurture it to maturity. In the summer of 1944, moves were afoot to place her in a more behind-the-scenes role at the BBC. She went on paid holiday to Jamaica, ostensibly for research purposes, but fearing for her position she travelled miles, visiting four Caribbean islands, frantically collecting scripts for her new programme.[98] She returned to London on 18 December 1945 in 'a serious mental state', refusing food and locking herself in her Hampstead flat.[99]

Research by James Procter for *Small Axe* has found that Marson was encouraged to see a specialist at Middlesex Hospital, where electric or insulin shock therapy was recommended as a cure. Marson did not undergo this treatment voluntarily and had to be certified. On 13 March

1946, she was transferred to St Andrews Hospital in Northampton where, despite insulin shock therapy, her prospects for recovery remained uncertain, with doctors concerned about 'delusions' and paranoia she was experiencing.[100] Her contract with the BBC was terminated in October 1946. It was a desperately sad end for the BBC's first Black radio producer and Marson's mental health never fully recovered.

In April 1946, her friend, the poet J.E. Clare McFarlane, offered to take her back to Jamaica but a comedy of errors ensued on the journey to Swansea docks. First, the group had to be split into two cabs because of luggage: McFarlane in one cab and his wife, daughter and Marson in the other. Unbeknownst to McFarlane, Marson became obstructive, causing her vehicle to break down, and McFarlane was forced to board the boat without his family. Several frantic phone calls from the boat deck later, an alternative vehicle was found to transport McFarlane's wife and daughter and Marson to the docks, where the ship had already departed. The ship was forced to drop anchor and the late passengers were taken to it by pilot boat. Marson was protesting all the while as she was pushed up the rope ladder to get on board.

Marson's spirit was broken. On her return to Kingston, she was admitted to Bellevue Hospital for rest and observation. The admission to a psychiatric hospital of one of Jamaica's most prominent artists and journalists carried considerable stigma and she dropped out of view for several years. In a final ignominy, her poem 'Towards the Stars' was aired on *Caribbean Voices* without attribution, simply stated as the work of a Jamaican poet, not a former producer.[101] The eponymous collection was published by the University of London Press in 1945.

When she got better, Marson kept in touch with Grenfell Williams, T.S. Eliot, Orwell and Swanzy. In a letter to BBC features producer Laurence Gilliam on 6 March 1957, Marson reflected: 'My years at the BBC now seem like a dream – an exciting dream which ended in a nightmare when I got ill. But it is the happy things that I constantly recall and the wonderful people with whom I was associated.'[102]

In 1949 she became organising secretary for Pioneer Press, the book publishing arm of Jamaica's *Gleaner* newspaper. Here she nurtured the careers of writers such as Salkey, who found her 'generous, gracious and supportive', and her contacts on the English literary scene proved indispensable.[103]

In her mid-50s, she outgrew Jamaica yet again, visiting cousins in Brooklyn, New York, and settling in Washington to write a book on everyday life on the island. The segregation and distinct racial hierarchy that existed in the city derailed Marson. She 'got a rude shock' when denied admission to the cinema, struggled to find restaurants that would serve her and was even barred from places of worship, where she was told to seek out 'coloured churches'.[104] A brief, ill-fated marriage to the American dentist Peter Staples followed. There is little in the archive about the marriage breakdown, but Marson's mental health had again taken a turn for the worse.

Back in Jamaica and living with her sister Ethel, Marson was delighted to receive an invitation from Israel's Foreign Minister Golda Meir to attend a seminar for female leaders in Jerusalem in October 1964. She had resumed her work with Jamsave and was also working to combat discrimination among Jamaica's Rastafari community.

Following her trip to Israel, she visited England on a stopover, attending many of her old haunts and noting that a new generation of Caribbean artists, such as Kamau Braithwaite, Salkey and Wilson Harris, who had got their breaks on *Voices*, were now forging their careers in the capital.

She would not live to see their Caribbean Artists Movement, the roots of which she had nurtured, flourish. The following year Marson was admitted to Kingston Hospital, suffering from severe depression and high blood pressure. She suffered a heart attack and died in hospital on 6 May 1965 at the age of 60. Her sister Ethel sadly recalled 'her heart gave out'.[105]

'Little brown girl in a white, white city'

For several years, Marson's contribution as a journalist, radio producer and feminist was erased from history. She is curiously absent from Peter Fryer's otherwise authoritative *Staying Power*, for example. And the Irish producer Swanzy was largely credited with the establishment of *Caribbean Voices*, which provided a launchpad for the careers of so many Caribbean artists.

A talented and versatile journalist and editor, Marson used *The Keys* to highlight the local and international issues facing people of colour as the Second World War loomed. Her intelligence and activism brought her to the centre of the world stage at a time of unceasing turbulence, as the League of Nations sacrificed the small African nation of Abyssinia on the altar of Fascist appeasement.

Marson was bold in her focus on women's rights and keen for cross-border co-operation between international feminist groups working to elevate women from their status as second-class citizens. Her work and that of Ashwood Garvey was pioneering in this regard. This torch would be passed on to Claudia Jones, whose publication along with Edward Scobie's *Flamingo*, elevated the work of those Caribbean artists Marson worked so hard to promote at the BBC. Finally, Marson's plays and her poetry stand as startling testimony to what it was like to be a person of colour at that time – how racial difference could generate subservience and abuse.

Marson's mental health issues may be the reason she was airbrushed from history. Unlike Padmore and James, she was not operating on the fringes: her work took her to the heart of the establishment, that of the Ministry of Information and the BBC. Operating inside establishment confines brought significant pressures. She was forced to be Janus-faced, glossing over the colour bar that she experienced personally, and promoting an image of a united, colour-blind Empire, proud to fight for 'the Mother country' during the Second World War. It was a position that would alienate her peers, and set her up for criticism from both the white West Indian elite and Black Londoners, who thought she should use her position to promote more diversity. The lack of allies in a war-ravaged London must have been particularly hard, and was exacerbated following the breakdown of her relationship with Thompson.

As the only Black woman producer, Marson's behaviour was constantly viewed in racial terms and she was always having to adapt her behaviour to that which was 'expected' of a woman of colour. This was the universal lens under which she was scrutinised, from petty work disputes to contract and salary expectations, and the inherent pressures and racism she endured from her co-workers undoubtedly had an adverse effect on her mental health. A twenty-first-century report links such racism to an increased likelihood of depression, hallucinations and delusions.[106] But unfortunately for Marson, understanding of mental health conditions in the early twentieth century was often wanting.

In her most famous play *Pocomania* (which translates as 'a little madness'): Marson touched on how society's norms promote refinement and decorum and conformity when in reality one wants to scream, shout and beat a drum at the unfairness of it all. In England, Marson suffered her own 'little madness', which pushed her considerable legacy into the shadows, but really who can blame her?

Her poems often revealed her most honest thoughts, free from editorial censure. In 'Black Burden', Marson summed up the pressures facing a person of colour in a position of white predominance: 'I am black/And so I must be/More clever than white folk/More wise than white folk,/More discreet than white folk/More courageous than white folk.'[107]

In truth, she strove to be.

REVOLUTION ABOVE A RECORD STORE

CLAUDIA JONES, editor, founder of carnival and anti-racist
campaigner (*West Indian Gazette and Afro-Asian Caribbean
News*, 1958–64). Preceded by career in US Communist newspapers:
Weekly Review, 1937–43; *Spotlight*, 1943–45; *The Daily
Worker*, 1945–46.

It was unlike Claudia Jones to miss a dinner party, especially one on
Christmas Day. The host Eric Levy, her friend, fellow Communist
Party colleague and close neighbour, was beginning to find her absence
concerning.

Jones loved parties. A tall, slender and elegantly dressed figure, she
was truly the life and soul of them, and Levy appreciated her vivacious
company. He was keen to learn more of Jones' interview with the great
civil rights leader Martin Luther King, and of her recent visit to China.
Her no-show was extremely perplexing.

Earlier when he had knocked on the door of her basement flat in
the building they shared in London's Lisburne Road to wish her Merry
Christmas, there had been no answer. Levy shivered as a fine mist gar-
landed the skeletal trees on nearby Hampstead Heath, a prelude to yet
another night of hard frost. He remembered the so-called Big Freeze of
1963 when brittle ice floes had paralysed the tides off the Kent coast and
6ft snowdrifts had transformed Kentish Town into an Arctic dunescape.
But the weather was not his main concern that evening.

Levy was aware that Jones suffered from cardiovascular disease
and had been hospitalised many times; she had been discharged from

St Stephen's Hospital in London earlier that month. He was also aware that his friend was suffering the strains and stresses of running a monthly newspaper at a loss. And he had some idea that Jones was encumbered by personal debt, which is the reason she had moved into 58 Lisburne Road that autumn after leaving her last property in arrears. He didn't know that Jones was so financially desperate that she had occasionally visited betting stores and, at least once, treated herself to a flutter on the horses at Kempton Park racecourse.[1]

The next day, Levy knocked on Jones' door again. Faced with silence, he made his way to the side of the red-bricked property and smashed a ground-floor window with a gloved hand to gain access to Jones' two-bedroom flat. Once inside, he saw the editor of the *West Indian Gazette* dead in her bed, her glasses intact and a book stubbornly open on her lap. The 49-year-old had suffered a fatal heart attack on Christmas Eve 1964.[2]

News reached the *Gazette* office in that gloaming period between Christmas and New Year. The devastated staff struggled to put together an issue in Jones' memory. Reporter Donald Hinds, one of Claudia's first hires, remarked years later: 'When Claudia died, a great hole was ripped in the fabric of our society. In December 1964 the black community was widowed.'[3]

The loss of Claudia was unfathomable. Said the activist Pearl Connor, a close friend: 'Claudia was one of the most charismatic Caribbean women I ever knew ... She linked her political stance with the artistic and cultural achievements of our people. Claudia was somebody really very important, a great stimulus to us all ... She made you fearless.'[4]

Hinds knew in his heart that the paper could not carry on without its erstwhile editor: the *Gazette*'s fate and hers were bound. At a symposium in 1996 he said: 'A lot of us had come to associate the *Gazette* with Claudia. They were almost inseparable, it was so much a part of her.'[5]

Febrile Atmosphere

Jones launched the *West Indian Gazette and Afro-Asian Caribbean News* in March 1958, proclaiming in its first editorial: 'There are at least 80,000 good reasons why we believe a West Indian newspaper is necessary. They are the 80,000 West Indians now resident here. Together we form a community with its own wants and problems, which our own paper alone would allow us to meet.'[6]

Jones could not have foreseen that this humble 'one-leaf flyer', as she described it, would go on to become a monthly paper with a substantial newsstand presence. Nor could she have prophesied that the likes of Martin Luther King, Malcolm X, W.E.B. Du Bois and Jamaican prime minister Norman Manley would grace the *Gazette*'s cramped offices above what was then Theo's Record Store at 250 Brixton Road, London.

The paper had been launched into a febrile atmosphere. A decade had passed since the 'open door' policy of the 1948 Nationality Act, which heralded the arrival of the HMT *Empire Windrush* and subsequently a large wave of migration from Britain's colonies in the Caribbean. Many of those who travelled were citizens of the UK and colonies, held British passports and equal rights of residence, and expected a warm welcome from what they termed 'the mother country'.

But as numbers of immigrants from the Caribbean grew, the rhetoric around the new arrivals turned hostile. Articles in the national media describing a 'flood of migrants' threatening scarce housing and jobs were common. In the 1961 census, 172,877 persons born in the West Indies were recorded in the UK (out of an overall population of 52 million). West Indians were largely concentrated in urban centres – London, Birmingham, Manchester, Nottingham and Derby.[7] The author G.C.K. Peach has argued that the 1961 census figure was possibly 20 per cent too low and at the beginning of 1964 the number of West-Indian born persons in Britain numbered around 300,000, a small but not insignificant number.[8]

Colour bars were operating openly in London and major UK cities, with many rented lodgings bearing signs in windows, saying, 'No coloureds' or 'No blacks, no dogs, no Irish'. Black and brown people were barred from all-white pubs and discriminated against in employment, where most were limited to heavy lifting and manual work, even if they had clerical qualifications from 'back home'.

Newly arrived West Indians were forced into overcrowded slum housing in some of London's poorest boroughs. Poor sanitation and heating bedevilled these properties – this was the era of the notorious slum landlord Peter Rachman – and West Indians had little choice but to take what they were given. In places such as Notting Hill, this created the perfect breeding ground for racism and fascist organisations such as Oswald Mosley's Union Movement and the White Defence League agitated in these areas. The new immigrants were made scapegoats for slum housing and accused of spreading disease, undercutting wages and living off social security.

In 1958, no mainstream media networks existed for the Black and brown community and, with many newspapers and politicians either ignoring or exacerbating their plight, they were in desperate need of a voice.

Into this vacuum stepped Jones, a dignified and accomplished orator, with an electrifying presence and a flair for poetry. 'She could command a rapt audience,' recalled friends, who had seen her speak at New York's Madison Square Gardens.[9]

Jones had been actively engaged in working for the improvement of Black people's conditions and rights in the United States on behalf of the Communist Party USA (CPUSA) before being deported to the UK in December 1955 as a high-profile casualty of J. Edgar Hoover's 'Red Scare' policy. The FBI director, an ardent anti-Communist, had seen it as his mission to weed out the more radical elements of left-wing labour groups in the late 1940s and early '50s and Jones, who had emigrated to the US as a child from Trinidad and never been fully naturalised, was an easy target.

At this point Jones was 40 and had spent three decades in the US. Born on 21 February 1915, she had arrived with her aunt and three sisters in 1924, two years after her parents, Sybil (known as Minnie) and Charles Cumberbatch. The family was middle class: in Jones' own words, her mother was a land owner and her father's family was in the hotel business. The drop in cocoa prices on the world market had adversely affected her parents' fortunes and, like thousands of West Indian immigrants before them, they had emigrated in search of the American dream, where 'gold was to be found on the streets' and their children could have more opportunity.[10]

Jones stated that this 'dream was soon disabused' as her family faced the 'special scourge of indignity stemming from Jim Crow national oppression'.[11] The family lived at 404 St Nicholas Avenue in Central

Harlem, an overcrowded building that housed other West Indian immi-grants, a few blocks from the famous Apollo Theatre. Charles worked as an editor for the *West Indian American News*, where he covered the African anti-colonisation campaigns. Jones would later credit her father with instilling in her and her sisters 'a pride and consciousness of our people [and] of our relation to Africa'. Her mother was employed as a dressmaker in a clothes factory. The girls attended an integrated school, PS 4 Duke Ellington on 160th Street, and settled in after initially suffer-ing some discrimination. In a matter of a few years, Jones was elected to the school's governing body as mayor along with her Chinese running mate in an early sign of her leadership qualities.

In November 1928, tragedy befell the Cumberbatch family when Jones' mother died suddenly after contracting spinal meningitis. The disease, which could kill those who contracted it in a matter of hours, spread among the poor, targeting those in overcrowded and unsanitary living conditions, and outbreaks were frequent in factories and schools in New York. Minnie, who had gone in to work for her shift, never made it home.

The experience rocked Claudia, who was only 13 at the time of her mother's death and would state in a 1952 speech that, whenever injustice came to mind, 'I would think of my mother'.[12] In America, the so-called land of the free, her mother had died at the age of 37, overworked, exhausted and sick.

As America teetered on the edge of the Great Depression, Charles lost his job at the newspaper. Now the family's sole provider, he worked as a furrier to make ends meet, but was unable to keep this job as the economic situation worsened. He later became a superintendent of the apartment building where the family lived.

Jones' youth was consequently blighted with poverty. She and her sisters spent their early years in a damp basement flat in direct view of an open sewer. A clever student, she did not attend her junior high school graduation as there was not enough money to pay for a gradua-tion gown. She 'bawled her eyes out in humiliation and self-pity'.[13]

At the age of 17, she contracted tuberculosis as a result of her impov-erished living situation and was hospitalised at Sea View Sanatorium for a year. Jones stated: 'I began to wonder why there was wealth and poverty, why there was discrimination and segregation, why there was a contradiction between the ideas contained in the Constitution and the Bill of Rights, which contravened its precepts of the pursuit for all of "life, liberty and happiness".[14]

The very system of capitalism was exploitative, surmised Jones, and she identified a connection between her own family's economic struggles and those of working-class people in general. Like McKay a decade earlier, she was beguiled by the Harlem street corner orators and how they railed against injustice.

By the time she graduated from high school, Jones had become politically active, joining the junior NAACP and the Urban League and writing a weekly column for the Harlem youth club's newspaper entitled 'Claudia's Comments'. Her experience working in a series of manual jobs after she graduated, in particular a laundry where she watched Black women co-workers faint from exhaustion in the insufferable summer city heat, further shaped her worldview. One of her friends recalled Jones was 'quick and clever at school, but along with 5 million other young people had to leave school during the depression and go to work. Seeking jobs, and on the job, she came smack up against discrimination at every turn.'[15]

At the age of 21, incensed by the miscarriage of justice in the Scottsboro Boys' trial, she joined the Communist Party, which had been instrumental in appealing the boys' plight. Just as Padmore had found decades earlier, Jones found the CPUSA's commitment to the rights of workers, women and people of colour a powerful draw. The rise of fascism in Europe, in particular the Italian invasion of Ethiopia and the Spanish Civil War, further radicalised her.

Meanwhile, her father was working as an editor for the Federal Writers' project that had also employed McKay in the depression years. His job was to collate information on the contribution of Black writers to the 'culture and development' of the city. One of these contacts, Ella Baker, was instrumental to Jones' development as a radical journalist. Baker had written an article in the NAACP's *Crisis* magazine in November 1935, exposing the street corner 'slave markets' in Bronx, New York, which Black women would frequent to secure domestic work on a zero-hour contract basis. In this piece Baker pioneered the use of the term 'triple exploitation'[16] to describe the situation of Black women workers exploited as workers, as women, and as Black citizens of a country where segregation was normalised. Jones later popularised this term in essays, most poignantly in reference to her mother.

Jones' intellect, organisational skills and talents as an orator meant that she quickly rose to prominence within the Young Communist League (YCL). She was at the forefront of conferences and significant party business, including the drafting of the constitution, and shared a stage with the National Chairman, Earl Browder, at the party's 18th birthday celebrations. In 1943 following several articles in *The Daily Worker* and YCL's *Weekly Review*, she became the latter's editor-in-chief.

In the run-up to the Second World War, Jones attended numerous anti-war rallies, reiterating that war was an imperialist project where people of colour were used as cannon fodder. The fact that the US Army was segregated was a case in point – why should Black people fight for an army and a country in which they were not afforded equal rights? From a feminist standpoint, Nazi Germany's triple K policy, *Kinder, Küche, Kirche* (children, kitchen, church), alarmed Jones. The Third Reich openly advertised its use of women's reproductive labour to supplement the military machine, and Jones was increasingly wary that a similar policy would be adopted in the US.

The Communist Party anti-war stance changed in June 1941 when the Soviet Union was invaded. Now the war against Nazi Germany was a war against fascism and racist policy in general. In a pamphlet entitled 'Lift Every Voice – For Victory (1942)' Jones looked back on Joe Louis' fight against the Nazi hope Max Schmeling on 22 June 1938 in New York's Yankee Stadium. Louis had delivered a 'knockout blow that was heard round the world ... in defiance of the Nazis' Aryan arrogance', she stated.[17]

Jones' rise through the party coincided with her marriage on 15 September 1940 to Abraham Scholnick, the son of Russian Jewish immigrants. Scholnick was a baking factory worker for the Tastee Bread Company, but little is known about how he met Jones or whether he was a fellow party member. In Jones' FBI file the couple are described as 'quiet tenants with no children' by their building superintendent.[18] Scholnick registered for the draft that his new wife had campaigned against and in

1943 began training with the 1060th Flying Squadron. Jones made her second application for US citizenship around this time. She was denied, despite being married to a US citizen; her sisters, Yvonne, Lindsay and Sylvia, were successful in their bids to be naturalised.

Her health was a major issue – she never fully recovered from TB, and would go on to suffer headaches, bronchitis and pneumonia. According to medical records, she underwent 'major gynecological' surgery in 1944 that triggered a premature menopause at the age of 29.[19]

This must have put a strain on her marriage and on 27 February 1947 Jones divorced Scholnick in the City of Juárez, Chihuahua, Mexico, citing incompatibility.[20] Travelling to Mexico for an inexpensive divorce was not uncommon at the time. Several years later, Scholnick appears as a two-sentence postscript in a long letter from Jones to Comrade Foster (William Z. Foster, General Secretary of the CPUSA), entitled 'autobiographical history'. To add insult to injury, Jones states in the same brief postscript that she plans to marry again in England within the next few months. How so little remains in the archive of Scholnick and of the man she was going to marry remains a mystery.[21]

The historian Marika Sherwood revealed that Jones had an extramarital affair with Howard 'Stretch' Johnson – a 'pencil thin' tap dancer, known for his Three Johnsons act with his siblings Winnie and Bobbie, the former a famed dancer at Harlem's Cotton Club.[22] 'Stretch' was a fellow member of Harlem's Young Communist League and the two remained close correspondents.[23]

Rising Star

What is known is that work and party business became Jones' main preoccupation. As well as being editor-in-chief of *Weekly Review*, Jones was from 1943 to 1945 editor of *Spotlight*, the magazine produced by the American Youth for Democracy, which had replaced the YCL during the Second World War. Towards the end of the war, she was appointed editor of the Negro Affairs desk at *The Daily Worker*. Following the end of her marriage, she also took an active role in national women's movements, such as the Congress of American Women. Her journalism work put her in contact with the actor and campaigner Paul Robeson and his wife Eslanda; she interviewed the actor in June 1943 for *The Daily Worker*. The three would become lifelong friends and the Robesons would support her when they lived briefly in London.

Jones' membership of the party and her work as editor of prominent party newspapers did not escape the attention of the FBI, which apparently held a 'copious' file on her.[24] Between 1948 and 1951, as McCarthyite hysteria took hold, she was arrested three times and interned on 'the McCarran Wing of Ellis Island', nicknamed after the notorious security laws. In lyrical prose, noting a homing pigeon's thirty-one attempts at flight, Jones described in a letter how the Statue of Liberty stood with her back to Ellis Island, and how the 'criss-cross light iron bars' interned the seventeen men and women of 'a virtual United Nations composition' on her wing.[25] She went on to relate how ordinary trade union activists from 'the electrical and maritime industries' found themselves incarcerated because of the government's hostile policies.[26]

Jones' attitude to her arrests was at first to deem them ludicrous. At the first arrest on 10 January 1948 at her apartment in 143rd Street in New York City, she 'ridiculed being arrested' and refused to sign an affidavit allowing the agents to search her apartment.[27] She was released on a $1,000 bail but the FBI, which had taken a while to realise that Jones was not a naturalised US citizen, was now working out how to deport her. The arrest failed to quell her activism: she had been assigned to work with working-class and Black women for peace and equality, and to this end she toured forty-three states, recruiting new members and holding mass rallies.

The FBI continued to keep a keen watch on Jones, logging the slogans chanted at rallies she attended, and even noting when Jones had a flare-up of bronchitis. On 20 June 1951, she was taken into custody for a third time, along with sixteen other Party leaders; she would later describe being woken at 7 a.m. by 'FBI characters', being searched for weapons and taken into custody.[28] Jones stated her bail was 'her weight in gold': it was set at $25,000, including deportation charges. Friends and family raised the funds for her to be freed, and for her future defence, with one committee stating it was 'bowled over' by the financial gifts and presents she received.[29] The support Jones received illustrated the high esteem in which she was held within the community.

In 1953 she was convicted under the Smith Act, which specifically targeted Communist Party sympathisers and made it illegal to advocate the overthrow of the US government. (The Bureau later admitted that Jones' speeches had never sanctioned such an action, instead focusing on equal rights for women and Black people.)[30] She was sentenced to one year and one day and fined $2,000. After a failed appeal, she was sent to Alderson Women's Penitentiary in West Virginia in January 1955 and threatened with deportation to either Trinidad or the UK.

US prisons at that time were often segregated and conditions were particularly harsh for people of colour. Jones was placed in a maximum security section with her friend Elizabeth Gurley Flynn, a white labour activist. On arrival they suffered the indignity of a routine strip and cavity search – and, as was standard practice, the now known carcinogen DDT was poured on their hair and left on for forty-eight hours in an attempt to delouse them. Flynn spoke about the first three days, acknowledging 'the heavy shadow of prison', and the sensation of the lock turning in the door and feeling dread 'like a trapped animal'.[31]

Their 'cottage', unlike the others, had steel-barred windows. Flynn said of the conditions:

> Picture if you will a room about eight feet in length and three and one half feet in width. This is your home for the duration of your unjust sentence ... Negro women prisoners got the worst jobs and were excluded from some classifications at that, so that the indignity was double in the case of [a] Negro Smith Act victim.[32]

Jones stated the routine was 'hectic': they were expected to rise at 6.30 a.m. and start work at 8 a.m. after cleaning their quarters. There was hardly any lunchbreak and the women worked until 7 p.m.[33]

The incarceration took its toll on Jones physically and she spent much of her prison time in the hospital sanatorium, where she was diagnosed with hypertensive cardiovascular disease. Dr Louise Miller, a hospital physician, noted Jones' poor health and tried to have her released, but the judge was unmoved. Jones was instead prescribed digitalis for her heart condition. She made the best of her time in prison; as well as weaving, she learnt pottery, jewellery making and other crafts.

Poetry became an outlet and a way of articulating her feelings at being imprisoned. She praised fellow jailed activists such as Puerto Rican nationalist Blanca Canales Torresola, who was serving a life sentence, and wrote touching poems about her friendship with Flynn. One of her most notable verses was 'Lament for Emmett Till', the 14-year-old child who had been brutally lynched in Mississippi in August 1955 while visiting relatives.

Jones secured an early release in October 1955 but the deportation order remained. In a press release dated 27 October 1955 from the National Committee to Defend Negro Leadership, details are given of Jones' fragile health and the decision to deport her immediately. Emphasising the unique nature of the situation, it stated: 'Miss Jones is the only Negro woman in the history of the US who has ever been imprisoned and threatened with deportation for her political beliefs and for her leadership in the struggle for peace and Negro rights.'[34] Official papers reveal that the UK and Trinidadian governments juggled Jones' fate between them. 'She may prove troublesome,' scrawled the governor of Trinidad in a document margin.[35]

The UK eventually agreed to take Jones and provide for her medical treatment (a factor may have been that they did not want Jones organising in the colonies), and she found herself aboard *Queen Elizabeth* bound for Southampton. A crowd of around 300 people gathered in the Skyline Ballroom in Harlem's Hotel Theresa on 7 December 1955 to wish her farewell.

Jones received several cards and letters from well-wishers and friends, including the editors and staff of *The Daily Worker* and W.E.B. Du Bois. Paul Robeson sent a poignant tribute, castigating 'the Smith Act, the McCarran Act, the jailings and deportations, the lynchings in Mississippi'. 'And Claudia will return to us – no doubt about it. She is on the winning side of history in our day – the side of peace, of justice, of liberation,' he wrote.[36]

William Z. Foster, the leader of the Communist Party USA, wrote to his British counterpart Harry Pollitt, general secretary of the Communist Party, on 9 December 1955, pleading with him to assist Jones as he had other comrades in similar circumstances. 'She was among the 150 Communist leaders who have been seized, framed and jailed … under … faked-up pretext,' he stated. He continued: 'Comrade Claudia, in ill health has been literally torn up by the roots … deported from the country where she has lived practically all her life, and compelled to begin life abroad all over again.'[37]

Jones wrote to her father from the ship on 19 December 1955. Although the thought of Shakespeare country excited her, her heart was still in the US. She wrote: 'My mind and deepest thoughts are still in the land I belong to and know and its people whom I have worked and struggled with for social progress.'[38]

There is no doubt that Jones was feeling nervous about the next steps. Her deportation from America had been protracted and had attracted significant attention, but she was, as her time in prison had illustrated, a strong character. Flynn would later state: 'Claudia's resilient spirit and resourceful ability to adapt to all circumstances, which made her unique in Alderson, sustain her in exile.'[39]

Jones took the boat-train from Southampton to Victoria Station and was met by her cousin Trevor Carter and Billy Strachan, a Jamaican RAF veteran. Carter's first impression of his cousin was that she looked 'successful' like 'a leader'. This smart, statesman-like woman had to fold herself into Carter's vehicle – 'a motorcycle within a bit of canvas thing like a tent' – in which he transported her through a smoggy, barely visible London.[40]

'Uprooted and ill'

That first year was hard for Jones. The smog was hazardous for someone with her health conditions. She spent two months in St Stephen's Hospital that winter and complained to Stretch that 'it is impossible to be both uprooted and ill'.[41] She was unable to find affordable accommodation and stayed with friends and fellow deportees, Mikki and Charlie Doyle, all the while concerned that she was a burden. The largely male, white-dominated Communist Party of Great Britain struggled to find a role for her. Jones was replete with American mannerisms – everyone was 'baby' or 'darling' – and the stuffed shirts were baffled by the appearance of this glamorous woman in their midst. Diane Langford stated, 'the upper-class lawyers and academics who controlled the dowdy Communist Party had no idea what to do with her', while 'the white working-class men ran the grassroots movement in their own interests, which rarely included solidarity with oppressed people of the colonies ... Claudia's sudden appearance among the left-wing beneficiaries of British imperialism was challenging'.[42]

Jones struggled to get work and this passionate, organised and brilliant leader had to resort to employment as a typist for the Chinese News Agency, work for which she was barely remunerated. Her beloved father, who had supported her throughout her incarceration, moving near Alderson so he could visit her regularly in prison, fell ill and died in the summer of 1956. Jones was unable to visit or attend his funeral. The US state department had blocked her travel and she wasn't approved for a full passport until 1962. A month after Charles' death, her sister Yvonne travelled to see her in London, which provided some comfort.

The cold, long, unforgiving British winters were taking a toll on Jones' health and it was only by writing to Dr Eric Williams in Trinidad for help in obtaining temporary travel documents that she managed to travel to Nice, France, in the summer of 1957. It was hoped the trip to warmer climes, paid for by friends, would improve her health.

Through party contacts, Jones managed to find rented accommodation at 6 Meadow Road, south London. Her landlord, the 'Red Dean of Canterbury', Rev. Hewlett Johnson, proved remarkably tolerant of her regular bounced cheques and non-payment of rent, and she stayed there until April 1960, when she moved to north London. The artist and activist Gertrude Elias, who lived near Jones, enquired if she was continuing her important work for the party by speaking on platforms around the country (much as she did in the US). Jones apparently laughed bitterly in response and stated she was doing 'donkey work', referring to the Chinese News Agency. Elias said she noted that Jones did not even have enough money for lunch.[43]

Poverty bedevilled Jones' time in London, but she continued to network, becoming active in many labour organisations set up to help the community, including the West Indian Workers and Students' Association and the Indian Workers' Association.

Through the latter organisation she met Abhimanyu Manchanda, known as Manu, who became a fixture in her life as a lover, friend and colleague. Jones sublet a room in her flat in Meadow Road to Manu to cover living expenses, and the two became extremely close. Pictures survive in his estate of the two holidaying in Cornwall and of Jones with his family. Manu's nieces used to call her Auntie Claudia.[44]

The labour groups that Jones worked with had been discussing launching a paper to serve the ever-expanding Caribbean community, and it was thought the *Caribbean News*, published by the Caribbean Labour Congress, with its limited, left-of-centre audience, would not have been sufficiently popular.

A new paper was needed and Jones, with her distinguished career in Black American newspapers, was chosen to head the launch. The decision was to prove monumental. The *Gazette* was launched at a time of increasing tensions on the streets of west London, where gangs of Teddy boys and far-right groups had been openly harassing residents of colour for months. Complaints to the police by non-white residents were ignored, despite local magistrates expressing concern at this increased level of intimidation.

Four months after the *Gazette* hit the newsstands, on a warm, fetid August bank holiday evening, the simmering prejudices boiled over on to the streets of Notting Hill. Hundred-strong white mobs, armed with improvised weapons – cudgels, iron bars, butcher's knives and leather belts studded with nuts and bolts – marched through the streets, chanting 'Keep Britain White'. PC Richard Bedford, on duty that night, heard the crowd shouting, 'We will kill all black bastards. Why don't you send them home?'[45]

Black and brown residents barricaded themselves in their homes, as milk bottles, Molotov cocktails and rocks hailed outside. Five Black men were beaten unconscious on the first night of violence and it wasn't long before the Black community responded in kind, with young Black men arming themselves with similar improvised weapons as a means of self-defence. Every night brought fresh atrocities, although no lives were lost. Ordinary civilians were swept up in the fray – people of colour who worked as plumbers and carpenters were arrested simply for toting bags of tools. In the end 108 people were charged with offences, seventy-two were white and thirty-six described as 'coloured'.

Although the violence eventually petered out, the acrid stench of petrol bombs was not the only thing that lingered in the air: non-white residents at the time reported the mood being thick with racial hatred and prejudice, 'an atmosphere you could slice like a knife. We felt unwanted.'[46]

As the writer and campaigner Gus John explained: 'Some of our relatives were impacted by the 1958 riots in Notting Hill. And so the picture that I had from being in school, both in Trinidad and Grenada [of a tolerant society], was falling apart. The Britain that was presented in the schooling and education system in those islands was not the Britain that we experienced when we got here.'[47]

The hate was not confined to London; St Ann's in Nottingham had witnessed similar violence that month. Emboldened, the far-right White Defence League and Oswald Mosley's Union Movement party moved their headquarters to London's Notting Hill a few weeks later. The White Defence League chose 74 Princedale Road, the Notting Hill home of the late Imperial Fascist League leader Arnold Leese, as its headquarters, and published an anti-immigration magazine, *Black and White News*, with a circulation of about 800.

Popular mainstream newspapers echoed the official narrative of events put out by the Metropolitan police and reported this episode of racial violence as merely 'disturbances', the fault of 'ruffians, both coloured and white'. It was only after four decades had elapsed and the release of secret papers that the true racially violent nature of the riots was revealed.[48]

In the fractious atmosphere post-riots, Jones' *Gazette* came to the fore. In truth there was no one who was better aware of how Black newspapers could galvanise a community and engender it with a sense of pride. The newspaper saw tackling racism as one of its central tenets. 'People without a voice were lambs to the slaughter,' Jones declared following the riots.[49]

Such forthright statements attracted foes. *The Daily Worker* reported on its front page of 28 August 1958 that the Ku Klux Klan of Britain had trashed the *Gazette*'s offices, smashing equipment and daubing graffiti on the walls. Racist correspondence was sent to Jones from the organisation that same month, addressing the editor as 'Mr B. Ape'.[50]

Jones wrote about the Klan letter in a 'London letter' in the US paper *The Daily Worker* and described how West Indians in the UK were being 'scapegoated' as a visible minority under the imperialists' tactic of 'divide and rule' in order 'to divert the people's anger into channels away from themselves'.[51] In the article, she spoke of holding several sessions with Manley and Dr Carl La Corbiniere (deputy president of the West Indies Federation). Alarmed at the violent nature of the riots, Manley had toured the UK in September 1958 and visited the *Gazette*'s offices; while Jones had met La Corbiniere at Amy Ashwood Garvey's house at 1 Bassett Road in London's Notting Hill.

Ashwood Garvey had recently returned from Ghana and established the Association for the Advancement of Coloured People (modelled on the US's NAACP).[52] Jones and Ashwood Garvey became firm friends – in a letter dated 2 July 1964, Ashwood Garvey refers to her as 'the luckiest and most loyal friend I have'.[53] Ashwood Garvey served as 'a major source of subsidies' for the *Gazette*[54] and Jones bestowed on the elder stateswoman the title of 'honorary president' of the paper.[55] The Ashwood Garvey connection directly linked Jones' work with those of earlier progressive actors of the 1920s and '30s: McKay, Pankhurst, James and Padmore, even Garvey himself. Jones' *WIG* took up the mantle of their activism and in many ways drove it forward with a wider community to represent. As the paper became more established, Padmore exchanged party correspondence with Jones from Nkrumah's headquarters in Accra.[56]

Jones became the spokesperson for her community and harassment from right-wing groups continued throughout the paper's existence, sometimes making headlines in the paper itself. 'UK Nazis call *WIG* offices', one of the news reports on page three of the January 1960 edition, states: 'WIG office was the recipient of an anonymous call earlier this month, saying: "this is the Nazi movement calling. We will get you tonight for the three policemen who were done in".'[57]

None of this swayed Jones' vision: she was intent on making the *Gazette* a success. The paper, she believed, would accompany the Caribbean community in London, bringing news from 'back home' and reporting on issues new arrivals faced adjusting to life in the capital. Hinds explained: 'During those months, from late summer to autumn 1958, the *Gazette*'s offices did more business meeting worried blacks than did the Migrants' Service Department.'[58]

Edward Pilkington, in *Beyond the Mother Country: West Indians and the Notting Hill White Riots*, sums up the *Gazette* as:

allowing West Indians to express their uncertainties and confusions in the wake of the riots. Their British identity had been jolted by the riots, for how could they call themselves British after being treated like unwanted strangers? This left a vacuum to be filled … Out of the ashes of the 'Mother Country' a new vision was born. The riots marked the dawn of a new West Indian identity for black people living in Britain.[59]

Gus John further explained:

I had never been to Jamaica … My two uncles were from Guyana … but I hadn't been to Guyana either. So in many respects, most of the Caribbean countries were totally alien to me. [In England] we were discovering one another as Caribbean people and that was pretty exciting for a whole number of reasons. What we leave we carry. So we carried our value systems, our belief systems. And it was really interesting to see how that gained expression in the country we had adopted as our future home … We began to develop an identity as Caribbean people.[60]

A Paper for its People

The *Gazette* office was so much more than just a newspaper office: in its role as both a community centre and liaison bureau, it acted as the central nervous system of a burgeoning West Indian community. Positioning itself in the heart of Brixton, it was a paper dedicated to its people and at its very centre was Jones.

The newspaper office was a crowded, claustrophobic and untidy space, with desks bulging with papers and telephones ringing off the hook. Hinds described it as a 'beehive of activity'.[61] The paper itself was a product of 'colossal human energy', mostly Jones', commented the historian Bill Schwarz, and it was evident that she poured her heart and soul into the venture.[62]

A queue would often snake from the cramped office all the way down the narrow stairway to the back of Theo's record store, much to the consternation of its owner, who would tut as the line of West Indians rumbled impatiently. Jones took her time with each client, who was likely to be preoccupied with matters such as job security, housing rights and education. When there were instances of discrimination or even racist attacks, Jones would make full use of her networking skills, mobilising her substantial contacts in local government, social services and the police, to see what she could do. Hinds explained: 'What they needed was a godmother ... That was the role Claudia Jones played best.'[63]

In the early days, the paper was run in an ad hoc and some would say chaotic manner. Anybody who wanted to write for it could – their copy just had to pass the muster of its critical editor. Jones, a seasoned wordsmith, had high standards, shouldering most of the editorial tasks, such as editing and rewriting copy, herself.

Jones and her partner Manu, who appeared on the masthead as general manager, were often found in the office at all hours sorting editorial business or community matters. Although the riots had highlighted the difficulties facing the community, it was also a time of hope, optimism and real possibility with anti-colonial struggles sparking around the world, and the two plugged in to this mindset, actively working for change. As Langford, who married Manu years after Jones' death, noted: 'They were both charismatic people and their personalities were needed.'[64]

What started as a love affair seemed to have evolved into more of a partnership by late 1959. In one quite haughty letter, Manu stated he was instructing solicitors to 'disassociate with both the *Gazette* and the Coloured Peoples' Publishing House', citing Jones' 'very chaotic, most inefficient, uneconomic and unsystematic working'.[65] Jones was an editorial powerhouse but was no accountant, and the advice sessions she insisted on giving ate into valuable work time. According to Langford, there were 'pressure points': Manu wanted the paper to be run in a more formal way so they would not keep going bankrupt.[66] Some of the advertising department's choices, such as hair or beauty products, did not align with the paper's political views and this also provoked clashes. Manu never did leave the *Gazette*, though, and Jones and he remained close – theirs also was a companionship based on common political goals, intellect and a shared colonial background. (Manu hailed from India.)

Other staff included Theo Campbell, the owner of the record store below the offices, who wrote the sports section, focusing on cricket and boxing, and who later introduced the young London Transport bus conductor Hinds to Jones. The talented Hinds was keen to write for the paper and was soon given the title of City Reporter. He often worked shifts on the buses and came to the *Gazette* wearing his bus conductor's uniform. Jones' assistant Alrick Cambridge joined much later (eighteen months before her death), as did the feature writer Ken Kelly, who later wrote for *Punch*. Inez Lachkan was the women's editor and both Ashwood Garvey and the Guyanese author Jan Carew are on the masthead as contributing editors. (Carew would later go on to launch *Magnet News* in 1965.) The staff was bolstered by a number of willing student volunteers.

Nobody was paid at the paper, including Jones. The enterprise had community very much at its heart and finances second. Everybody wanted to be a part of it and strove to make it a success. Hinds said:

> Those who were politically aware knew that it had to be done ... I knew that a West Indian paper was needed, and also there was a carrot that if the *West Indian Gazette* did get on its feet, I was going to be the first full-time employee ... [The office] was a place alight with optimism for both the individual and the community as a whole.[67]

Jones had captured a mood. She was living in exile from her family and friends in the US and the *Gazette* became very much her calling. John added:

> It was a rare thing to have a Black newspaper with radical politics run by a declared Communist in London, but it also spoke to the issue of Black people as a displaced pool of labour coming from the Caribbean to Britain, particularly in relation to rebuilding the place after two world wars ... It spoke to the community and it spoke to our experience as former colonial people in those islands.[68]

The paper thrived in those early days after the riots, regularly outselling its print run. Its circulation hit 30,000 during the winter of 1958.

Jones wanted the paper to reach and serve the community in multiple ways. To this end she brought her extensive connections from the Harlem community to bear. The Robesons performed two benefit concerts for the paper, while Flynn championed Jones' work in the CPUSA's *Sunday Worker*, explaining how the *Gazette* challenged British racism and imperialism. Distinguished US writers such as Du Bois and James Baldwin were also featured frequently in the paper.

In its heyday, the *Gazette* attracted politicians such as Martin Luther King, Manley, Cheddi Jagan, Phyllis Allfrey and David Pitt, and writers such as George Lamming, Carew, Salkey, Namba Roy, Sam Selvon and John La Rose through its doors.

Said Hinds: 'As we went into 1959, politicians from what was referred to as the British Caribbean were seen going up the stairs to talk to Claudia ... The British media also sought Claudia's opinions ... Claudia was one with the finger on the pulse of British society.'[69]

International Focus

Jones' editorials and reporting in the *Gazette* were stridently Pan-African in nature, linking the issues faced by newly arrived West Indians in Britain to the international struggle against racism and colonialism. In October 1961, she wrote: 'We oppose colonialism, we stand for the unity of West Indians and Afro-Asian Caribbean people; we stand for peace and disarmament and oppose nuclear weapons, we want to build friendship and understanding of all ... world peoples, based on the recognition of equality and dignity of all peoples and nations.'

Styled as a tabloid over twelve pages, the paper carried news and analysis, popular features, film and book reviews, and sport.[70] Its cover price was sixpence. A number of classifieds added bulk, with small ads featuring anything from hair salons and tailors to grocers that catered for the Black community. Grimaldi Lines, Encona and Mount Gay rum regularly took out full-page ads.

The *Gazette*'s geographical scope and reach rivalled that of the British mainstream media, which devoted few column inches to the Global South. Such was the intellectual heft of its columns, particularly the editorials penned by Jones, that readers were fully informed on the horrors of apartheid, including the Sharpeville massacre, where police fired on a number of Black anti-apartheid demonstrators, killing or wounding up to 250 civilians, and the Rivonia trial, where a number of anti-apartheid activists, including Nelson Mandela and Walter Sisulu, were convicted of treason and imprisoned.

The *Gazette* regularly ran cover stories and editorials on the progress of the anti-apartheid movement. In January 1960, it called for boycotts of South African goods as a means of putting economic pressure on the government.

Indeed Jones and the *WIG* kept the pressure on the South African government when the British media's silence could be seen as being complicit with a racist regime. In August 1960 a news story by S. Stewart outlined Trinidad's boycott of South African goods, with dockers refusing to unload South African corn and Trinidadian women mobilising and marching in the streets against apartheid. The article stated: 'The callous and inhuman treatment of Africans at Sharpeville served to arouse the indignation and resentment of peoples all over the world thereby crystallising world resentment against Dr Verwoerd's slave state.'

The paper's words were matched with actions. A year on from the Sharpeville massacre, Jones organised a protest in Trafalgar Square to mark the anniversary on 21 March 1961. Her good friend Eslanda Robeson spoke, reminding the audience that 'the reason the Murders at Sharpeville are important to the world is because they exposed once again, the evils and dangers of racial discrimination, segregation and oppression'.[71] While in May 1964, Manu and four other activists took part in a seventeen-day hunger strike calling for economic sanctions against South Africa.

Readers were regularly kept abreast of international decolonisation movements. In Hinds' words, 'It shook its fist at the Congo civil war and the abandonment of Patrice Lumumba.'[72] The paper took the bold decision to print the last photograph of Lumumba on the back of a truck, bound without his spectacles, about to be delivered to his rival Moïse Tshombe's henchmen, and the last letter of the first democratically elected leader of the Congo was printed on the cover in April 1961. Meanwhile, a triumphant cover story in November 1960, 'And Now

Nigeria – 35 Million Africans Free', is illustrated with a beautiful picture of turbaned women smiling and celebrating Nigerian independence the previous month.

Serving as an information repository on the Black world at a critical juncture, the *Gazette*'s contribution to history was invaluable, although staff did not realise it at the time: 'I don't think I really grasped the true fact that I was in the presence of history,' surmised Hinds.[73]

Closer to home, a public house in Ladbroke Grove operating a colour bar was a front-page splash in April 1961: 'Archie Spencer asked for a pint of bitter and was told "we don't serve coloured people here".' While the controversial Commonwealth Immigrants Bill, which was pushed for by Conservative Home Secretary Richard Butler and became law in July 1962, was also tackled. In November 1961, Jones informed her readers in perspicacious terms of how Butler's 'colour bar bill' would establish 'a second-class citizenship status for West Indians and other Afro-Asian peoples in Britain'. The *Gazette* continued to complain loudly about the act, with Jones consistently outlining its racist design and intention.

In a sign of its political clout, the *WIG* also organised a demonstration in London outside the US embassy to coincide with the historic march on Washington for civil rights in August 1963. Cambridge stated that Jones, as the chief organiser, 'managed to bring together groups of people from many different walks of life, Asians, Africans, West Indians and British, from different political persuasions and even from different faiths'. He argued that in doing so Jones extended her 'internationalist understanding to a struggle against the national oppression of black America which her imagination had never left behind'.[74]

A long colour piece gives a real insight into Jones' life and that of non-whites in Britain at the time. In 'I Spend a Night in a Notting Hill Police Station', Jones recounted an incident where she went to the opening of the Red Stripe House – 'a gay party with lots of people present' – and was given a lift home by friends, the Bartholomews. The husband George was stopped by police and arrested for drink-driving. The reason for the suspicion is lame: the group had been seen leaving a noisy party. Jones accompanied George to the police station and naturally got into a long discussion with the inspector about the treatment of West Indians in the UK, eventually doling out copies of the *Gazette* 'which I carry everywhere. Thereupon, the station became a reading room', with 'Officer 367' and others perusing the paper.[75]

When people of colour were a rarity on stage and screen and scarcely reviewed in mainstream newspapers, the *WIG*'s review pages championed writers and artists from the community. In December 1961, Pearl Prescod's role as Harriet Tubman in the BBC documentary *Come Along to Freedom* was reviewed, while work by actors such as Cy Grant, Corinne Skinner-Carter, Sydney Poitier and Nadia Cattouse was profiled regularly.

Jones reviewed James Baldwin's *The Fire Next Time* and Hinds interviewed the great writer following the publication of *Another Country* in 1962; novels by George Lamming, Roy, V.S. Naipaul, Andrew Salkey and E.R. Braithwaite were also critiqued.

Philanthropic causes were also on the paper's radar. A benefit concert was organised by the *Gazette* for victims of Hurricane Flora, which devastated the Caribbean in 1963.

But perhaps the most memorable institution the *Gazette* and Jones established was that of carnival in the UK. In November 1958, a Caribbean carnival committee was set up by the paper for the purposes of showcasing West Indian talent and culture, in the aftermath of the Notting Hill riots.

According to Pearl Connor: 'Everyone wanted to run away and leave. The fear was in the area and she [Claudia] was thinking about how to do something about it.'[76] No one on that committee was aware that they were witnessing the origins of what would become the largest annual street event in Europe – the Notting Hill carnival – attracting crowds of more than a million over the August Bank Holiday.

On Friday, 30 January 1959, the first carnival took place indoors in London's St Pancras Town Hall to coincide with the annual carnival in Trinidad, and it was televised by the BBC. Tickets were priced 7*s* 6*d* and could be obtained from the *Gazette*. Jones and her committee had taken great care with the decorations, decking the hall out in palm fronds, colourful shell mobiles and other memorabilia from the Caribbean. The dress code was smart: the men's suits featured knife-edge creases, while the women rocked full-circle swing skirts and ballgowns with long elbow-length gloves, their waists cinched in with wide belts. There was the odd tropical shirt, despite the winter chill.

In her introduction in the carnival's brochure, entitled 'A People's Art is the Genesis of their Freedom', Jones stated that she was determined that the events of Notting Hill and Nottingham should never occur again. She goes on to extol 'the role of the arts in bringing people together for common aims, and to its fusing of the cultural, spiritual as well as political and economic interests of West Indians in the UK and at home'.[77]

Jones wanted to celebrate and restore pride in West Indian culture – a culture that had been seriously baited by the events of August 1958. The carnival, with its dances and Carnival Queen beauty contests (the feminist Jones knew how important it was to celebrate Black beauty), was a means of linking the cultural with the political.

The carnival was a huge success, featuring costume mas players, the Trinidad All Stars and Hi-fi steel bands, dance troupes, and artists such as Cleo Laine and calypsonian Mighty Terror, and culminating in a Grand Finale Jump-Up. It became an annual occurrence, always sponsored by the *Gazette*, and in 1962 Jones managed to secure the great calypsonian, the Trinidadian Mighty Sparrow, as a headline act.

Despite carnival and the harmony it attempted to restore to a battered community, the racist murder on 17 May 1959 of young Antiguan Kelso Cochrane, who was stabbed by white youths, forced a reassessment. In a display of unity, more than a thousand mourners, of all races, attended his funeral in Kensal Green cemetery. According to Hinds: 'After Cochrane's death, we had to rethink everything, we had to revise our faith in the Union flag.'[78]

Jones and the *Gazette* tried to get justice for the young Black carpenter and his family, but they were thwarted at every turn. There were accusations of police complacency in dealing with the racist killing, treating it initially like a robbery, and claims of a cover-up. Cochrane's killers were never found, although Oswald Mosley's Union Movement was heavily implicated.

Labour of Love

In her editorials for the *Gazette*, a weary Jones continually campaigned against racism in Britain, the colour bar and the insidious spread of extreme right-wing parties, but this campaigning fervour did little to assuage the paper's financial difficulties.

Despite its high-profile and starry supporters, the *Gazette* was unable to turn a profit. Circulation flatlined at a disappointing 10,000 in late 1959 and advertisers, which were more often than not small businesses in the Black community, were often late with subscriptions as they suffered from financial difficulties themselves. The paper was constantly struggling to pay the monthly printing bill and was often late. It was not unusual for two editions of the monthly paper to merge in order to save costs. Hinds said: 'Looking back it seems preposterous that the only coherent voice from the black community in Britain was a monthly paper so strapped for cash, it often could not find the £100 to pay the printers.'[79]

In 1962 fractures began to appear among the *Gazette*'s most loyal and committed staff. Hinds had started a young family and had less time to devote to the paper, while Kelly had opted to go freelance. Personal circumstances changed for much of its volunteers and the *Gazette*, very much a labour of love, was the first casualty. To compound things, the relationship with Campbell had become strained and the paper had to find new premises off Brixton's Coldharbour Lane. Hinds recalled: 'We all loved Claudia and respected her, but we were not always there for her. Some people were very cautious of her Communist connections at a time when the cold war was at its hottest. The majority had families and all had their livings to make ... I was not as readily accessible to the cause and the great woman as I would like to think.'[80]

Jones was well aware of the fragility of the paper. As early as February 1961 the *Gazette*'s accountant was preparing to sue her over unpaid fees. Jones had written to her friend Eslanda Robeson in June 1960 that she was at 'a point where the exhaustion and the weight of the problems are weighing me down a bit. WE CANNOT FAIL. Too much has gone into the establishment of this paper – too much in terms of work, concepts and sacrifice, personal and otherwise for this to happen.'[81]

She went on to expound the need for investors and a printing press. Sadly none of this came to fruition and a bruised *Gazette* limped on, an increasingly stretched Jones taking on most of the work. In a situation that mirrored that of Edwards' a century earlier: this charismatic and bold editor was struggling against the odds to keep her vision afloat.

Letters to Manu outlined the grievous state of both Jones' and the paper's finances. In October 1962, she wrote that she was not relishing the prospect of flat hunting again. Her health required a place on higher ground 'with central heating, if not too costly'. Other letters focused on bills – phone, electric, printers – before moving on to editorial issues such as the 'absence of Donald's column', the need for lighter features and Manu's preponderance for long sentences '70 words or more'.[82]

Celebrity friends occasionally came to her aid. Pablo Picasso, whom she had met in France in 1957, gave her two drawings to sell to raise money. (It is not known if they were actually sold or what happened to them after her death.) As Hinds stated, 'Claudia loved and understood people, more than she did the balance sheet.'[83]

As the *Gazette* struggled, so did the woman who embodied it. By now Jones was seriously ill and being hospitalised regularly. Furthermore she had been threatened with eviction for rent arrears. Money worries plagued her. She received a little money from her sisters in the US but this and a £4 a week stipend she paid herself in expenses could hardly sustain her. In 1963, she narrowly avoided prison for outstanding debts owed to a travel company, while in the year of her death, she was being sued for non-payment of council rates. Letters from the bank habitually papered her doormat, each missive the same: the *Gazette*'s overdraft had not been paid. In the last year of her life, she refused to slow down – participating in protests outside the South African embassy in London, working with the ANC to organise a hunger strike against apartheid and travelling to Japan for a conference against atomic bombs at which she gave a keynote speech, and then on to China in the autumn, fitting in an interview with Martin Luther King on the way.

It is not known what she thought about Khrushchev's secret speech in February 1956 outlining Stalin's abuses of power, which led to many Communist Party members' disillusionment, but six months before her death, she wrote: 'I am certain that mankind will take the high road to a socialist future.'[84] According to Cambridge, it was Jones' loyalty and commitment to Communist principles avowed by Lenin that informed her 'deep ethical compass'.[85]

Following Jones' death, a grief-stricken Manu managed only four more issues of the paper, publishing her posthumous editorial on Martin Luther King's receipt of the Nobel Peace Prize in the December–January 1965 issue, which reported her death on the front page under a huge portrait photograph. The subsequent February–March issue is packed with tributes: 'Africa mourns'; 'Belgian Friends Lament Claudia'; 'World's Liberation Movement Loss'. The shock at the sudden loss of the *Gazette*'s editor reverberated across the world.

Hinds wrote of Jones' funeral, which took place on the morning of Saturday, 9 January at Golders Green crematorium: 'Unconcerned at the wet, cheerless day, hundreds had been waiting, in groups, for the bier to arrive from the chapel of rest. One African with deep emotion sighed, "We have lost the only person who qualified as the national leader of the Afro-Asian Caribbean peoples in Britain."'

The coffin, draped in red, gold and black, was preceded by a long funeral procession, with many international dignitaries in attendance.

The *Gazette* folded five months after Claudia's death. The final issue of April–May 1965 is nine pages long with an article on Malcolm X's assassination and a posthumous piece by Jones. The paper feels cobbled together and poorly edited; Manu was also ill and depressed. In the end the *Gazette* simply couldn't continue without its dynamic editor at the helm. Her revolutionary spirit, her dynamism and her dedication to racial justice was what made it soar.

Jones' ashes were interred in a plot to the left of Karl Marx's grave in the journalist section of Highgate Cemetery. For two decades, disputes over ownership of her grave plot and lack of finance meant it was left unmarked and untended until a headstone was erected in 1984, almost two decades later.

Langford stated that Manu 'kept all her [Jones'] stuff: passport, papers, betting slips' and ballgowns that were ruined when their flat flooded. She added that 'there was a cabin trunk full of worn, pointy shoes, costume jewellery, baubles, depleted perfume bottles, an electric contraption for relaxing her hair and an alarm clock with a large bell'.

Also saved was a 'wooden cube with a Perspex lid, lined with vermillion felt, [it] contained blood-drenched pebbles gathered from a beach on which dozens of Chinese Communists had been murdered by the Kuomintang ... [a] relic of revolutionary martyrs' presented to 'either Manu or Claudia'. In a way, this list of items gives a unique snapshot into this remarkable woman's character.[86]

In one final ignominy, Jones' contribution to the anti-racist struggle as editor of the *Gazette* and founder of the Notting Hill Carnival was not memorialised for many years. In August 2008, a blue plaque was finally unveiled on the corner of London's Tavistock Road and Portobello Road commemorating Claudia Jones as the 'Mother of the Caribbean Carnival in Britain'. She was so much more – an accomplished poet, freedom fighter and campaigning activist and editor.

In her last published essay 'The Caribbean Community in Britain', for the African American journal *Freedomways*, Jones assessed the *Gazette*'s contribution:

This newspaper has served as a catalyst, quickening the awareness, socially and politically, of West Indians, Afro-Asians and their friends. Its editorial stand is for a united independent West Indies, full economic, social and political equality and respect for human dignity for West Indians and Afro-Asians in Britain, for peace and friendship between the Commonwealth and all world peoples.[87]

Hinds was more scalpel like in his summation: 'The *West Indian Gazette*, like a child from the insalubrious part of town, was born into a struggle and its life was destined to be short, tortuous and somewhat bruising.'[88]

In its short life, the *Gazette* did much to serve the Caribbean community in Britain. While its founder's grave lay neglected, choked with weeds and bramble in Highgate cemetery, progressive movements flourished from the roots the paper had established in the UK.

The *Gazette*'s newest recruit Cambridge, who had taken the call of Jones' death that fateful day, founded the journal *Black Liberator* in 1973, which carried on much of Jones' work, focusing on the needs of the UK's growing Caribbean community. Cambridge, along with George Joseph and Sonia Chang among others, was also involved in the establishment of the Black Unity and Freedom Party, part of the British Black Power movement. A young Leila Hassan Howe was on the editorial board of its newspaper *Black Voice*. She stated: '*Black Voice* was part of the legacy of Claudia Jones ... When we had our education classes or when we would do our political discussions, we would be made aware who Claudia Jones was and the fact that she was a Communist and the fact that she really was one of the first people ever to stand up for rights for Black people in this country.'[89] Hassan Howe, with her husband Darcus Howe, would go on to be part of the editorial team of *Race Today*, a magazine and political movement that would span more than a decade and place at its heart the struggle for equal rights and justice for people of colour in the UK.

The *Gazette* proved a rich incubator of talent: many of the writers it promoted – Salkey, Selvon, Hinds – went on to work with magazines such as Edward Vivian Scobie's *Flamingo* and Carew's *Magnet News*, while John La Rose set up the hugely influential New Beacon Books and chaired the New Cross Massacre Action Committee.

In the dark days of the riots, Jones could not have foreseen that the revolutionary spirit she started in the offices above a record store was to have such an enduring legacy. Her struggle to give her people a voice became in the end her greatest achievement.

THE RENEGADE PANTHER

DARCUS HOWE, writer, broadcaster and civil rights campaigner, founder of the Race Today Collective (the *Black Eagle*, 1968; the *Black Dimension*, 1969; *Race Today*, 1973–86; *The New Statesman*, 1995–2008)

Darcus Howe could not take his eyes off the man on the Roundhouse stage. He was captivated by his childhood friend Stokely Carmichael's performance. It 'was so brilliant, the change of tone of voice, commanding the audience'.[1]

The year was 1967. It had been three years since the death of Claudia Jones. Inside the Roundhouse, a former steam engine repair shop that resembled a vast concrete circus tent in Camden, north London, a Congress on the Dialectics of Liberation was taking place featuring leading intellectuals and thinkers. The symposium's theme was to 'demystify human violence in all its forms'. The conference's backdrop was the bloody, brutal and intractable Vietnam War.

Prominent speakers invited included beat poet Allen Ginsberg, German philosopher Herbert Marcuse; C.L.R. James and Carmichael; the latter urged the conference organisers to move beyond 'intellectual masturbation'.[2]

Howe wasn't the only person impressed by the passion and clarity of Carmichael's speech that day; several of those assembled found the words of the 'Black Power Prophet' intensely moving.[3] Marcuse's student Angela Davis wrote several years later: 'In the enormous barnlike structure, its floor covered with sawdust, the air reeked heavily of marijuana and there were rumors that one speaker, a psychologist, was high on acid ... As I listened to Stokely's words, cutting like a switch-blade, accusing the enemy as I had never heard him accused before. I admit I felt the cathartic power of his speech.'[4]

Along with Ginsberg, the father of flower power, Carmichael was the star draw at the conference, which ran from 15 to 30 July 1967. The 26-year-old chairman of the US-based Student Nonviolent Coordinating Committee (SNCC) had in a few short years gone from a college senior at Howard University to running two major civil rights campaigns and rubbing shoulders with Martin Luther King. Following his twenty-seventh arrest, he summarised the frustration of an emerging generation of black liberation activists subjected to the heavy hand of the law by calling for 'Black Power'.[5] 'Black Power' became a rallying call for his supporters, and would mark his political evolution as leader of the Black Panther Party. It was in this atmosphere that Carmichael arrived in London, mobbed like a rockstar by press and public alike when he toured the multicultural enclaves of Notting Hill, Brixton and Hackney in his trademark sunglasses and silk dashiki.

Flanking him on the Roundhouse stage on 18 July were the civil rights activist Michael X (who was eager to grab some of Carmichael's stardust, despite his own rather dubious past[6]) and Obi Egbuna, a Nigerian-born playwright and the president of the Universal Coloured Peoples' Association (UCPA), and his deputy Roy Sawh. The UCPA was barely a month old, having been established on 5 June 1967 following a meeting of seventy-six people in Notting Hill. The fact that they were anointed Carmichael's tour guides was a significant coup for the fledgling organisation.

Carmichael's speech identified western imperialism as the main threat to human rights, social justice and racial equality, and the root cause of institutional racism. The solution, he asserted, was greater unity among the peoples of the Global South.

'We have to extend our fight internationally ...' he said. 'Not only because we're against black men fighting their brothers in Vietnam, but also because we are certain that the next Vietnam will be in the Congo, in South Africa, in Zimbabwe, Bolivia, in Guatemala, in Brazil, in Peru, or indeed the West Indies. And we are not going to fight our brothers.'[7]

Referencing Claude McKay's *If We Must Die*, which he argued had been misappropriated by Winston Churchill during the Second World War, Carmichael pointed out that any attempt by Black people to peacefully coexist with white people had been met with violence and oppression.[8] 'We can no longer accept this oppression without retribution,' he said to rousing applause.[9]

Said Egbuna: 'It was one of the best speeches I have ever heard Stokely make, and his impact on the audience, both black and white was electric ... A new phase of black history had begun.'[10]

Carmichael's UK visit chimed with race riots that were spreading across Detroit, Newark and New Jersey in the US, and Roy Jenkins' jittery Home Office was keen to halt similar uprisings in the UK. Newspapers reported that police in provincial cities with high multicultural populations were on high alert.[11] Instead of a planned speaking appearance in Rainbow Hall in Reading two days later, Carmichael hastily left the country. According to Sawh, his departure had been prompted by a visit from Special Branch. Michael X, who took Carmichael's place in Reading, was subsequently arrested and charged with inciting racial hatred under the 1965 Race Relations Act. He was jailed for a year on 9 November 1967, and thanks to the British state's intervention, his social cache grew considerably.

Impressed with his friend's turn at the conference, Howe vowed to learn more about revolutionary movements, their style and tactics. Born Leighton Rhett Radford Howe in the village of Moruga in the far south of Trinidad on 26 February 1943, Howe was James' second cousin and referred to his older relative as 'Uncle Nello'. He moved from Eccles village, a rural outpost in the south of Trinidad to Belmont, a suburb of Port of Spain, with his parents (his father, Cipriani, was the village school's well-respected headmaster and Anglican priest and his mother, Lucille, the local teacher) and seven siblings at 10 years old. He had won a scholarship, like James before him, to the island's elite Queen's Royal College.

Belmont was the birthplace of steelpan, calypso and carnival, and Howe was fascinated by the working-class neighbourhoods of the north, and the gangs that carved up the territory. Unbeknownst to his family, he became close to the leader of the Renegades gang, who went by the nickname Gold Teeth. The contradictions inherent in attending the island's equivalent of Eton and then liming with the Renegades as an impressionable teenager was not lost on Howe. 'I've always lived a reckless life, flying close to the sun like Icarus,' he stated years later.[12]

The streetwise Carmichael, who was the first person in the neighbourhood to own a pair of roller skates, made a huge impression on his younger friend. The two lost touch when Carmichael moved to New York to join his parents, but became reacquainted at the conference, hanging out for the four days that the sylph-like, shade-wearing messiah was in London.

Although Carmichael's visit to UK shores was dramatically cut short, it proved to be the catalyst for the British Black Power movement. In September 1967, a mere six weeks after Carmichael's visit, Egbuna's and Sawh's UCPA set out its philosophy in a fifteen-page pamphlet entitled *Black Power in Britain: A Special Statement by Universal Coloured People's Association*. Borrowing heavily from the movement across the Atlantic, the pamphlet had a picture of a black panther on the front and Stokely Carmichael on the inside cover.

Black power was now a global export.

Howe, who had arrived in England in 1961 at the age of 18 to study law at Middle Temple, along with a number of Queen's Royal College schoolfriends, was drawn to the ideology of Black Power. Settling in Notting Hill, which only a few years earlier had been scarred by race riots and the murder of Kelso Cochrane, he was warned by his compatriots not to go out late at night and told that if he courted a white girl, he was to walk a few paces behind her so that onlookers would not realise they were together.

Such racism shocked him. For two years Howe studied law, while in the evenings he spent his time at the Rio café and the area's shebeens. The Trinidadian barrister Desmond Allum regarded Howe as his protégé: 'He was very, very bright … He had also come from a background of the steel bands, the Renegades … and fancied himself as a bad John.'[13]

Allum recalled Howe not standing for the National Anthem in the local Swiss Cottage cinema. After the film, he was followed and severely beaten by a gang of Teddy boys who were also in the audience. Defiant, he stated: 'Nobody was born to reign over me.'[14]

Howe eventually quit his law studies, eager to start a career in the civil service for which he was amply qualified, but at a job interview they refused to believe his exam certificates were not forged. Struggling to get work, he accepted a position as a postman on a weekly wage of £7 15s 6d. In September 1965 he married English art student Una Hedy Martin, who gave birth to their first child Tamara a couple of months later; the pair would have another daughter, Taipha, and money would become even more of a priority.

Howe had always been politically conscious: as a youth he had distributed the People's National Movement paper and attended speeches by its leader Eric Williams on the effects of British colonialism in Trinidad. But the racial discrimination he encountered in England in terms of housing, employment, and even when out socialising awakened a fury in him and an acknowledgement of a desperate need for societal redress.

In the bars and clubs of Notting Hill Howe crossed paths with European radicals eager to share ideas and tactics with Black Power groups. In May 1968, Paris was burning: the student protests against capitalism and imperialism had turned violent and President Charles de Gaulle had gone into hiding. Howe took up an invitation to visit the French capital and the chance to see a revolution in action. Familiar with the anti-colonial writings of Fanon and Césaire, he believed there was much to learn from the student occupiers, later calling the strike 'a political manifestation of the first importance'.[15]

Following his visit to Paris, Howe set up his own Black Power group, The Black Eagles, in the summer of 1968, operating from Notting Hill. Egbuna, who had formed the British Black Panther movement in April 1968, following a split with Sawh, had been jailed for twelve months in July 1968 for publishing a pamphlet entitled 'What to Do if Cops Lay Their Hands on a Black man at The Speakers Corner', which allegedly incited the murder of policemen.[16] At a benefit concert for Egbuna at the Roundhouse on 25 August, Howe launched himself on to the Black Power stage, making his first speech as a Black Power radical in front of a crowd of a thousand people. It was an impressive debut: Howe, with his large brooding eyes, was a magnetic presence. As Leila Hassan Howe, who became his wife, stated years later, 'He had that slow, deliberate way of talking. That Trinidadian lilt ... which he never gave up ... He spoke sense. He always articulated an idea … It was that combination of his intellect and his charisma and the fact that he was uncompromising. Darcus was uncompromising on the issue of race.'[17]

The lifespan of the Eagles was brief – only five months – but it was influential. Howe made full use of his legal training, setting up street patrols 'with the aim of policing the police' in Notting Hill to make sure justice was being administered transparently and fairly.[18] Writing in *Black Dimension*, he stated that 'the ghetto patrol' was working and that 'it would seem that the police are taking a little more care before approaching to harass us black people'.[19]

Two short-lived publications were associated with the Eagles, the *Black Eagle* and the later *Black Dimension*. Both only ran for three issues. The *Black Eagle* appeared from October 1968 to January 1969 and, although Howe was out of the country during much of its production (Michael X managed the first issue), he had input in the reading list and its content. By the third issue Howe had full control of its editorial reins. He also was the sole editor of *Black Dimension*, which ran from February 1969 to March–April 1969.

Like many Black Power publications, the *Black Eagle* was very much a DIY affair – produced on an old Gestetner machine, densely typewritten, photocopied and stapled together, then distributed at London's Speakers' Corner and on the tube. Una's artwork defined the publication and the later twelve-page *Black Dimension*. One particularly eye-catching illustration in the latter entitled 'Disembowel Enoch Powell' shows Powell lifting up his coat and shirt as a procession of right-wing enablers, from judges to thugs with rolled-up sleeves, emerge from his stomach cavity.[20] Powell had made the controversial 'Rivers of Blood' speech the previous year, arguing about levels of uncontrolled immigration into the country. This inherently divisive polemic by a mainstream politician succeeded in emboldening the National Front and other far-right groups.

The cover of the first issue of *Black Dimension* published in February 1969 features a large black-and-white drawing of Constable Frank Pulley, notorious for harassing Black people in Notting Hill, or The Grove as it was known to locals. A crowd of people gather behind him, as a speech bubble with the words 'We accuse you' floats above his head.

The activist Gus John, who was working in Notting Hill as a youth worker, recalled the tensions at the time: 'We youth workers had to regularly escort the young people either to bus stops or their homes because of the harassment from the Notting Hill police. This hideous fellow, PC Pulley, he made a career out of abusing his power as a policeman.'[21]

Both of these publications, although brief, encapsulate the embryonic stirrings of Howe's later activism. Notable articles in *Black Dimension*'s limited print run included a cover story on Egbuna's release, the Anguillan Revolution, and in an article entitled 'Police State in West London', the attempt to crush Black Power in Britain by arresting activists. In *Black Dimension*'s inside front cover, Howe published six 'people's demands', which included an end to discrimination and police brutality and persecution. Crucially, one of the demands stated that 'black people be tried by their own peer group as is written in the Magna Carta'.[22] Reading lists were also published, featuring Fanon, James, the autobiography of Malcolm X and, interestingly, Michael X's polemic.

Howe spent time with Michael X in late 1968. Howe's biographers state that this was 'largely through economic necessity as he was unemployed and Michael X offered him a place to stay'.[23] Howe fiercely guarded details of his private life, but it is possible that at this point his relationship with Una had broken down. Michael X was cresting a wave of Black Power popularity following his incarceration and surrounding himself with intellectuals such as Howe, whom he could pump for information on the movement to make up for his own shortcomings.[24]

In October 1968, Howe travelled to Montreal to take part in the Congress of Black Writers. Here prominent intellectuals and thinkers, including James (a tangible link to the 1930s activists), Guyanese activist Walter Rodney and Carmichael, met to discuss the history and struggles of peoples of African descent and the meaning of Black Power. From there Howe travelled to Brooklyn, New York, where he worked with the SNCC on the Ocean Hill-Brownsville education campaign, helping Black and Puerto Rican parents organise for better education and facilities for their children. At both the congress and at the education protests, Howe learned valuable lessons about the importance of grassroots organisation. In fact, the knowledge he gleaned in Paris, New York and at the Congress of Black Writers was instructive, shaping his development as a prominent Black Power journalist, activist and orator.

At the congress, James warned him of associating with Michael X and on his return to the UK at the end of 1968, Howe took full editorial control of *Black Dimension* and expunged all references to Michael X from the editorial content. This was a bold step to make, as it was controversial to disrespect a fellow activist.[25]

Black Dimension's focus on police had not gone unnoticed and Pulley threatened to bring charges of criminal libel. The magazine was shut down and Howe, who was worried about being arrested, sought the advice of James, who urged him to go to Trinidad to avoid libel action. James put Howe in touch with Trinidadian labour leaders Stephen Maharaj and George Weekes, the leader of the Oilfields Workers' Trade Union (OWTU). Weekes recognised Howe's talent and asked him to join the staff of the *Vanguard*, the union's newspaper.

Howe arrived at a critical time: one of economic turmoil and high unemployment when a series of industrial actions was rippling across the twin state, and the government was trying desperately to use legislation to curtail the union's organising.

Howe worked with the editor, Wally Look Lai, to cover the protests and took an active role in stoking disaffection against Eric Williams' post-colonial government, which was still allowing the economic and social constructs of white power – foreign oil companies such as Texaco and Tesoro – to control and exploit Trinidad's natural resources. He began making speeches to crowds on the bed of East Dry River, where he'd played cricket and practised steelpan as a child, reading Fanon by candlelight and arguing for the country's natural resources to be owned and controlled by its people.

When Trinidad's Black Power Revolution started on 26 February 1970 at the University of the West Indies, Howe played a pivotal role, addressing crowds in the capital's cathedral, which briefly became the eye of the storm of the protests.[26] He also took part in and reported for the *Vanguard* the 'long march', a 28-mile walk from Port of Spain to the sugar belts of Caroni County on 12 March, an impressive show of African and Indian unity. Howe had grown up among indentured Indians in Eccles village and was keen to stress the political kinship between the two groups. Following an army mutiny, Williams' government declared a state of emergency on 21 April 1970 and Howe returned to the UK to avoid being arrested as one of the protest's main agitators.

The Battle of the Mangrove

In Howe's absence Black Power activism in Britain had simply moved underground; it had not disappeared. This new generation of activists included PhD chemistry student Altheia Jones-LeCointe, who had revitalised the Black Panthers after Egbuna's incarceration; Cambridge graduate Farrukh Dhondy; Leila Hassan Howe; Mala Sen; Linton Kwesi Johnson; Barbara Beese; Olive Morris; Tony Soares; Zainab Abbas; Sonia Chang and Alrick Cambridge. While most of these were associated with the Black Panthers, others were associated with the Black Unity and Freedom Party, the Black Liberation Front or the Fasimbas: in fact, Black Power networks were mushrooming all around the country.

On his return to the UK, Howe returned to his familiar haunt of Notting Hill and got a job on the till at Frank Crichlow's all-night restaurant, the Mangrove in All Saints Road. Decked out in black leather furniture, and decorated with a mural of mangrove trees on the wall, the Mangrove acted as a sanctuary for London's West Indian community. Constable Pulley and his police force were still roaming The Grove, looking to arrest people of colour on the flimsiest of evidence. In this context, as the writer and activist Ambalavaner Sivanandan put it, the restaurant was 'a resting place in Babylon'.[27]

Patrons remembered the delicious home-cooked Trinidadian food — the spiced chicken and rice and peas and Crichlow's trademark pineapple punch. Barbara Beese, who was Howe's partner at the time and mother of his third child, a baby son, said it was the 'go to' place for Black people in the area, providing much-needed community support.[28]

The restaurant's laidback ambience attracted celebrities such as Bob Marley, Jimi Hendrix and Vanessa Redgrave. It even had its own short-lived community magazine, *The Hustler*, to which Howe contributed. The fortnightly magazine's exposés on police, though, curtailed its promise. Howe recalled: '[t]he paper was printed by an old Polish émigré who operated from a base in Fulham. A visit from the Notting Hill police brought the arrangement to an end. We had to fold.'[29]

Despite Crichlow's insistence that the Mangrove was a respectable establishment, it was subject to continuous police raids. The restaurant, which was originally open from 6 p.m. to 6 a.m., with the bulk of the trade after midnight, had its all-night licence revoked late in 1969 and Crichlow was told he could serve only takeaway food after 11 p.m. One of the reasons given for the licence's removal was that 'people with criminal records, prostitutes and convicted persons used the Mangrove'. Crichlow stated he was the victim of unlawful discrimination and complained to the Race Relations Board. He wrote: 'My restaurant is patronised by respectable people.'[30]

Between January 1969 and July 1970, police raided the Mangrove Restaurant twelve times, alienating customers and staff and severely impacting trade. Crichlow had taken the traditional route of writing letters, meeting the local MP and approaching lawyers to bring an end to the police harassment; however, Howe saw this action as limited and persuaded Crichlow to reach out to the local community for help. Crichlow viewed Howe as a 'red-hot little trouble-making kind of fellow', but having exhausted all other avenues he followed his advice.[31]

Howe created a group called the Action Committee for the Defence of the Mangrove and preparations for a protest march on 9 August began, with the restaurant premises used to fashion placards. Before the protest, barrister Tony Mohipp, on behalf of the Mangrove committee, wrote an open letter to Prime Minister Edward Heath. It stated: 'We, the Black People of London have called this demonstration in protest against constant police harassment which is carried out against us, and which is condoned by the legal system. In particular, we are calling for an end to the persecution of the Mangrove Restaurant of 8 All Saints Road, W11, a restaurant that serves the Black community.'[32]

In the high summer sunshine, Howe made a rallying speech to 150 demonstrators outside the Mangrove, placing Notting Hill's Black community at the forefront of the struggle for Black rights in the UK. He stated with typical aplomb: 'We have become the shapers of our own destiny as from today ... What our objective is today and what it's going to continue to be is a concerted, determined attempt to prevent any infringement of our rights.'[33]

With Howe's words echoing in their ears, the marchers, outflanked by 200 police officers, made their way along All Saints Road. The march was to take in a route that passed three local police stations. As they were marching, demonstrators thought they spotted PC Pulley's car and the crowd chanted 'We want Puller', in reference to his habit of 'pulling' local Black people off the street.[34] Alarmed by the chants, police called for reinforcements. The blare of sirens antagonised the crowd and the seething tensions erupted around Portnall Road, where enraged protesters battled the police for fifteen minutes. Howe stated: 'We gave as good as we got. Bricks, stones, bottles, any ammunition at hand we threw at police. Whole building skips were emptied at them.'[35] Nineteen arrests were made. Howe was actually arrested in a police raid of the Mangrove following the demonstration.

The press coverage was alarmist: the spectre of race riots on Britain's streets, which had haunted the Home Office since Carmichael's visit, had come true. The press concentrated on violence against the police. The *Scotsman*'s front-page headline was '17 police hurt in Black Power clash',[36] while the *Mirror* splashed with 'Policemen may be killed in race clashes'.[37]

Howe and eight other defendants, including Jones-LeCointe, Crichlow and Beese, who became known as the Mangrove Nine, faced charges including riot and incitement to riot, affray and possession of offensive weapons. At an earlier hearing at Marylebone Magistrates' Court, the more serious charges of riot and incitement to riot were thrown out, with the magistrate concluding that the protesters' shouts did not constitute 'evidence of either intent to riot or incitement'.[38] Furthermore, the magistrate ruled a large number of comments in the police statements inadmissible as 'they clearly equated black radicalism with criminal intent'.[39] However, in a highly unusual step, the Director of Public Prosecutions reinstated the charges and called for the case to be heard at the Old Bailey.

Dhondy and his wife Mala (née Sen), who had both been active in the Indian Workers' Association in Leicester, had recently moved to London. Dhondy remembered being impressed with a 'wonderful' speech Jones-LeCointe gave at the National Conference on the Rights of Black People in Britain at London's Alexandra Palace on 22–23 May 1971. He recalled that she said of the Black Panthers: 'We take our fierce name from the military. But really what we are is a group of immigrant workers who oppose the injustice of this country.'[40]

Dhondy, who was now working as a school teacher in Deptford, offered his services to Jones-LeCointe's Black Panthers and she encouraged him to serve his apprenticeship reporting on the Mangrove trial. He recalled: 'I would go straight after school to the Old Bailey. A few people would tell me what had gone on in the day and we'd return to the Black Panther headquarters in Barnsbury Road and write up the trial.'[41] Jones-LeCointe was concerned about sensationalism in the mainstream media's coverage and in an astute move wanted the group's own reports on the trial to get out to their supporters.

The trial began in the Old Bailey on 5 October 1971 and lasted fifty-five days, attracting substantial national and international press coverage. A lawyer had recommended to Howe that he plead guilty, but he and Jones-LeCointe took the unusual step of defending themselves. 'I told him to go to hell,' said Howe.[42] Beese was represented by the barrister Ian Macdonald, who liaised with the legal counsel for the other defendants.

Howe and Jones-LeCointe made representations for an all-Black jury; since his Black Eagle days Howe had upheld the position that defendants should be tried by their peers to ensure a fair trial, as enshrined in the Magna Carta. The request was refused, but defence challenges ensured that two jurors were Black and the rest – eight men and two women – were drawn from working-class backgrounds.[43]

Howe was an impressive presence throughout the trial. Dhondy recalled:

It was quite brilliant to see these people in court. Darcus said, 'Can you give me some Shakespeare quotes?' So I used to think of Shakespeare quotes for him to use. And one of them was: 'The time is out of joint. Oh cursed spite, nine West Indians were born to put it right.'

He was an extremely good speaker. He would understand the tenor of his audience and spoke to them in the language that they would applaud. And that was quite a talent.[44]

The inability of police to recall key incidents and information, as well as contradictions inherent in their evidence, was pounced on by Howe, whose defence lurched towards the theatrical. Both PC Graham Rogers and PC Pulley said on numerous occasions that they could not remember events.[45] Chief Inspector Michael Trotman, who claimed to have been 'punched, kicked and trampled on' could not recall seeing Howe when violence broke out. He asserted: 'Obviously I can't account for each person's movements along the whole length of the procession during the hour and a half.' Howe's response elicited laughter from the courtroom: 'I agree. I agree. Nobody could do that. That's my case.'[46]

A core group consisting of Howe, Crichlow, Jones-LeCointe and Beese met each evening in the Mangrove to outline defence strategy. James advised Howe that in order to win the case 'the devil was in the detail'; his biographers note that 'copies of witness statements preserved at Columbia University are covered in red pen and marginalia in Howe's hand, a testament to the forensic analysis of the case against them'.[47]

A eureka moment came when officers claimed to have seen the defendants inciting the crowd to riot from the van's observation window. Howe proved that this was impossible as the view was greatly restricted from the slit-like aperture. He drew on foolscap paper to show jurors that this was the case. When Pulley made the preposterous suggestion that each officer had a single eye pressed to the window, Howe retorted, 'Where was your face?'[48] Howe's cross-examination of the four officers who had been stationed in the police observation van was a turning point in the trial, essentially demolishing the evidence on which the riot charge was based.

After fifty-five days of high drama, all nine were acquitted of incitement to riot and five, including Howe, Beese and Crichlow, were acquitted of all other charges. Acknowledging it was the season of 'peace and goodwill', the judge suspended the sentences of the four defendants convicted of lesser offences including affray and assault. No one would be going to jail. In his summation, the judge concluded that the trial 'had regrettably shown evidence of racial hatred on both sides'.[49]

It was a historic moment: an official legal reckoning that racial hatred existed within the Met. Beese stated in an interview with the *Guardian* in 2020: 'The case was groundbreaking and a defining moment for Black people because it gave real meaning to the term "Black power". We were doing it for ourselves, taking on the establishment and winning, exposing its racism and hypocrisy.'[50]

A Natural Leader

After the trial, Howe joined the Panthers, but it wasn't a natural fit and tensions arose between him and Jones-LeCointe. As Hassan Howe explained:

> Darcus was a leader ... Even in the Panthers, there was a lot of resentment to Darcus because, as Linton [Kwesi-Johnson] would tell you, all the youth used to gather around Darcus. When Darcus would speak, the way he had of speaking, that tone, that ability to just touch you by what he's saying ... Eddie, who was Altheia's husband, hated Darcus because he just had *it* ... that charisma. Linton said: 'In the Panthers, all the youth, all they wanted to hear was Darcus.'[51]

Mala and Dhondy were invited to be part of the Panthers' central core but Beese and Howe were not. One of the roles assigned to both Howe and Dhondy, who had become close friends, was to give lectures to young people at Oval House opposite the cricket ground. 'About 200 people would gather,' said Dhondy. 'Darcus would speak about Caribbean history and books by Angela Davis. I spoke about E.P. Thompson's *The Making of the English Working Class* because we weren't for racial revolution. We were for socialistic, Marxist revolution.'[52]

Dhondy recalled that the Black Panther Movement was an extraordinary commitment – 'it took over our lives' – with meetings, demonstrations, pickets, strikes, and penning pamphlets, leaflets and journalism for the group taking considerable time.[53]

The Panthers had a small newspaper, *Freedom News*, which was produced fortnightly in north and east London.[54] Billed as the community's voice, it advertised several outreach activities such as advice on housing, education, employment, immigration and general legal advice. It was part of the Panthers' network, with other centres in Birmingham,

Nottingham and Bristol, and was a concerted effort to organise around Black people's rights. Reports covered in *Freedom News* included Islington Council's slum housing,[55] a thousand-strong march against the 1971 Immigration Act; and a firebomb attack on the Panthers' own bookshop, also called Freedom News, in 74 Railton Road.[56] Dhondy, who had been living above the shop at the time of the attack, recalled the exit blocked by flames and being forced to jump from the first floor to the ground 'as the glass front of the bookshop exploded outwards with bangs and crashes'.[57]

In an indication of how frequent such attacks were and the lack of seriousness with which they were dealt with by police, the Met did not even interview Dhondy, who was the only occupant of the house when the fire happened, and the only mainstream press report was a small news item that said five Black and Asian houses had been firebombed in the capital that day, 15 March 1973.

James, although pleased that the group had a community-oriented publication, criticised its lack of focus. He insisted that the group should write about their own lives and experiences rather than focus on political rhetoric. Dhondy recalled:

> I was fascinated by the penetrating accuracy of his words. He was saying: devote the newspaper to the experiences that you as immigrants – Black and Asian people – in this country have … The public we were trying to reach and encourage to accompany us in the movement for justice, equality and social and political rights would respond to experiences parallel to or evoking their own.[58]

Both Howe and Dhondy followed James' advice, with the latter writing anonymous pen portraits about his time as a school teacher – the series was so successful that Dhondy was awarded a publishing contract with Macmillan.

Better news was to come: the author John Berger shared half his 1972 Booker Prize winnings for the novel *G* with the Black Panthers. In his acceptance speech he said: 'The London-based Black Panther movement has risen out of the bones of what Bookers and other companies have created in the Caribbean; I want to share this prize with the Black

Panther movement because they resist both as Black people and workers the further exploitation of the oppressed.'[59]

The Panthers used the money to buy a house in north London at 37 Tollington Park Road. (The cheque and mortgage was put in Dhondy's account as he was the only person with a full-time job.) Jones-LeCointe rented out the rooms to fellow Panthers and managed the monthly payments, but it was several months later, when the group were almost comfortable financially, that fissures began to appear.

A central core meeting that Dhondy witnessed and later relayed to Howe involved a young tenant of the house being castigated for sneaking his white girlfriend into the commune. Dhondy was enraged and astonished by this moral policing, as was Howe, who claimed the group were acting 'pseudo religiously'. The two decided to leave, along with Beese and Mala, who were disappointed with the direction the movement was taking. When Eddie LeCointe, along with two other Panthers, turned up at Dhondy's school with machetes, demanding with menaces that Dhondy sign over the deeds of Tollington Park to them, the violent and unnecessary incident left a huge schism in the Panthers' ranks and the group disintegrated soon after.[60]

Race Today and a New Dawn

Howe and Dhondy debated starting another Black activist organisation, but as luck would have it, a mini mutiny was taking place at the Institute of Race Relations (IRR), which was based in London's King's Cross. The staff – a number of whom, including Hassan Howe, were drawn from Black activist organisations – were concerned that the government advisory body was more a bureaucratic entity than an organisation actively working for racial justice. It produced two dry academic journals, the quarterly *Race & Class* and the monthly *Race Today*, but as Dhondy emphasised: 'Essays from universities and polytechnic institutes on the "dialectics of class" and recondite arguments about the cultures of race might have had a function, but whatever the pretensions of its writers, they were contributing nothing to social and political change.'[61]

The decline of the Black Power movement had left a vacuum when people of colour in the country were in desperate need of representation. The early 1970s was a time of industrial discontent and economic hardship, with racial tensions crudely exploited by career-hungry politicians. Aware of this climate and wanting to take the organisation in a more radical direction, the institute's librarian, Sivanandan, launched a coup against the white management. One of his first actions was to appoint Howe as editor of *Race Today* on 6 November 1973. The appointment of the well-known Black Power activist and one of the Mangrove Nine raised eyebrows, with the *Guardian* noting that his editorship 'promises to steer the magazine yet further from its academic origins towards the frontline of racial politics'.[62]

Sivanandan later stated:

> The reason we had asked him to edit the journal was not specifically because of that [Mangrove trial] … The kinds of things that made me think Darcus could be a right kind of editor for *Race Today* was that he was well-informed, well-read on political issues and most importantly that he like us saw the concept of 'Black' as inclusive of Asians (very important then), he also saw class as well as 'race' as an important determinant and he was interested in the struggles of the Third World, especially in former colonies. In other words he was not a black nationalist.[63]

Race Today was not unique in this stance – Black was a 'unifying political identity' among Black and Asian radicals in Britain in the 1970s and '80s, and was used as a moniker for several integrated groups.[64]

Howe was determined to take the magazine in a more activist direction, reporting how minority communities in the UK were furthering their own rights, politically, socially and culturally; furthermore, he was determined to push the boundaries of journalism by contributing to the organisation of that activism himself. In a January 1974 editorial, 'From Victim to Protagonist – The Changing Social Reality', he stated:

> Our task is to record and recognise the struggles of the emerging forces as manifestations of the revolutionary potential of the black

population. We recognise too the release of intellectual energy from within the black community, which always comes to the fore when the masses of the oppressed by their actions create a new social reality.[65]

This was radical even by the 'new IRR's' standards. According to Howe, Sivanandan wanted to retain control of the journal. Howe stated: 'I had just come out of the Old Bailey, for 55 days, fighting for my freedom … I wasn't going to go and be manipulated.'[66]

The contrast in ideology led to him instigating a physical as well as ideological break with the IRR, moving from the institute's office in the dead of night in the summer of 1974.

Dhondy recalled: 'Darcus asked me to drive him and two others in my dark-green, rattletrap, ex-post-office van to King's Cross at midnight. From the *Race Today* office, we emptied out and loaded into the van all the equipment, photocopiers, typewriters, library of books, stationery and everything else apart from the furniture and drove to Brixton.'[67]

The next morning Sivanandan and others arrived to find the magazine offices in King's Cross stripped bare. Howe's departure had also created a funding headache, with some of the IRR's donors backing *Race Today* to the disadvantage of the organisation. In 1974, the World Council of Churches gave a $10,000 grant to *Race Today*, increasing its support to $15,000 in October 1975. Cadburys was also a major donor.[68]

Former Black Panther Olive Morris sourced a squat for the journal's new offices at 74 Shakespeare Road, Brixton, in the heart of London's Black community and the liberated equipment was placed there. The nascent Race Today Collective, comprising of editor Howe, Hassan Howe (the paper's deputy editor in 1973), Jean Ambrose, Barbara Beese, Michael Cadette, Eden Charles, Dhondy and Mala, Patricia Dick, Claudius Hillman, Kwesi Johnson, Akua Rugg, Marva Spencer and Lorine Stapleton now had a new home. As the Collective grew, a wall was broken between that house and premises on 165 Railton Road, which would later become its permanent home.

'The people who formed the Race Today Collective already had a history of activism in the Black Power movement,' stated Hassan Howe. 'We were well versed in campaigning. We were well versed in publishing … so all of us were seasoned activists.'[69]

Howe followed the stance of his uncle and mentor James (who would soon occupy the top-floor flat of the building in Railton Road).[70] James believed in uniting groups that had a common enemy in both capitalism and racism, and *Race Today*, now free of its former shackles, would follow this lead to the letter. In Howe's editorial of April 1974 he set out *Race Today*'s commitment to 'record and recognise' the struggle of the Black and Asian working class, citing Marx's *A Worker's Inquiry*, which stated that workers 'alone can describe with full knowledge the misfortunes that they suffer'.[71]

The majority of the Collective had other jobs and came to the offices in the evening (Dick worked for the Citizens Advice Bureau, Mala for Air India, Cadette was a bus driver, Johnson a student, and Beese and Dhondy were both teachers). The only full-time members were Howe, Hassan Howe and Stapleton, and, as in much of the arts in those days, the Collective's activities were funded by the dole. Once the magazine turned a profit, it was agreed to pay Howe a £30 weekly wage. In the early days the magazine was put together laboriously using a cut-and-paste technique. Howe urged subscribers to spread the journal's message. In 'A Dozen Ways to Help Us Build', published in April 1974, he acknowledged its 'stormy past' but showed how readers could get involved in sustaining its future through fundraising activities and even helping with layout, printing and managing the telephone switchboards. Once the magazine was established, a £250,000 grant from the Greater London Council (GLC) paid for better in-house production facilities.[72]

The squat was a lively, bustling informative place, where people from all walks of life congregated. Hassan Howe commented: 'The politics of the hour were thoroughly analysed, dissected and discussed.'[73]

Dhondy, who said James was the journal's 'ideological guide', recalled visitors weren't just politicians or activists. James' purview straddled the world of cricket and Ian Botham and Viv Richards and other celebrities visited him. 'He would always ask: "Farrukh, where is the claret, man?" I would reply: "You drank it yesterday, boss." He said: "Well go and get some more. Can't you see the people here? And he wouldn't want any old Sainsbury's claret. He wanted Saint Emilion."'[74]

The late professor Harry Goulbourne described Howe's relationship with James as one of 'nephew and protector'. He stated in Howe's biography: 'Darcus provided CLR with care, he made sure that visitors didn't exhaust the old man, and one got the impression that he felt very privileged to be in that position, to take care of him in the last leg of his life.'[75]

The thirty-page monthly journal's new direction was reflected in an eye-catching, forward-thinking layout by designer Julian Stapleton. The cover's banner headlines in large pump font were accompanied by bold illustrations, which now bear a striking visual testament to two turbulent decades of racial politics and a fitting tribute to Howe's vision as editor.

As well as news of a national concern, such as immigration round-ups; industrial action; police brutality; education and health issues, such as sickle cell, that affected the community, there was also an extensive focus on the Global South. *Race Today* covered the Grenadian revolution, the struggle against apartheid South Africa, the Middle East situation and the Caribbean trade union movement, as well as the FBI's hand in the breakdown of Black Power in America. By emphasising the international shared struggles of Black and oppressed communities, Howe hoped to illustrate to readers that liberation and racial justice were part of a much broader global fight.

The journal broke new ground in publishing, with its attitude towards journalism and its subjects. A colleague of James' had coined the term 'full fountain pen' to describe a more rounded process of recording working people's lives in their own voices, rather than the journalist's voice.[76] An insightful article on industrial action at Ford's, 'We Are the Majority at Ford's', November 1976, featured an intimate diary of a rebellion at the plant from the worker's perspective. *Race Today* also encouraged dynamic engagement with readers through its letters page.

Women's issues feature heavily in the publication: Selma James wrote an incisive piece in the January 1974 issue, 'Sex, Race and Working-Class Power', centring Black women's struggles at the heart of the labour revolution, while a cover feature on Black nurses, 'Black Women and Nursing: A Job Like No Other', explained how such work was rooted in a colonial legacy and gender and class discrimination, hence its low pay and poor status (August 1974).

In Howe's thirteen years as editor, the journal ran a number of significant campaigns, most notably in support of the Leicester Imperial

Typewriters strike in July 1974, where the majority Asian workers downed tools because of discriminatory pay. Howe travelled to Leicester and spoke on the picket line. He argued that it was 'one of the most powerful strikes of the time. The newly arrived Asians organised themselves skilfully with community support, with women in the vanguard.' The strikers' victory indicated that 'black power was coming to industry'.[77]

Race Today also supported the Grunwick dispute a few years later (1977) when pejorative working conditions at the film-processing plant forced the majority Asian women workers to demand union recognition. Mala and Dhondy were involved in a long-running campaign with the Bengali community in their struggle for better housing in the mid-'70s, uncovering large-scale corruption and organising the largest squat in Britain's history in London's East End to draw attention to poor housing stock. As Hassan Howe explained, it wasn't a short-term offensive: 'We were in the East End for almost three years, working with families.' The campaigning and picketing of council buildings by the Bengali Housing Action Group, which was set up in February 1976 with the Race Today Collective, led to all the families being suitably rehoused.

Alliances were also formed with the Republican struggle in Ireland, with IRA hunger striker Bobby Sands penning a short story, 'Black Beard in Profile', published in *Race Today* in 1981 while Sands was on hunger strike, and a humourless Gerry Adams visiting the offices in 1983. Howe described his presence as 'icy – he spoke literally without a blink'.[78]

National justice campaigns were also on *Race Today*'s radar, including that of George Lindo, who was framed for robbing a betting shop in Bradford in 1978 by the local police, and the 'Oval Four' – young men who were accused of 'nicking handbags' on the tube and jailed for two years; after fifty years their convictions were overturned as the original evidence was found to be suspect.[79]

The magazine even campaigned on behalf of its editor. After the Mangrove trial, Howe was being surveilled by Special Branch and was arrested several times, although in almost every case he was acquitted.[80] An incident at Notting Hill Gate station when Howe was racially abused by the ticket inspector led to another arrest after he retaliated and a passerby got involved in the ensuing fracas. Howe was found guilty of actual bodily harm at Knightsbridge Crown Court on

5 September 1977, sentenced to three months in jail and fined £100 (the charge related to the passerby, not the ticket inspector). The Race Today Collective petitioned politicians, while every evening a core of twenty activists picketed Pentonville prison, where Howe was being held. Howe was released after a week in a triumphant and 'memorable campaign' stated Hassan Howe, who was now officially Howe's partner after he broke up with Beese.[81] The pair began a relationship in 1977, marrying in 1989.

For Howe, politics and culture were inseparable. The journal's 'Creation for Liberation' section profiled arts in the community and the Basement sessions, held at the magazine offices, where artists were invited to talk about their work, were hugely popular. In 1980 the annual *Race Today Review* was published, giving, as Howe explained, an insight into the 'creative activities which flow from the terrain on which we do political battle'.[82] The magazine also provided a vital platform for the influential Caribbean Arts Movement, founded by John La Rose, Kamau Braithwaite and Andrew Salkey, and regularly profiled art, poetry and literature from the group's members. It was also a key partner in the International Book Fair of Radical and Third World Books with New Beacon Books and Bogle-L'Ouverture.

Race Today consistently lobbied to keep carnival on the streets, with The Race Today Mangrove Renegade Band a regular participant at the Notting Hill Carnival. Howe chaired the Notting Hill Carnival development committee for a number of years.

Under Howe, the magazine, which was distributed through independent bookshops and available to individual subscribers worldwide (the cover price was 10p in 1974, rising to 70p in 1988), quadrupled its subscription from 1,500 to 6,000.[83]

Thirteen Dead and Nothing Said

In 1981, *Race Today* launched its most definitive campaign, the New Cross Massacre Action Committee, following a house fire on 18 January 1981 that claimed the lives of thirteen young Black people and injured twenty-seven others (a young man, Anthony Berbeck, who had escaped from the fire, would subsequently take his own life two years later, bringing the total number of deaths as a result of the incident to fourteen).

The tail-end of the previous decade had been marred by racial tensions. The National Front had made significant gains in a 1976 by-election in Lewisham, campaigning on a ticket of repatriation for all people of colour, and there were a number of racist murders. The list was lengthy and shameful, and Howe and *Race Today* campaigned to keep the spotlight on such crimes. In June 1976, Gurdip Singh Chaggar was murdered in Southall. Two years later, in April 1978, 10-year-old Kenneth Singh was stabbed to death in Canning Town; while mere weeks after that incident, on local election night, 4 May 1978, 24-year-old Altab Ali was murdered – his assailants saying in court that they attacked him because he was 'a P---'. One month later, Ishaque Ali, 45, died of a heart attack shortly after another racially motivated attack in Hackney.

In November 1977, the Moonshot club in New Cross, a well-known venue for young Black people, was targeted by a firebomb attack, which many locals believed was in retribution for the NF's humiliation in the Battle of Lewisham that year when crowds of counter-protesters, including Howe, had prevented right-wing extremists marching through the streets. The following year, in July 1978, Deptford's Albany Empire, which had hosted fifteen Rock Against Racism benefit gigs, was gutted by fire. A note saying 'Got you' signed 88, 88, which was widely believed to be from Column 88, a fascist paramilitary splinter group, was left at the venue but police never found the arsonists. Tensions were also high following the murder of Blair Peach in April 1979. Peach took part in an Anti-Nazi League demonstration against a National Front election meeting in the mostly Asian area of Southall and was hit by a Special Patrol Group truncheon in the ensuing violence.

So when a house fire at 16-year-old Yvonne Ruddock's birthday party at 439 New Cross Road, in Lewisham, not far from the Moonshot, killed thirteen young Black people that fateful January night, and the subsequent police investigation ruled out a firebomb, despite a wealth of evidence to the contrary, the Black community had had enough.

The blaze started in the ground floor of the three-storey house and spread rapidly. Witnesses spoke of their skin peeling off in the intense heat, of being engulfed in thick black smoke within seconds and having to leap out of a second-floor window to escape the flames. Many of those at the party, including Armza Ruddock, Yvonne's mother, were convinced that the fire was the result of an incendiary device being thrown into the ground-floor front window.[84] The shock, sorrow and anger in the community was compounded when some of the bereaved received anonymous racist letters. Two days after the fire, 300 people gathered along with Howe and the Race Today Collective at the Moonshot at an impassioned meeting. The New Cross Massacre Action Committee (NCMAC) was formed to ensure justice for the horrific murders of the thirteen young people and La Rose installed as its chair.[85]

With police advancing the theory that the fire had been started by youngsters at the party, which the press colluded in with misleading reports, a fact-finding commission was established to interview survivors, with operations co-ordinated from the *Race Today* offices. The community did not believe that the police could be trusted to do a proper investigation. A fundraising body was set up and a Black People's Day of Action mooted for Monday, 2 March 1981.

'It was such a momentous event, everyone was very clear that something had to be done about it and then of course going down and meeting the parents … you'll never forget the level of grief that was going on in the community at that time,' said Hassan Howe. 'The Black community could not just stand by and allow this to happen to them.'[86]

The tragedy, which should have invoked national mourning, was met with silence by the establishment. When the Queen sent her condolences after forty-five people were killed at a Dublin disco a month later, the Black community felt they had been snubbed. 'We didn't feel that Britain owned that tragedy as something that had happened to a section of itself,' said John. 'The state saw us as a race apart, a people apart. We did not matter.'[87]

The march, which took place two months after the fire on a Monday to cause maximum disruption, was an organisational feat by Howe and the Race Today Collective, and ensured the Black community was a visible force to be reckoned with. Operations were organised out of the *Race Today* offices with Black groups, including John's Black Parents Movement. Howe travelled tirelessly to Manchester, Leeds, Liverpool, Bristol and other cities, aided by John, rallying the community. 'Howe's organisational prowess was a significant factor in the mobilisation,' stated Kwesi Johnson.[88]

On the day of the march, Hassan Howe recalled standing in Fordham Park in London's New Cross under a leaden sky. 'It was drizzling and I was thinking "Oh my God" but then of course the coaches started coming in and people started pouring off them and then we knew, we just knew, we'd done it.'[89]

The march was a resounding success, with up to 20,000 people marching through the streets of London, chanting 'Thirteen Dead and Nothing Said' and demanding justice for the young people who had perished in the fire. 'It got bigger as it marched through the city. People were just jumping off buses, people would come out of supermarkets, see the coffins and the banners of the children's faces and just join when they realised what it was for. Schoolchildren jumped over fences, they left their classes [to join],' said Hassan Howe.[90] Hassan Howe added that Howe's four children – Tamara, Taipha, Darcus and Rap – were present.

Marchers walked along Fleet Street, as certain sections of the press had amplified the police's disinformation campaign, claiming it was Black on Black violence. The march was largely peaceful – the only altercation a scuffle on Blackfriars Bridge after police blocked part of the agreed route. Unfortunately, the press coverage amplified this rather than the largely peaceful nature of the gathering: the *Daily Express* called it 'the rampage of the mob'; while the *Evening Standard* published a picture of Howe next to a photograph of a policeman with a bloodied face, blowing up a quote from him stating, 'It was a good day'. *The Sun*'s coverage was racist and alarmist in nature and 'The Day the Blacks Ran Riot in London' was later found to be inflammatory and 'damaging to good race relations' by the Press Complaints Council. Commenting later on the negative backlash, Howe stated: 'We can only draw this fight, can't win it.'[91]

Inquests were held into the fire in 1981 and 2004. The police failed to convince the jury at the first inquest that the fire was a result of 'Black on Black' violence, and open verdicts were recorded at both inquests.

Still Kwesi Johnson, who was a steward on the day, summarised: 'The Black People's Day of Action was the most powerful expression of Black political power this country has ever seen. Black people were no longer prepared to be marginalised.'[92]

'Temperature rising'

A month after the march, an uprising began in Brixton as a direct result of police targeting young Black people using 'stop and search' powers. In a police exercise termed 'Operation Swamp' – 1,000 people were stopped and searched in Brixton over five days. Riots spread across Britain's inner cities, including Toxteth in Liverpool and Manchester's Moss Side, that summer because of such provocative policing. Said Hassan Howe:

> At that time, Brixton, although very deprived and poor, was a strong Black community. I remember they stopped me and Darcus on Railton Road and asked us where we were going. And they said, 'We need to search you.' And Darcus said: 'Try and search me.' It was a power thing. You could feel the temperature rising. And you knew it was going to blow.[93]

The uprising started in Brixton on the evening of 10 April. After a routine stop and search outside a mini cab office, a crowd of youths gathered. Tensions were further inflamed after false rumours spread that police had failed to help a young Black man earlier that day who it was alleged had later died of stab wounds.[94] This spontaneous gathering morphed into a well-organised revolt and the police lost control of Brixton for three days. A bus was hijacked and 415 police officers and 172 members of the public were injured. Numerous vehicles and premises were destroyed or damaged by fire. Rioters burnt down the George pub, in an act of revenge for years of racial discrimination by the landlord, while thousands of police were drafted in as a response.

Hassan Howe recalled the youth 'using military tactics, knowing when to retreat. It was brilliant.'[95] Bricks, bottles, slates – everything was used against the police. And *Race Today* and Howe were there reporting it all. 'We'd go out periodically and report back to Darcus – "they're using petrol bombs now",' said Hassan Howe. 'In fact they brought so many reservists [officers] in, they would be lying in the road outside [the] *Race Today* offices and we would have to climb over them to get inside.'[96]

'It was the fightback, I was for that 100 per cent,' said Hassan Howe. 'Finally you're [the police] getting what you deserve for how you've treated us all these years. We were at one with the community and it was about time it stopped.'[97]

Howe later catalogued the historical roots of the uprising in a series for *Race Today* in February 1982, entitled 'Bobby to Babylon: Brixton before the Uprising', describing how action manifested following a decade or more of 'malpractices carried out against Brixton's Black Community by the police'.[98]

Following the uprising, Lord Scarman was appointed to hold an inquiry into the riots. His report, published on 25 November 1981, rejected a further crackdown in the area advocated by right-wing politicians and called for an improvement in community relations and more community redevelopment and planning.[99]

Howe was commissioned to write a 1,500-word response to Scarman's report for *The Times* – his first for the mainstream press. In 'My Fears after this Failure', published on 26 November 1981, Howe stated that Scarman failed to identify the systemic racism inherent in the force that led to the revolt. He also highlighted that the report failed to recommend safeguards against physical abuse and forced confessions of detainees.

In the wake of Scarman's report, a new code for police behaviour and an independent Police Complaints Authority was established in the Police and Criminal Evidence Act of 1984.

Race Today continued to be at the forefront of activism. In October 1985 the death of Cynthia Jarrett following a police search of her home in Broadwater Farm, Tottenham, and the shooting the previous week of Dorothy 'Cherry' Groce during another police search in Brixton triggered another wave of uprisings in the community in those areas of London. Again Howe's *Race Today* provided a much-needed voice.

Hassan Howe took over as editor in 1986 and the final issue of *Race Today* was in 1988. Howe wanted to keep the Collective alive, but this changed with James' death in 1989, which created a 'pall over everything', according to Kwesi Johnson. Howe's energies were diverted towards broadcasting commitments and he was forced to admit that *Race Today* had 'exhausted the moment'. The Collective formally disbanded on 7 April 1991.[100]

Howe had occasionally been making brief appearances on TV news programmes in the early 1980s, usually in tandem with *Race Today*'s campaigns. Dhondy, who had staged successful plays in the West End in the early '80s, was now cultivating a career as a TV dramatist. In 1983, he was asked to be commissioning editor of multicultural programmes for Channel Four. Dhondy was instrumental in bringing Black and Asian producers to the broadcaster. He also employed his old Black Panther friend on *The Bandung File*, with journalist Tariq Ali. The programme ran from 1985 to 1991 in an early evening slot and was hugely popular. Howe's programmes reflected his journalism in *Race Today*: police harassment; the significance of the Grunwick dispute a decade on and the aftermath of decolonisation. Inspired by James, he covered Haiti in the *Unfinished Revolution*, chronicling the island's history of revolt, its crippled economy (the island was forced to pay France, its former slave masters, reparations for more than a century following the 1804 revolution) and the dire living standards of its citizens.[101] His biographers stated that he 'cried himself to sleep' following the programme.[102]

A successful career in television followed. Howe came to Dhondy with the format for *The Devil's Advocate*, which subjected invited guests to intense and uncomfortable scrutiny from Howe. The programme ran for six seasons from 1992 to 1996 and catapulted him into mainstream celebrity. He relished his newfound fame, which involved a number of appearances on talk shows, current affairs programmes and even comedy shows such as *Shooting Stars*. Documentaries including *England My England*, *White Tribe* and *Slave Nation* followed, where Howe took an almost anthropological stance to Englishness. For a new generation, the often sensational nature of these documentaries overshadowed his earlier journalism as activism work. In fact, celebrity was often a double-edged sword. Howe had the platform to reach a mainstream audience but the medium of television allowed no room for nuance.

From the mid-1990s Howe became a regular columnist for *The New Statesman* and was awarded Columnist of the Year at the 1998 Race in Media awards for his opinion pieces in that journal. He also penned opinion pieces for *The Voice*, which was established in 1982 and served the UK's Black community, and for London's *Evening Standard*.

In April 2007 Howe was diagnosed with prostate cancer. His article for the *Guardian* in which he recounted his visit to the clinic was undeniably moving. When he was told he had the disease, his consultant pointed out that 'West Indian men are three times more likely to die of prostate cancer than white men in the UK', adding the disease was prevalent in the Black Atlantic. Early testing, urged the consultant, would save lives.[103]

Howe, a seasoned campaigner, did not miss the political significance of a disease that affected Black men disproportionately. He worked with the NHS and Channel 4 to encourage men in the community to have regular check-ups and the programme *What's Killing Darcus Howe?* was broadcast in 2007.

'A lethal combination'

On 1 April 2017, Howe died in his sleep at the age of 74.

His funeral cortege set off from Brixton from the site of the former *Race Today* offices to All Saints Church, Notting Hill, where the former Renegade was laid to rest. His eldest daughter Tamara and best friend Dhondy gave a speech. Howe's seven children joined his widow there.[104] *The Voice* newspaper stated: 'Only a man with the legacy of Darcus Howe could unite with such ease and sombre celebration The Nation of Islam, UK Black Panthers, Rastafarian hornsmen and Nyabinghi drummers, teenaged steel pan players, elderly Irish west Londoners and manicured political dignitaries to name a few.'[105]

Howe had worked tirelessly for half a century for the cause of racial justice in the UK. In *Black Dimension* he'd written (with a high dose of irony) of a payback 'civilising mission' – of the kind the British Empire had employed. 'The British had travelled the globe to civilize Africa, India and the Caribbean, now it was time to return the favour.'[106]

Years later, his biographers noted: 'Howe and the Black Power Movement would civilise Britain by challenging the state-licensed barbarism of the Metropolitan Police (Met), by teaching Britain to become a harmonious multiracial society, by bringing "reason to race".'[107]

Through his consistent activism, Howe made sure the issue of racial justice was always on the agenda, as the sheer endurance of his *Race Today* project testifies. '*Race Today* started in 73 and lasted more than 14 years,' said Hassan Howe. 'People find that amazing. And that is to Darcus's credit hugely, that he was able to build and sustain an organisation for so long.'[108]

Howe illustrated the inherent inequalities that people of colour faced in the UK – in employment, in housing and in the criminal justice system. As a member of the Mangrove Nine, he challenged that injustice head on, taking on the repressive might of the establishment and shining a harsh light on its inherent prejudices. He was tenacious, consistently highlighting how the state, media and police colluded to perpetuate an unjust society. He was resilient in the face of constant surveillance, police harassment and the mainstream media's attempts to demonise his efforts.

Howe could not have foreseen that a few years after Fleet Street journalists had leaned out of their office windows and catcalled the Black People's Day of Action, he would be welcomed into their midst, becoming a regular commentator for the mainstream press.

'If there was one word to describe Darcus, it was courage,' said Hassan Howe. 'Darcus was a very courageous person ... that courage and the fact he didn't care was quite a lethal combination.'[109]

CONCLUSION

It is fitting that this book ends with Darcus Howe, whose forty-year career took him from journalism's fringes – where he was essentially producing densely typewritten Black Power fanzines on a Gestetner machine, hand stapled and distributed in London's parks and on the tube – to the heart of Fleet Street as an award-winning columnist for *The New Statesman*. In many ways, his story arc embodies the collective trajectory of the seven journalists I have chosen to profile in this book. These journalists operated on the margins of society, but it was the steady accretion of their thoughts, ideas and values, ultimately their worldview, that permeated the mainstream of British society and changed it for the better.

In a speech in 1967, C.L.R. James identified the roots of Black Power in earlier decades, stating that, 'Stokely and the advocates of Black Power ... stand on the shoulders of all that has gone before.' He nodded to the work of Garvey, Césaire, Padmore and Fanon as critical in this regard. He continued:

> Too many people here in England, and unfortunately people in the United States too ... see Black Power and its advocates as some sort of portent, a sudden apparition, as some racist eruption from the depths of black oppression and black backwardness. It is nothing of the kind. It represents a high peak of thought on the Negro question which has been going on for over half a century.[1]

I would argue that these discussions have been taking place since before the dawn of emancipation, with individuals both here and in the US putting pen to paper in order to advocate for a fairer society for all.

It is no coincidence that this book is helmed with the extraordinary story of Samuel Jules Celestine Edwards. In his short life, Edwards was brave enough to criticise the legacy of the slave trade and imperialism. With an almost eerie foresight, he asked why British slave owners were compensated for £20 million lost capital (approximately £150 billion in today's money) when the enslaved received nothing.[2] Englishmen 'boast about the Empire over which the sun never sets,' proclaimed Edwards. 'How many have been murdered, robbed and enslaved to acquire dominion?'[3]

Edwards posed these prescient questions when the British Empire was at its height, when the scramble for Africa had carved the continent between European powers, and more than a century before the Rhodes Must Fall and the reparative justice campaign. His position was a lonely one in late Victorian Britain when politicians, press and public opinion viewed the Empire's architects as paragons of virtue and patriotism.

Long after the ink on Edwards' papers had faded, his astute analyses would prove immortal, both here and in the US. His and Catherine Impey's influence on the young American journalist Ida B. Wells was a powerful legacy. Wells' autobiography *Crusade for Justice* describes her experience in the UK as formative; while the genesis of *The Red Record* (published in 1895), her potent study that raised awareness of the alarming rates of lynching in the US, can be traced back to the book *United States Atrocities* (1892), authored by Wells, and published and promoted by Edwards here in the UK. Wells' and Edwards' anti-lynching tours galvanised British public opinion, pressurising the US government to halt this barbaric practice. Her later anti-segregation activism and suffrage campaigns in the US marked her out as an influential civil rights and feminist campaigner. In 2020, nearly a century after her death, Wells was posthumously awarded a special citation by the Pulitzer Prize for her 'outstanding and courageous reporting on the horrific and vicious violence against African Americans during the era of lynching'.[4]

In the UK, Edwards' audacious and visionary editorials inspired the actor and journalist Dusé Mohamed Ali to establish the *African Times and Orient Review* in 1912. This progressive organ was a thorn in the side of British imperialism, promoting the perspectives of people of colour in the Edwardian age, and critically linking African, Asian and

Arab communities together in the struggle against prejudicial British colonial policies. It campaigned for home rule in Egypt and consistently highlighted the contribution of the colonies to the First World War effort, stressing that self-government should naturally follow what Ali termed the ultimate sacrifice. Ali's advocacy was noted at the heart of government, with his Indian Muslim Soldiers' Widows and Orphans' War Fund (1915) attracting Lloyd George and other prominent members of the British Cabinet as patrons.

Ali's mentoring of a young Marcus Garvey proved equally consequential. Garvey, 158 Fleet Street's bona fide handyman, eagerly immersed himself in the world of the *Review*. Its charismatic editor imparted crucial knowledge that would help mould one of the twentieth century's foremost Black leaders. Garvey's ideology would later influence the US civil rights movement during the 1950s and '60s and the future proponents of Black Power, both in the US and the UK.

It was Ali's influence on Garvey's indomitable first wife, Amy Ashwood Garvey, however, that was of even deeper significance on these shores. The first Mrs Garvey was no pushover: legend has it that she shielded Garvey from an assailant's bullets at his offices in New York, and she was keen to build her own reputation as an activist following their divorce. Proving that imitation was the sincerest form of flattery, Ashwood Garvey produced a fleeting US clone of the *Review*, the weekly *West Indian Times and American Review*, in the early 1920s. Ashwood Garvey's campaigning work with James and Padmore for the International African Friends of Ethiopia directly linked Ali's earlier progressive work to that of the 1930s campaigners. Her life story intersected with some of the most consequential actors of that time. She is credited with organising and nurturing the Nigerian Progress Union in 1924, the bedrock of the West African Students' Union, which actively campaigned for self-determination of the colonies in the UK during the 1930s and '40s. Bestowed with the title *Iyalode*, or mother, by the West African students, Ashwood Garvey's role was that of a facilitator: her International Afro Restaurant and Florence Mills Social Parlour acted as important venues, inspiring networks and collaborations that would transform Britain post-war. Her friend Sylvia Pankhurst, who had tutored a young Claude McKay in the rudiments of journalism, was Ashwood Garvey's staunch ally in the Ethiopian cause, opening her home to campaigners and establishing the *New Times and Ethiopian News* in 1936. Later in life, Ashwood Garvey would collaborate with Claudia Jones in her role as managing editor on the *West Indian Gazette and Afro-Asian Caribbean News* and, following the racist murder of Kelso Cochrane and the Notting Hill Riots, lobby Westminster for better race relations to be enshrined in policy.

The advanced journalist spirits of the 1930s – Padmore, James and Marson – consistently campaigned to rout discrimination in housing, education and employment – whether it was in nursing, the armed forces or on the Cardiff docks. They highlighted the untenable economic situation in Britain's colonies, demanding the British state act to install 'the same constitutional rights and the same civil liberties enjoyed by the people of Britain'.[5]

Schooled in the US civil rights protest movement, the talented and astute Jones would take up this baton in her role as editor of the *Gazette*, using her journalism to advocate for better rights for the country's growing non-white population in the 1950s and '60s, deliberately adding an important global dimension by linking this struggle with the heritage of anti-colonial protest. Her activism ultimately led to the first act prohibiting discrimination on racial grounds – the Race Relations Act 1965.

The intellectual scaffold for Black Power had been wrought in earlier decades: the significant journalism and activism of Edwards, Ali, McKay, Padmore, Marson and Jones had sown the seeds of a movement that would permanently alter British history. Howe inherited this ideology and with typical steel advanced it. In his role as *Race Today* editor, Howe shrewdly identified journalism as a force for change: it was not there merely to record, it was there to harness 'intellectual energy' and demand better rights for all.[6]

His campaigns provoked important changes in the constitution, notably with regard to institutional racism within the police and criminal justice system; however, it was his role as the chief organiser of the Black People's Day of Action that truly transformed the UK. This watershed moment was a significant expression of Black political power: it highlighted the alarming increase in racist attacks and murders in the 1970s and '80s, drawing attention to police cover-ups and inaction, and demanded appropriate legislation to curb these actions. Its historical significance was summed up by John La Rose, the chair of the New Cross Massacre Action Committee, who stated following that day: 'Black struggles became centre stage in British politics.'[7]

The significant gains accrued as a result of this journalism as activism cannot be underestimated. The gift that these journalists gave us was a better society for all: a society where it was enshrined in law that no one would be discriminated against because of the colour of their skin. Their ultimate hope was for a thriving, multicultural Britain. Our gift to them is to ensure this hope is realised.

TIMELINE OF SIGNIFICANT UK PUBLICATIONS ASSOCIATED WITH *INK!*[*]

August 1892 – *Lux* – Editor, Samuel Jules Celestine Edwards (last issue 13 July 1895; nearly a year after Edwards' death on 25 July 1894)

July 1893 – *Fraternity* – Editor, Samuel Jules Celestine Edwards (last issue 1897)

July 1912 – *African Times and Orient Review* – Editor, Dusé Mohamed Ali – (last issue December 1920)

September 1919–December 1920 – *Workers' Dreadnought* – labour correspondent, Claude McKay; Editor Sylvia Pankhurst (est. May 1914 as the *Woman's Dreadnought*; became the *Workers' Dreadnought*, July 1917; last issue June 1924)

October 1931–August 1933 – *The Negro Worker* (Hamburg) – Editor, George Padmore (established 1928, last issue 1937)

August 1933–January 1935 – *The Keys* – Editor, Una Marson (launched July 1933; last issue July 1939)

July 1937–October 1938 – George Padmore's International African Service Bureau publications – *Africa and the World* (Editor, I.T.A. Wallace-Johnson, July 1937); *The African Sentinel* (Editor, I.T.A. Wallace-Johnson, October 1937); *International African Opinion* (Editor C.L.R. James, July 1938)

March 1958–April/May 1965 – *West Indian Gazette and Afro-Asian Caribbean News* – Editor, Claudia Jones; there were only three more bi-monthly issues published after Jones' death in December 1964

---

[*] Please note this list is by no means comprehensive; it features those publications associated with the journalists featured in *INK!*

October 1968–January 1969 – *Black Eagle*, editor Darcus Howe
February 1969–March/April 1969 – the *Black Dimension*, editor
  Darcus Howe
November 1973–1985 – *Race Today*, editor Darcus Howe (last
  issue January–February 1988; editor Leila Hassan Howe, January
  1985–88). The journal was founded in 1969 by the Institute of Race
  Relations

NOTES

Introduction

1   The British Library holds Vol. 2, No. 5 (November 1959)–Vol. 8 No. 2 (February/March) 1965 on microfilm (some fragments, some copies missing). There is also a print copy of Vol. 8, No. 3 April/May 1965 stored in Yorkshire. IRR holds Vol. 2, No. 5 (November 1959)–Vol. 8, No. 2 (February/March) 1965 on microfilm, as does the University of Oxford (it is the same microfilm as the BL) and a print copy of Vol. 8, No. 3 (April/May 1965). IRR has print copies from November/December 1959–February 1965: some fragments; some duplicate, some missing. Lambeth Archives holds the same issues on microfilm as the IRR. Reporter Donald Hinds also donated a number of print issues to Lambeth archives (dates span September 1959 to December/January 1965 but this is not a complete run)

2   Note this is an ongoing journalism project, so the situation may change

3   The Library of Congress in Washington DC has digitised the *African Times and Orient Review*, 1912–18; Vol. No. 1 (July 1912)–Vol. 2, no. 17 (December 1913); Vol. 1 No. 1 (March 1914)–Vol. 6 (October 1918) and the Daniel Murray Collection: Vol. 1 No. 1 (July 1912), Vol. 2, Nos 17–18 (November–December 1913) are all available online, www.loc.gov/item/98650713

4   Pettiano, Tony, 'Newspapers the Rough Draft of History,' Readex blog, 10 April 2010, www.readex.com/blog/newspapers-rough-draft-history [accessed 20 December 2024]

5   Du Bois, W.E.B., *The Souls of Black Folk* (Chicago: AC McClurg & Co., 1903), p.10

6   Manjapra, Kris, *Black Ghost of Empire* (London: Penguin Random House, 2022), p.4

7   Manjapra, *Black Ghost of Empire*, p.4; Ellison, Ralph, *Invisible Man* (New York: Vintage International, 1995), p.3

8   Manjapra, *Black Ghost of Empire*, p.4; Ellison, *Invisible Man*, p.94

9   James, C.L.R.; Hall, Stuart; Braithwaite, Phoebe, '"A Microcosm of the World": C.L.R. James, the Complete Unaired 1976 BBC Interview', *The New York Review of Books*, 21 December 2024, p.2

10   Rashotte, Vivian, 'Steve McQueen on Blitz and How It Tells a Different Kind of war Story', 12 November 2024, www.cbc.ca/arts/q/steve-mcqueen-on-blitz-and-how-it-tells-a-different-kind-of-war-story-1.7380939 [accessed 6 January 2024]

11   Bostanci, Annie, 'How was India Involved in the First World War',
       30 November 2014, www.britishcouncil.org/voices-magazine/how-was-
       india-involved-first-world-war [accessed 6 January 2024]; 'Remembering
       Indian Soldiers', www.india1914.com/Price_of_war.aspx [accessed
       6 January 2024]

12   Women in Journalism website, 'Shocking Lack of Media Diversity Across
       Newspapers', 16 September 2024, www.womeninjournalism.co.uk/
       research/lack-diversity-british-newsrooms [accessed 6 January 2024]

13   *West Indian Gazette*, June 1960, Vol. 3 No. 4, p.2

14   *West Indian Gazette*, August 1960, Vol. 3 No. 1, p.3

15   Howe was technically C.L.R. James' second cousin but referred to him
       as Uncle Nello; the tendency to refer to elders as uncles and aunties is
       common in West Indian culture

16   James, Hall, Braithwaite, 'A Microcosm of the World', p.2

17   Sherwood passed away on 16 February 2025

18   St Clair Knox, 'In Memoriam of Celestine Edwards', *Fraternity*, Vol. II
       No. 8, 1 March 1895, p.3

Chapter One

1   *The Weekly Dispatch* (London), 24 October 1880, p.13

2   'Outline Sketch of the Life of Celestine Edwards', *Fraternity*, Vol. II No. 11,
       1 June 1895, p.3 (from Celestine Edwards' – now lost – logbook). This is a
       true story from Edwards' logbook reprinted in *Fraternity*. The author has
       also used for detail a newspaper article from the *South London Press*, 'Raglan
       Music Hall', 23 December 1882, p.4, an account of Rev. B. Senior and his
       friends at Surrey chapel opening the hall and the reception they received

3   Ibid.

4   *Eastern Argus and Borough of Hackney Times*, 25 May 1889

5   Poulsen, Charles, *Victoria Park: A Study in the History of East London*
       (London: Journeyman, 1976), p.99

6   *Shields Daily Gazette*, 25 September 1895, p.3

7   Edwards was 5ft 10¾in. The average height for an 1870s male was 5ft 6in.
       He was said to be such a magnificent public speaker that it elevated his
       physical presence

8   'The End of a Remarkable Career', *Shields Daily Gazette*, 25 September
       1895, p.3; 'Feeding the Children', *Justice*, 1 September 1890 – this is a
       composite of Wailey's obituary published in several newspapers and an
       article of one of the regular collections Edwards would make in Victoria
       Park

9   Schneer, Jonathan, *London 1900: The Imperial Metropolis* (New Haven and
       London: Yale University Press, 1999), p.207

10   One report in the *Eastern Argus* was extravagant in its praise for Edwards'
       rhetorical abilities: 'The audience in front of Mr Celestine Edwards could

never complain of being wearied, for his abilities as an eloquent speaker are, if anything, equalled by his wit, pointed sarcasm and fullness of assurance in which he endeavours to teach.' (*Eastern Argus*, reported in the *Bristol Magpie*, 8 April 1893); 'Coat and hat stolen, Who stole the coat?', *Sunderland Daily Echo and Shipping Gazette*, 23 September 1890, p.3

11   'Remarkable Accident at Landport, Several Persons Hurt', *Hampshire Telegraph*, 18 February 1893, p.7

12   Fryer, Peter, *Staying Power: The History of Black People in Britain* (London: Pluto Press, 1984), p.282

13   Edwards was never sure if he was born in 1857 or 1858

14   Letters, *Fraternity*, 1 November 1894

15   'Outline Sketch of the Life of Celestine Edwards', *Fraternity*, Vol. II No. 5, 1 December 1894, p.3. NB 'this chapter is taken almost ad verbatim from our sailor's logbook, the faded MSS which is in our [*Fraternity*'s] possession.'

16   Ibid.

17   'Outline Sketch of the Life of Celestine Edwards', *Fraternity*, Vol. II No. 6, 1 January 1895, p.3

18   'Outline Sketch of the Life of Celestine Edwards', *Fraternity*, Vol. II No. 8, 1 March 1895, p.3

19   'Outline Sketch of the Life of Celestine Edwards', *Fraternity*, Vol. II No. 9, 1 April 1895, p.6

20   'Outline Sketch of the Life of Celestine Edwards', *Fraternity*, Vol. II No. 10, 1 May 1895, p.8

21   Ibid.

22   'The city was something of a mecca for West Indians and Africans, a number who were enrolled at Edinburgh University medical school', (Moses Da Rocha and Jeffrey P. Green); Schneer, *London 1900*, p.206

23   It also should be noted that Henry Williams, the main organiser of the 1900 Pan-African conference in London, also got his start in Britain by lecturing for the temperance movement. The historian Jonathan Schneer has theorised that it was easier for Black members to be accepted into an organisation whose main aim was to salvage drunkenness rather than unions who were concerned about the threat of foreign-born workers

24   Grenfell, Wilfred, 'To My Friend', *Fraternity*, Vol. II No. 7, 1 February 1895, p.3

25   *Fraternity*, Vol. II No. 10, 1 May 1895, p.3

26   Schneer, *London 1900*, p.208; *Lux*, 17 November 1894

27   *Fraternity*, Vol. II No. 13, 1 August 1895, p.17 (from Celestine Edwards' – now lost – logbook)

28   *Fraternity*, 1 August 1895, pp.93, 94

29   Schneer, *London 1900*, p.209

30 Booth, Charles, *The Life and Labour of the People of London* (London: Macmillan & Co., 1902, first published 1889); summary accessed digamoo. free.fr/booth1969.pdf (quote found under Chapter 1, Poverty, The Eight Classes) [accessed 17 January 2025]

31 *Fraternity*, Vol. II No. 13, 1 August 1895, p.17 (from Celestine Edwards' — now lost — logbook)

32 Grenfell, Wilfred, 'To My Friend', *Fraternity*, 1 February 1895, Vol. II No. 7, p.3

33 Ibid.

34 Ibid.

35 *Portsmouth Evening News*, 25 September 1894

36 Editorial, *Lux*, Vol. 1 No. 1, 6 August 1892, p.1 (Edwards published the contents of the circular in *Lux*'s first issue)

37 Ibid., p.1

38 A Clerkenwell institution that supported 300 people and provided Bible school and sewing classes for up to 1,000 children

39 Editorial, *Lux*, Vol. II No. 29, 18 February 1893, pp.1–3

40 RH Anti-Slavery Papers. Brit Empire. S20E5/7 Minute Book of C. Impey for the Society of the Brotherhood of Man, Frederick Douglass to Catherine Impey, 9 July 1888

41 Bressey, Caroline, *Empire, Race and the Politics of Anti-Caste* (London: Bloomsbury, 2013), p.133

42 *Fraternity*, 1 August 1893, p.1

43 Ibid., p.3

44 *Fraternity*, 1 March 1894, p.6

45 'Cruel Barbarities in an English Town', *Fraternity*, 1 April 1894, p.11

46 'Murder will Out', Editorial, *Fraternity*, Vol. VI No. 7; Vol. 1, 1 January 1894, p.1

47 'Sparks', *Lux*, 16 September 1893

48 Wells, Ida B., *Crusade for Justice* (Chicago: University of Chicago Press, 1970), p.90

49 Ibid., p.91

50 'Outline Sketch of the Life of Celestine Edwards', *Fraternity*, 1 November 1895, Vol. III No. 29, p.53

51 Ibid.

52 Dates of his death differ, from 25 July 1894 (Fryer et al.) to 27 July 1894. Later issues of *Fraternity* repeat the latter

53 Lorimer, Douglas A., 'Legacies of Slavery for Race, Religion and Empire: S.J. Celestine Edwards and the Hard Truth (1894)', *Slavery & Abolition* Vol. 39 No. 4, 2018, pp.731–755

54 Thomas, Theodore, *Hard Truth* (London: Lawrence & Symcox, 1894), pp.52–3

55 Ibid., p.60

56   'The Female Accusation', *Fraternity*, 1 August 1894, p.4

57   Schneer, *London 1900*, p.212; *Lux*, 12 January 1895

58   Schneer, *London 1900*, p.224

59   Ibid., p.223

60   Ibid., pp.399–407. Ali claimed to be a student at King's College London, the same alma mater as Edwards, but there are no records of him attending this school

Chapter Two

1   Ali, Dusé Mohamed, *Leaves from an Active Life: The Autobiography of a Pioneer Pan African and Afro-Asian Activist*, compiled with an introduction by Mustafa Abdelwahid (New Jersey: The Red Sea Press, 2011), p.87

2   *The Times*, 22 April 1905, p.10

3   Ali, *Leaves from an Active Life*, p.89

4   Ibid., p.89

5   Ibid., p.91

6   Duffield, Ian, *Dusé Mohamed Ali and the Development of Pan-Africanism, 1866–1945*, Vol. 1 (Edinburgh: Edinburgh University Press, 1971), p.53

7   Although Ali's early life is decidedly shaded, an MI5 file from the First World War mentions a Captain Dusé (deceased) as being his guardian – (MI5 files FO 371/2355/15047/15, 7 February 1914). Ali wrote various biographical accounts of his early life in the *Hull Lady*, June 1902, p.43. He outlines his family connections to Urabi Pasha in *The New Age*, 14 July 1910, p.10. This is also in *The Land of the Pharaohs* (London: 1911). A letter he sent to the Foreign Office in 1919 also elucidates his claim to be an Egyptian national, Dusé Mohamed Ali to Rt Hon. A.J. Balfour, S. of S. for Foreign Affairs, 9 August 1919, FO 371/3728/114805/19. But, as Duffield states, there is a vagueness and lack of chronology between these various reports (mostly produced by Ali). For more information see Duffield, Ian, *Dusé Mohamed Ali and the Development of Pan-Africanism*, Vol. 1, pp.1–3

8   *The New Age*, 14 July 1910, p.263

9   Mahmud, Khalil, *In the Land of the Pharaohs* (London: Frank Cass & Co. Ltd, 1968), p.10

10   Chamberlain, M.E., 'The Alexandria Massacre of 11 June 1882 and the British Occupation of Egypt', *Middle Eastern Studies*, Vol. 13 No. 1, January 1977, pp.14–39

11   *Aberdeen Press and Journal*, 8 September 1882, p.5. A report with an English engineer stating that he 'was warned by a vegetable seller that Christians were to be massacred on the morrow'

12   Ali, Dusé Mohamed, *In the Land of the Pharaohs: A Short History of Egypt* (London: Stanley Paul & Co., 1911), pp.100–101

13   Ibid.

14 Ali writes in his autobiography *Leaves from An Active Life* that his mother and sisters were sent away to Sudan for safety and 'I never saw nor heard of them again despite my efforts to discover their whereabouts for a period extending over some 15 years', p.33

15 *Nigerian Daily Times*, 10 March, p.7

16 New York Passenger arrival lists, Ellis Island, 1892–1924, 'Wm Rand' on vessel *Wyoming*, 6 October 1886, arrival: New York, US; microfilm serial M237, microfilm roll M237_4999, line 46, list number 1219, quoted from Dorman, Jacob S., 'Western Civilization through Eastern Spectacles Dusé Mohamed Ali, Black Orientalist Imposture and Black Internationalism', *The Journal of African American History*, Vol. 108 No. 1, p.33, *Wyoming*'s passenger manifest; p.34, analysis of Ali/Rand lecture circuit in 1888

17 Duffield, *Dusé Mohamed Ali and the Development of Pan-Africanism*, Vol. 1, p.38

18 Ali, *Leaves from an Active Life*, p.42

19 Duffield, *Dusé Mohamed Ali and the Development of Pan-Africanism*, Vol. 1, p.36

20 In the marriage certificate to Brunyee, Ali is described as a widower. However, this author can find no reference to a first wife. 'African Stories in Hull & East Yorkshire', 2017, www.africansinyorkshireproject.com/duse-mohamed-ali.html [accessed 14 September 2021]

21 Records show marriage between April and June 1901 – Civil Registration Indexes 1901 of the General Register Office of England and Wales, in district of Knaresborough, Yorkshire, Vol. 9A 241

22 Killingray, David, 'Rights, Land and Labour: Black British Critics of South African Policies before 1948', *Journal of Southern African Studies*, Vol. 35 No. 2, June 2009. Sapire, H., 'Liberation Struggles, Exile and International Solidarity', *Journal of Southern African Studies*, Vol. 35 No. 2, June 2009, pp.375–398

23 Matera, Marc, *Black London: The Imperial Metropolis and Decolonization in the Twentieth Century* (California: University of California Press, 2015), p.7

24 Duffield, *Dusé Mohamed Ali and the Development of Pan-Africanism*, Vol. 1, p.376

25 'White Women and Coloured Men: The Other Side of the Picture', *The New Age*, 21 January 1909, pp.262–263; Ali, *In the Land of the Pharaohs*, p.264

26 The series commissioned in *The New Age* was 'Western Eyes through Eastern Spectacles', all authored by Ali, 4 February 1909, p.301; 18 February 1909, pp.341–342; 4 March 1909, p.381; 25 March 1909, p.443; 22 April 1909, p.519

27 Orage would invite new contributors to weekly Monday meetings he would hold in the ABC tearooms in London's Chancery Lane. Duffield, *Dusé Mohamed Ali and the Development of Pan-Africanism*, Vol. 1, p.91

28 *The Times*, 1 June 1910, p.9

29 Ali, *Leaves from an Active Life*, p.107

30 Ali, Dusé Mohamed, 'The Situation in Egypt', *The New Age*, 16 June 1910, p.147

31 Ibid.

32 Pickthall, Marmaduke, 'The Situation in Egypt. A Reply to Dusé Mohamed Ali', *The New Age*, 30 June 1910, p.196

33 *The Scotsman*, 16 February 1911, p.2

34 *The World*, 14 February 1911, pp.249–250

35 Blunt, Wilfred Scawen, 'My Diaries', entry for 19 April 1911, p.759, quoted in Duffield, *Dusé Mohamed Ali and the Development of Pan-Africanism*, Vol. 1, p.140. Duffield elaborates in detail the plagiarism allegations against Ali and the consequences for his career

36 Duffield, Ian, 'Dusé Mohamed Ali: His Purpose and His Public', Niven, A. (ed.), *The Commonwealth Writer Overseas*, Marcel Didier, 1976, p.165

37 Duffield, *Dusé Mohamed Ali and the Development of Pan-Africanism*, Vol. 1, p.143

38 'Quo Vadis', *The New Age*, 23 February 1911, p.388

39 Ali, Dusé Mohamed, 'The Coloured Man in Art and Letters', *T.P.'s Weekly*, June 1911, pp.399–407

40 On page 35 there is a list of market prices for natural resources such as gold, diamond, rubber

41 *African Times and Orient Review*, September 1912, p.101

42 Mohamed, Beatrice, 'Unity', *African Times and Orient Review*, April 1920, p.76

43 Ibid., p.14

44 Garvey's piece appeared in the *Review* in October 1913, pp.158–160. Ferris' response in the *African Times and Orient Review*, 14 April 1914

45 Garvey Papers, I, p.5

46 Duffield, *Dusé Mohamed Ali and the Development of Pan-Africanism*, Vol. 1, p.191

47 *African Times and Orient Review*, December/January 1913, p.197

48 *African Times and Orient Review*, January 1920, pp.33–34.

49 'India and the War Contribution', *African Times and Orient Review*, January 1917, p.59

50 *African Times and Orient Review*, April 1917, p.2

51 *African Times and Orient Review*, January 1918, p.132

52 *African Times and Orient Review*, October 1917, p.75 – states the *Review* had asked permission to send W.F. Hutchinson to the front as war correspondent

53 James Baird FO to Lt Col Raymond Greene WO, 18 September 1917, FO 395/130/186216/58

54   Duffield, *Dusé Mohamed Ali and the Development of Pan-Africanism*, Vol. 1, p.4; quoted in notes Dusé Mohamed Ali to Rt Hon. A.J. Balfour, S. of S. for Foreign Affairs, 9 August 1919, FO 371/3728/115805/19

55   Ali was born in Egypt when it was under Ottoman suzerainty, Ali, *In the Land of the Pharaohs*, p.7

56   TNA: PRO CO 554/35/55259; also quoted Grant, Colin, *Negro with the Hat* (London: Vintage 2009), p.39

57   Gundara, Jagdish S. and Duffield, Ian, *Essays on the History of Blacks in Britain* (London: Avebury, 1992), 'Duse Mohamed Ali, Afro-Asian Solidarity and Pan-Africanism in Early Twentieth Century London', pp.124–149; quotes FO 371/2355/15047/15, P. Nathan MI5, War Office to G. Clarke, Foreign Office, 7 February 1915, *Confidential Report on Dusé Mohamed*

58   TNA: PRO CO 554/35/55259

59   Duffield, *Dusé Mohamed Ali and the Development of Pan-Africanism*, Vol. 1, p.196

60   Ali, Dusé Mohamed, 'Yesterday, Today and Tomorrow', *African Times and Orient Review*, 30 June 1914, p.2

61   Duffield, *Dusé Mohamed Ali and the Development of Pan-Africanism*, Vol. 1, p.200

62   *African and Orient Review*, December 1920, p.54

63   Several times Ali states he went to the US in 1920, for example in his obituary of Marcus Garvey in *The Comet*, 6 August 1940, p.4, but Duffield places him at the APU meeting on 20 July 1921. He surmises Ali left Britain after this date. Duffield, Ian, *Dusé Mohamed Ali and the Development of Pan-Africanism, 1866–1945*, Vol. 2 (Edinburgh: Edinburgh University Press, October 1971), p.650, see note 1

64   Duffield, Ian, 'The Business Activities of Dusé Mohamed Ali: An Example of the Economic Dimension of Pan-Africanism, 1912–45', *Journal of the Historical Society of Nigeria*, Vol. IV No. 4, June 1969, p.574

65   *The Comet*, 17 August 1940, p.4

66   *The Comet*, 5 March 1938, p.4

67   Morrison, Lionel, *A Century of Black Journalism in Britain* (London: Truebay, 2007), p.3

Chapter Three

1   Historians are still arguing about the number of First World War casualties with estimates between 6 and 13 million military lives lost. Online BBC Report, 'The War to End all Wars', 10 November 1998 news.bbc.co.uk/1/hi/special_report/1998/10/98/world_war_i/198172.stm [accessed 14 January 2025]. Source www.100letprve.si/en/world_war_1/casualties/index.html

2   McWhirter, Cameron, *Red Summer* (New York: St Martin's Griffin, 2011), p.15

3   Ibid., p.13

4   McKay, Claude, 'Claude McKay Describes His Own Life: A Negro Poet', *Pearson's Magazine* (New York), Vol. 38 No. 3 (September 1918), pp.275–276

5   Tillery, Tyrone, *Claude McKay: A Black Poet's Struggle for Identity* (Massachusetts: University of Massachusetts Press, 1992), p.33

6   Cooper, Wayne F., *Claude McKay: Rebel Sojourner in the Harlem Renaissance* (Louisiana: Louisiana State University Press, 1987), p.101

7   The date has often been given as 1889 but, according to his biographer Wayne F. Cooper and letters from McKay, the 1889 date is disputed. McKay claimed 15 September 1889 as his birthday until 1920. He had actually been born a year later on 15 September 1890. His family had apparently set his birthday back a year so he would be eligible a year earlier than was legally permissible to become a student teaching assistant in his brother U'Theo's school. The clearest statement of the correct date of Claude McKay's birth is in McKay to Alain Locke, 4 June 1927, in Alain Locke's Papers. See Cooper, *Claude McKay*, pp.525–526

8   McKay, Claude, *A Long Way from Home* (New York: Lee Furman Inc., 1937; Harcourt, Brace & Word, Inc., 1970), p.36

9   Ibid., pp.40, 59

10 Ibid., p.41

11 Ibid., p.51

12 Ibid., p.47

13 Ibid., p.101

14 Ibid., p.110

15 Cooper, *Claude McKay*, p.108

16 Ibid., p.217

17 Ibid., pp.110–111

18 McKay, *A Long Way from Home*, p.4

19 Cooper, *Claude McKay*, p.31

20 James, Winston, 'Letters from London in Black and Red: Claude McKay, Marcus Garvey and the Negro World', *History Workshop Journal* 85 (spring) pp.281–93, DOI: 10.1093/hwj/dby002 [accessed 13 January 2023]

21 Rogers, J.A., *Pittsburgh Courier*, 18 June 1927

22 McKay, *A Long Way from Home*, p.32

23 Cooper, *Claude McKay*, p.132

24 Tillery, *Claude McKay*, p.41

25 McKay mentions a pair of siblings, the Grays, funding his trip. James, Winston, 'Letters from London in Black and Red', *History Workshop Journal*, p.285; Tillery, *Claude McKay*, p.42

26 McKay, Claude, *Claude McKay: Complete Poems, Edited and with an Introduction by William J. Maxwell* (Urbana and Chicago: University of Illinois Press, 2004), p.45

27 Jenkinson, Jacqueline, *Black 1919: Riots, Racism and Resistance in Imperial Britain* (Liverpool University Press, 2009), p.23

28 'Racial Riot in South Wales': report of the Chief Constable Cardiff City Police, regarding rioting in Newport, Cardiff, Barry and Swansea, 6–13 June 1919, National Archives, CO323/816/40

29 *The Globe*, 6 June 1919, p.1

30 *Liverpool Echo*, 6 June 1919, p.5

31 James, Winston, 'A Race Outcast from an Outcast Class: Claude McKay's Experience and Analysis of Britain', Schwarz, Bill (ed.), *West Indian Intellectuals in Britain* (Manchester: Manchester University Press, 2003), p.74

32 McKay, *A Long Way from Home*, p.69

33 The paper had originally been called *The Woman's Dreadnought* in 1914–17 but Pankhurst had changed its title following the Russian Revolution

34 McKay, *A Long Way from Home*, p.68

35 Cooper, *Claude McKay*, p.164

36 Ibid., p.171

37 Pankhurst published five poems by McKay in *Workers' Dreadnought*: 'The Barrier', 'After the Winters', 'The Little Peoples', 'A Roman Holiday' and 'If We Must Die', 6 September 1919

38 Cooper, *Claude McKay*, p.171

39 James, 'A Race Outcast from an Outcast Class', *West Indian Intellectuals in Britain*, p.76

40 Pankhurst, Sylvia, 'Stabbing Negroes in the London Dock Area', *Workers' Dreadnought*, 7 June 1919, p.6

41 James, 'A Race Outcast from an Outcast Class', *West Indian Intellectuals in Britain*, p.76

42 '[P]erhaps I could dig up something along the London docks from the coloured as well as the white seamen. And write from a point of view which would be fresh and different', McKay, *A Long Way from Home*, p.76

43 McKay, Claude, 'Socialism and the Negro', *Workers' Dreadnought*, 31 January 1920, p.1

44 Morel, E.D., 'Black Scourge in Europe/Sexual Horror Let Loose by France on the Rhine', *Daily Herald*, 10 April 1920, p.1

45 McKay, Claude, 'A Black Man Replies', *Worker's Dreadnought*, 24 April 1920, p.2

46 Few records exist about its circulation but it was distributed at the docks and working men's clubs as well as Pankhurst's various enterprises

47 *Workers' Dreadnought*, 14 August 1920, p.2

48 C.E.E.: 'The Martyrdom of Ireland', *Workers' Dreadnought*, 9 October 1920, p.7

49 He compared Smillie to a 'powerful ash towering over saplings', Cooper, *Claude McKay*, p.178

50 McKay, *A Long Way From Home*, p.79
51 James, 'A Race Outcast from an Outcast Class', *West Indian Intellectuals in Britain*, p.75
52 *Workers' Dreadnought*, 16 October 1920, p.7
53 Ibid., p.1
54 Pankhurst papers, reel 254, 'Appeal of Miss Sylvia Pankhurst', 28 October 1920 (trial transcript), p.1
55 Cooper, *Claude McKay*, p.186
56 Pankhurst's six-month prison sentence was upheld on her 5 January appeal and she was sent to Holloway to serve it. On 31 May 1921, she was released for 'good behaviour'
57 McKay, *A Long Way from Home*, pp.150, 206 – here expresses yearnings and desire to see 'Lenin's opinion out of his own mouth'
58 Tillery, *Claude McKay*, p.51
59 Cooper, *Claude McKay*, p.198
60 Ibid., p.201
61 Ibid., p.213
62 Ibid., p.226
63 Ibid., p.236
64 Ibid., p.241
65 McKay, *A Long Way From Home*, p.79
66 Ibid., pp.162–164
67 McKay told this story of being tossed along Tverskaya Boulevard in 'Soviet Russia and the Negro', *The Crisis*, XXVII, December 1923–January 1924; quoted in Cooper, *Claude McKay*, p.254
68 McKay, Claude, 'Speech to the Fourth Congress of the Third Communist International', November 1922, published in *International Press Correspondence*, Vol. 3, 5 January 1923, pp.16–17 www.marxists.org/history/usa/groups/abb/1922/1100-mckay-cominternspeech.pdf [accessed 14 October 2023]
69 McKay, *A Long Way From Home*, pp.223–225; McKay, Claude, 'Petrograd: May Day', 1923
70 Cooper, *Claude McKay*, p.276
71 FBI files 12/16/21;123/23;2/3/23 (61-3497). Quoted in Tillery, *Claude McKay*, p.69
72 Evans, Richard J., 'A Middle-Class Revolt', *Prospect Magazine*, 21 August 2013, www.prospectmagazine.co.uk/culture/51370/a-middle-class-revolt [accessed 14 October 2023]
73 A brief note he left for Alain Locke at a Paris hotel makes it plain that McKay was already acquainted with the Nardals. It was dated 10 February but the year, unfortunately, was omitted: it might have been as early as 1923 or as late as 1928. Cooper, *Claude McKay*, p.307
74 Ibid., p.307

75 Harney, Elizabeth, *In Senghor's Shadow: Art, Politics and the Avant-Garde in Senegal, 1960–95* (Durham, NC: Duke University Press, 2004), p.25

76 McKay, *A Long Way From Home*, p.277

77 Du Bois, W.E.B., 'Review of Home to Harlem', *The Crisis*, September 1928, p.202

78 Bowser, Aubrey, 'Review of Banjo', *New York Amsterdam News*, 8 May 1929, p.366

79 Garvey, Marcus, 'Home to Harlem, Claude McKay's Damaging Book Should Earn Wholesale Condemnation of Negroes', *Negro World*, 29 September 1928

80 Langston Hughes to Alain Locke, 1 March 1928; Hughes letters, Locke Papers, Howard University, quoted in Tillery, *Claude McKay*, p.88

81 Tillery, *Claude McKay*, p.174

82 Antarah ben Shedad el Absi (Antar the Lion, the son of the Tribe of Abs), or Antar, was born in the middle of the sixth century in Arabia and feted for his poetry. His mother was an African princess taken as a slave; his father a nobleman. Stafford, A.O., 'Antar, the Arabian Negro Warrior, Poet and Hero', *The Journal of Negro History*, Vol. 1 No. 2, April 1916, pp.151–162

83 Cooper, *Claude McKay*, pp.424–425

84 In 2009, a doctoral student came across a typewritten manuscript while going through boxes in a rare book library at Columbia University. It turned out to be the long lost novel by McKay, *Amiable with Big Teeth*. In it he makes no secret of the cynicism with which he viewed the Communist Party. McKay, Claude, *Amiable with Big Teeth* (London: Penguin, 1917)

85 Review of ALWFH in *New Challenge*, quoted in Cooper, *Claude McKay*, p.450

86 Cooper, *Claude McKay*, p.467

87 Ibid., p.484

88 Ibid., p.490

89 Tillery, *Claude McKay*, p.176

90 McKay, 'When I Have Passed Away' (1922), *Claude McKay: Complete Poems*, p.166

91 McKay, *Claude McKay: Complete Poems*, p.xi

Chapter Four

1 The German police raided its office at least three times, the first during the harbour workers' strike in Hamburg in October 1931, the second in December 1931, when the police confiscated pamphlets and other propaganda material, and the third time in February 1933, resulting in the cessation of all of its activities in German. Weiss, Holger, 'The Road to Moscow: On Archival Sources Concerning

the ITUCNW in the Comintern Archive', *History in Africa*, Vol. 39, (Cambridge University Press, 2012), pp.361–393. See also Padmore to 'Dear Comrades', add: 'für Otto Huiswood', Hamburg, 16.11.1931, 534/3/668, 120r, RGASPI. See further Weiss, 'Framing a Radical African Atlantic', *Studies in Global Social History*, Vol. 14 (Brill, Leiden, etc., 2014), pp.302–303

2   Murray-Brown, Jeremy, *Kenyatta* (New York: E.P. Dutton, 1973), p.166
3   Other birth dates have been recorded. Special branch list 28 June 1900 but 28 June 1903 widely reported, while 28 July appeared on his passport. Author has opted for 28 June 1903. Secret Padmore papers CO968/1193, 7 February 1952
4   Hooker, James R., *Black Revolutionary: George Padmore's Path from Communism to Pan-Africanism* (London: Pall Mall Press, 1967), p.6
5   Ibid., p.3
6   Schwarz, *West Indian Intellectuals in Britain*, p.132. Schwarz states Padmore left 'days' after the marriage. Dr Leslie James states he arrived in NYC on 29 December 1924, see James, Leslie, '"What We Put in Black and White": George Padmore and the Practice of Anti-Imperial Politics' (LSE thesis, London, 2012), p.50. Quotes Ellis Island Record Collection, www.ellisisland.org (search passenger lists for Malcolm Nurse; shows the arrival date, etc.)
7   James, 'What We Put in Black and White', p.53
8   Hooker, *Black Revolutionary*, p.5
9   Ibid., p.7
10 James, C.L.R., *At the Rendezvous of Victory* (London: Allison & Busby, 1984), p.254; James, 'What We Put in Black and White', p.41
11 Makonnen, Ras, *Pan-Africanism from Within* (Oxford: Oxford University Press, 1973), p.120
12 Padmore, George, 'Awakened Negro Youth', *Negro Champion*, 22 June 1928
13 Hooker, *Black Revolutionary*, p.14
14 Lewis, Rupert, 'George Padmore: Towards a Political Assessment', Baptiste and Lewis (eds), *George Padmore: Pan-African Revolutionary* (Kingson, Jamaica: Ian Randle Publishers, 2008), p.204
15 Posgrove, Carol, *Ending British Rule in Africa* (Manchester: Manchester University Press, 2009), p.2
16 Hooker, *Black Revolutionary*, pp.13, 14
17 Ibid., p.15
18 Ibid., p.24
19 Adi, Hakim, *Pan-Africanism: A History* (London: Bloomsbury Academic, 2018), p.153
20 RGASPI 495/155/86: 290, 294, quoted in Miller, Pennybacker and Rosenhaft, 'Mother Ada Wright and the International Campaign to Free

the Scottsboro Boys', *The American Historical Review*, Vol. 106 No. 2, April 2001, pp.399, 387–430

21   James, Leslie, *George Padmore and Decolonization from Below* (London: Palgrave Macmillan, 2015), p.27

22   Hooker, *Black Revolutionary*, p.20, Letter Y. Berger to Hooker, 7 March 1967

23   George Padmore to James Ford, 17 March 1931. RGASPI 534/3/668, item 46; quoted in James, 'What We Put in Black and White', p.73

24   Posgrove, *Ending British Rule in Africa*, p.3; James, C.L.R., Notes, p.290

25   Pennybacker, Susan D., *From Scottsboro to Munich* (New Jersey: Princeton University Press, 2009), p.75; RGASPI 534/3/755 Padmore to Maxton, 1 June 1932; 165; Maxton to Padmore, 23 June 1932

26   Miller, Pennybacker and Rosenhaft, 'Mother Ada Wright and the International Campaign to Free the Scottsboro Boys', *The American Historical Review*, p.395

27   Pennybacker, *From Scottsboro to Munich*, p.24

28   *The Negro Worker*, August–September 1933, p.17; Cunard, Nancy, *Negro Anthology* (London: Wishart & Co., 1934), p.565

29   Vaughan, David A., *Negro Victory* (London: Independent Press Ltd, 1950), p.14

30   *The Negro Worker*, Vol. 2, No. 7, 15 July 1932, p.13

31   Posgrove, *Ending British Rule in Africa*, p.26

32   Ibid., p.3

33   Chisholm, Anne, *Nancy Cunard: A Biography* (London: Sidgwick & Jackson, 1979), p.267

34   James, *George Padmore and Decolonization from Below*, p.27. Historian Susan Pennybacker argued that while in Hamburg in 1932, Padmore suffered from 'a spiralling pattern of frustration with Comintern arrangements or their absence'

35   Nancy Cunard to Dorothy Padmore, November 1959. Cunard MSS 17/10, quoted in James, 'What We Put in Black and White', p.89

36   Weiss, Holger, 'Framing a Radical African Atlantic', *Studies in Global Social History*, Vol. 14 (Brill, Leiden etc., 2014), p.579. Quotes 26 Bill, Über die Festnahme und Ausweisung des Gen. Padmore [Report on the arrest and deportation of Comrade Padmore], no date [filed: 20.4.1933], 534/4/461, 124, RGASPI

37   Padmore to comrades, 6 March 1933. RGASPI 534/3/895, item 111-16. Pennybacker, *From Scottsboro to Munich*, p.77

38   Hooker, *Black Revolutionary*, p.30

39   Weiss, 'Framing a Radical African Atlantic', *Studies in Global Social History*, p.579

40   Padmore to Comrades, 6 and 7 March. RGASPI 534/3/895. Quoted in James, 'What We Put in Black and White', p.90

41 'Fascist Terror Against Negroes in Germany', *The Negro Worker*, Vol. 3 Nos 4–5, April–May 1933, p.1; Posgrove, *Ending British Rule in Africa*, p.4

42 Lewis, 'George Padmore: Towards a Political Assessment', Baptiste and Lewis (eds), *George Padmore: Pan-African Revolutionary*, p.206

43 'A Betrayer of the Negro Struggle', *The Negro Worker*, Vol. 4 No. 2, June 1934, p.6. Please note October 1933–34 *The Negro Worker* suspended

44 James, 'What We Put in Black and White', p.21

45 George Padmore letters 1930–45 [Padmore's correspondence with Cyril C. Ollivierre], Padmore to Ollivierre, 28 July 1934, SCMG624, Schomburg Center for Research in Black Culture, MS, Archives and Rare Books division; Posgrove, *Ending British Rule in Africa*, p.4.

46 James, C.L.R., *George Padmore: Black Marxist Revolutionary – A Memoir*, edited text of a talk given in north London in 1976 libcom.org/article/george-padmore-black-marxist-revolutionary-memoir-clr-james [accessed 12 April 2024], James, *At the Rendezvous of Victory*, pp.254–256

47 Ibid.

48 Trewelha, Paul, 'The Death of Albert Nzula and the Silence of George Padmore', *Searchlight South Africa*, Vol. 1 No. 1, September 1988, pp.64–69

49 James, C.L.R., Notes, pp.24–25; Minkah Makalani, *In the Cause of Freedom* (Carolina: University of North Carolina Press, 2011), states Kenyatta in slightly different version, p.193

50 Hooker, *Black Revolutionary*, p.42

51 Ibid., p.43

52 Solanke would state that the NPU had been 'conceived, born and mothered by Amy'. Martin, Tony, *Amy Ashwood Garvey: Pan-Africanist, Feminist and Mrs Marcus Garvey No. 1, Or, A Tale of Two Amies* (Massachusetts: The Majority Press, 2007), p.86. 'In 1946 in a lecture in Kano, Nigeria, Solanke described WASU as a direct outgrowth of the NPU', ibid., p.86

53 Martin, *Amy Ashwood Garvey*, p.106. Amy's newspaper tribute to Ali was published between 1926 and 1928 in Harlem

54 Padmore to Solanke, 21 February 1934, quoted in Adi, Hakim, *West Africans in Britain: Nationalism, Pan-Africanism and Communism* (London: Lawrence & Wishart, 1998), p.77

55 'The Truth About Aggrey House: An Exposure of the Government Plan for the Control of African Students in Great Britain', *Wasu*, London, 1934. Also *Wasu*, Vol. 3 No. 1, March 1934, p.3

56 *The Negro Worker*, August–September 1933, p.17

57 Vischer to A. de Wade, 8 July 1935, PRO CO323/1342/6652 pt2

58 Makonnen, *Pan-Africanism from Within*, p.146

59 Both these terms (Abyssinia/Ethiopia) were used interchangeably at the time

60   'Signor Mussolini and Abyssinia', *Spectator* archive, p.1 archive.spectator.
      co.uk/article/17th-may-1935/1/signor-mussolini-and-abyssinia-the-
      speech-of-signo [accessed 12 April 2024]
61   Posgrove, *Ending British Rule in Africa*, p.12. Padmore, 'Ethiopia and World
      Politics', *The Crisis*, May 1935, p.139
62   Posgrove, *Ending British Rule in Africa*, p.29. Padmore papers, Padmore to
      Ollivierre, 30 March 1938, SCMG624, Schomburg Center for Research in
      Black Culture, MS, Archives and Rare Books Division
63   The International Friends of Ethiopia: a public meeting. Record held
      in TUC archives, Modern Records Centre, University of Warwick.
      MSS.292/963/2, www.layersoflondon.org/map/records/the-international-
      friends-of-ethiopia-a-public-meeting/gallery/1 [accessed 12 April 2024]
64   Pankhurst set up her own paper, *The New Times and Ethiopian News*, in
      1936 and became a friend and adviser to Haile Selassie, eventually moving
      to Addis Ababa in 1956. When she died there in 1960, she was given a full
      state funeral. Ashwood Garvey later called Pankhurst 'the outstanding
      feminist of the century'
65   Report in *The Scotsman*, 29 July 1935, p.10
66   Makonnen, *Pan-Africanism from Within*, p.114
67   Ibid., p.114
68   Ibid., p.119
69   Padmore, George, *How Britain Rules Africa* (London: Wishart, 1936), p.8
70   Posgrove, *Ending British Rule in Africa*, p.18; 'Books and Publications', *The
      Economist*, 26 September 1936
71   Posgrove, *Ending British Rule in Africa*, p.31; UK/TNA,
      mEPO38/91/99495, Metropolitan Police, Special Report: Wallace-
      Johnson, 6 July 1937
72   *International African Opinion*, issue 1, July 1938, p.1
73   Padmore, George, 'Hands off the Colonies', *Controversy*, Vol. 2 No. 17,
      February 1938, www.marxists.org/archive/padmore/1938/fascism-colonies
      [accessed 11 March 2024]
74   Grant, Colin, *Negro with a Hat: The Rise and Fall of Marcus Garvey* (London:
      Vintage, 2009), p.441
75   Ibid., p.443
76   Ibid., p.2. C.L.R. James later eulogised Garvey, in an interview on
      BBC Radio 4 'Up, You Mighty Race', 1987, James acknowledged that
      ideological differences should not have obscured their common cause.
      Notes Grant, pp.1, 2
77   Matera, Marc, *Black London: The Imperial Metropolis and Decolonization in the
      Twentieth Century* (California: University of California Press, 2015), p.93
78   Ryan, Selwyn D., *Race & Nationalism in Trinidad and Tobago* (London:
      Faber & Faber, 1952), pp.60, 66–68; eprints.whiterose.ac.uk/90060/2/
      SXCaribbean%5B1%5D%5B1%5D.pdf [accessed 12 February 2024]

79   In 1944, in a heavily censored letter to Ollivierre, he mentioned 'the ordeal of air attacks' and of sending stamps as a present to Blyden – the letter was returned by the censor, illustrating the difficulties of maintaining the relationship. George Padmore letters, 1930–45, SCMG624, Schomburg Center for Research in Black Culture, Manuscripts, Archives and Rare Books Division

80   Posgrove, *Ending British Rule in Africa*, p.29

81   Bourne, Stephen, *Mother Country: Britain's Black Community at the Home Front, 1939–45* (Cheltenham: The History Press, 2020), pp.21–22

82   Padmore to Ivar Holm, 23 July 1946, Nkrumah MSS/Howard/154-41, folder 14; quoted in James, 'What We Put in Black and White', p.160

83   James, Hall, Braithwaite, '"A Microcosm of the World": C.L.R. James, the Complete Unaired 1976 BBC Interview', *The New York Review of Books*, 21 December 2024, p.13

84   Padmore, George, 'The British Empire is Worst Racket Yet Invented by Man', *The New Leader*, 15 December 1939, www.marxists.org/archive/padmore/1939/worst-racket.htm [accessed 12 February 2024]

85   Posgrove, *Ending British Rule in Africa*, p.55

86   James, C.L.R., Notes, p.82

87   Thompson, Vincent B., 'George Padmore: Reconciling Two Phases of Contradictions', Baptiste and Lewis (eds), *George Padmore: Pan-African Revolutionary* (Kingston, Jamaica: Ian Randle Publishers, 2009), p.204

88   James, *George Padmore and Decolonization from Below*, p.81

89   Report, *Daily Mirror*, 3 September 1943, p.8

90   Hooker, *Black Revolutionary*, p.62

91   Padmore, G., and Cunard, N., *White Man's Duty* (London: W.H. Allen, 1943). Sold for 9p and was reprinted. Chisholm, Anne, *Nancy Cunard: A Biography* (London: Sidgwick & Jackson, 1979), p.267

92   'Atlantic Charter', History.com, www.history.com/topics/world-war-ii/atlantic-charter [accessed 13 July 2023]

93   Vaughan, David A., *Negro Victory* (London: Independent Press Ltd, 1950), p.121

94   Sherwood, Marika, *World War II: Colonies and Colonials* (London: The Savannah Press, 2013), pp.89–90

95   Hooker, *Black Revolutionary*, p.77

96   Killingray, David, 'To Do Something for the Race: Harold Moody and the League of Coloured Peoples', Schwarz, *West Indian Intellectuals in Britain*, p.66

97   Adi, Hakim, 'George Padmore and the 1945 Manchester Conference', Baptiste and Lewis, *George Padmore: Pan-African Revolutionary*, p.109

98   James, *George Padmore: A Black Marxist Revolutionary – A Memoir* libcom.org/article/george-padmore-black-marxist-revolutionary-memoir-clr-james [accessed 12 February 2024]

99   Makalani, Minkah, *In the Cause of Freedom* (Carolina: University of North
      Carolina Press, 2011), p.224

100   Padmore, George, *Pan-Africanism or Communism? The Coming Struggle for
      Africa* (London: D. Dobson, 1956), pp.148–149

101   *Daily Herald*, 17 October 1945, p.3, quoted in Adi, Hakim, and Sherwood,
      Marika, *The 1945 Pan-African Conference Revisited* (London: New Beacon
      Books, 1995), p.44

102   Posgrove, *Ending British Rule in Africa*, p.101

103   Ibid., p.89

104   CO968/1193 FCO Secret Padmore Papers. Whitehall 3781/2. Letter from
      Maj. Gen. Sir Edward Louis Spears to Henry Hopkinson, 22 May 1953.

105   Posgrove, *Ending British Rule in Africa*, p.106

106   Padmore authored, along with numerous pamphlets: *The Life and Struggles
      of Negro Toilers* (1931); *How Britain Rules Africa* (1936); *Africa and World Peace*
      (1938); *How Russia Transformed Her Colonial Empire* (1946); *Africa: Britain's
      Third Empire* (1949); *The Gold Coast Revolution* (1953); *Pan-Africanism or
      Communism?* (1956)

107   Posgrove, *Ending British Rule in Africa*, p.126. Quotes Wright's
      biographer Hazel Rowley on this 'act of betrayal' (Rowley, *Richard
      Wright*, p.437)

108   Wright papers, Padmore to Richard Wright, 5 December 1955; quoted
      also in Posgrove, *Ending British Rule in Africa*, p.149

109   James, C.L.R., Notes, p.55

110   James, C.L.R., MSS ca 1942–1974, LMC 1552, Folder 1, Carbon letter
      James to friends (not identified, 11 March 1957), Lilly Library, Indiana,
      quoted in Posgrove, *Ending British Rule in Africa*, p.155

111   The US Embassy in Accra reported to the Department of State on
      9 August 1958, quoted Posgrove, *Ending British Rule in Africa*, p.162

112   Drake in Shepperson and Drake, 'The Fifth Pan-African Conference, 1945
      and the All-African People's Congress, 1958', *Contributions in Black Studies*,
      Vol. 8, Article 5, p.63. scholarworks.umass.edu/cibs/vol8/iss1/5 [accessed
      12 February 2024]

113   Posgrove, *Ending British Rule in Africa*, p.163. Wright Papers (D. Padmore),
      Pizer to R. Wright, 31 October 1959

114   Ibid., p.164; Cunard Collection, Box 17, Folder 10, D. Padmore to
      Cunard, 24 October 1959

115   James, *George Padmore: A Black Marxist Revolutionary – A Memoir* libcom.
      org/article/george-padmore-black-marxist-revolutionary-memoir-clr-
      james [accessed 12 February 2024], part of unpublished MS

116   Adi, Hakim, and Sherwood, Marika, *Pan-African History: Political Figures
      from Africa and the Diaspora Since 1787* (London: Routledge, 2003), p.152

Chapter Five

1   *The Keys*, Issue 1, Vol. I, July 1933, p.8
2   Scobie, Edward, *Black Britannia: A History of Blacks in Britain* (London: Johnson Publishing Company, 1972), p.146
3   Jarrett-Macauley, Delia, *The Life of Una Marson 1905–65* (Manchester: Manchester University Press, 2010), p.51
4   Ibid., p.51
5   *Daily Gleaner*, 28 September 1936, p.5
6   *The Daily Mirror*, 26 February 1936, p.11
7   Jarrett-Macauley, *The Life of Una Marson*, p.1
8   Ibid., p.11
9   Ibid., p.8
10   Ford-Smith, Honor, 'Una Marson: Black Nationalist and Feminist Writer', *Caribbean Quarterly*, Vol. 34 No 3/4, *Women in West Indian Literature*, II (September/December 1988), p.26
11   Reckord, Michael, 'Marcus Garvey and the Performing Arts pt 2' feat. Rupert Lewis, UWI Professor Emeritus in Political Thought jamaica-gleaner.com/article/entertainment/20161027/marcus-garvey-and-performing-arts-pt-2, 26 October 2016 [accessed May 2024]
12   Jarrett-Macauley, *The Life of Una Marson*, p.30
13   Ibid., p.32
14   Ibid., p.39
15   Killingray, David, Downie, James Alan, 'Race, Faith and Politics: Harold Moody and the League of Coloured Peoples' (Goldsmiths College 1999), p.13
16   Ibid., p.13
17   *The Keys*, the official organ of the League of Coloured Peoples (Vols 1–7, 1933–39), with an introductory essay by Roderick Macdonald (New York: Millwood, NY, Kraus Thomson Organisation Ltd, 1975), p.9. Makonnen, Ras, *Pan-Africanism from Within* (Oxford: Oxford University Press, 1973), pp.126–7
18   Vaughan, David A., *Negro Victory* (London: Independent Press Ltd, 1950), p.56
19   Morris, Sam, 'Moody – The Forgotten Visionary', *New Community*, 3.1, Spring 1972, p.192; Harold Moody, The League of Coloured Peoples and African Issues, Biennial conference – African Studies Association UK
20   Ibid., p.192
21   Killingray, Downie, 'Race, Faith and Politics', p.15
22   *The Keys*, Issue 1, Vol. I, July 1933, p.1
23   Ibid., p.13
24   *The Keys*, Issue 1, Vol. III No. 1, July–September 1935, p.4
25   *The Keys*, Issue 1, Vol. I No. 2, p.28, October 1933
26   *The Sphere*, January 1934, p.61

27 *The Keys*, April 1934, Vol. 1 No. 4, p.66

28 *The Keys*, Vol. 2 No. 3, January–March 1935, pp.45–46

29 Report: 'The Keys, Concert at Indian Students hostel', *The Keys*, Vol. 1 No. 3, 1 January 1934, p.48

30 Jarrett-Macauley, *The Life of Una Marson*, p.68

31 Posgrove, *Ending British Rule in Africa*, p.36

32 Jarrett-Macauley, *The Life of Una Marson*, p.48. Interview with Sylvia Lowe by Delia Jarrett-Macauley

33 Jarrett-Macauley, *The Life of Una Marson*, p.69. Biographer Jarrett-Macauley reprinted a letter (possibly by Marson to Atta). It was discovered by the historian Richard Rathbone in the Akyem Abuakwa State Council Archives, Kyebi, Ghana, AASA 9/57

34 Matera, *Black London*, p.53

35 Jarrett-Macauley, *The Life of Una Marson*, p.53

36 Matera, *Black London*, p.295.

37 Ibid., p.293

38 Jarrett-Macauley, *The Life of Una Marson*, pp.94–5; 'Race Enemy No. 1', *Wasu*, Vol. 4 No. 2, August 1935

39 'Winifred Holtby As I Knew Her', *Jamaica's Public Opinion*, 1937; Donnell, Alison (ed.), *Una Marson: Selected Poems* (London: Peepal Tree Press, 2011), p.180

40 Matera, *Black London*, p.126

41 Marson, Una, *The Moth and the Star* (self-published Kingston, Jamaica: 1937), p.79; Marson, Una, *Towards the Stars* (London: University of London Press, February 1945), p.47

42 Jarrett-Macauley, *The Life of Una Marson*, p.87; Report, *Cumheriyet*, 24 April 1935

43 Ibid., p.89

44 Snaith, Anna, *Modernist Voyages: Colonial Women Writers in London, 1890–1945* (Cambridge: Cambridge University Press, 2014), p.171; quoted from papers of Margery Corbett Ashby, who received extensive press coverage at the conference (Margery Corbett Ashby Papers, Box 484, The Women's Library)

45 Ibid., p.90

46 Ibid., p.90; *The Keys* Vol. III No. 1, July–October 1935, p.13

47 Marson, *The Moth and the Star*, p.80; Marson, *Towards the Stars*, p.47

48 Weldon Johnson Collection, Marson to Weldon Johnson, 27 January 1938, quoted in Matera, *Black London*, p.137

49 Jarrett-Macauley, *The Life of Una Marson*, p.92

50 The battle of Magdala, a daring escape plan, had been precipitated after the then Emperor Tewodros had taken a number of British hostages when his protestations for help against the Ottoman Empire were ignored by Queen Victoria

51 Marson, 'Racial Feelings?', *Public Opinion*, p.3, quoted in Umoren, Imaobong D., *Race Women Internationalists* (California: University of California Press 2018), p.44

52 Jarrett-Macauley, *The Life of Una Marson*, p.100

53 James, C.L.R., 'Abyssinia and the Imperialists', *The Keys*, January 1936, Vol. III, No. 3, p.32

54 'The Rape of a Black Empire', *The Keys*, Vol. IV, July–September 1936, p.2

55 Du Bois, W.E.B., 'Inter-Racial Implications of the Ethiopian Crisis', *Foreign Affairs*, 1 October 1935, www.foreignaffairs.com/articles/ethiopia/1935-10-01/inter-racial-implications-ethiopian-crisis [accessed October 2023]

56 'Ethiopia: Man of the Year: Haile Selassie', *Time*, 6 January 1936, pp.14–15

57 Bowers, Keith, 'Review of Imperial Exile', *Ethiopian Review of Books* ethiopianreviewofbooks.wordpress.com/2016/05/09/1023/ [accessed 24 May 2024]

58 Reported in 'The League: Capitulation', *Time*, 29 June 1936, content.time.com/time/subscriber/article/0,33009,770199-1,00.html [accessed 7 October 2024]

59 Jarrett-Macauley, *The Life of Una Marson*, p.102

60 Selassie's speech to the League of Nations in Amharic and French, tile.loc.gov/storage-services/service/gdc/gdcwdl/wd/l_/11/60/2/wdl_11602/wdl_11602.pdf [from French translation, accessed 24 September 2024]

61 Jarrett-Macauley, *The Life of Una Marson*, p.103. Quoted Nancy Cunard, for the Associated Negro Press; Cunard Papers, Chicago Historical Society, Chicago

62 Robinson, Harriet and Mutanda-Dougherty, Anoushka, 'How an Ethiopian Emperor Ended Up Living in Bath', BBC news online, 10 September 2024, www.bbc.co.uk/news/articles/c8jl2l8p.3klo [accessed 18 September 2024]

63 'Jamaican Girl Who Was Personal Secretary to Haile Selassie', *Daily Gleaner*, 25 September 1936, p.17

64 'Racial Prejudice in London Not Improving Says Miss Marson', *Daily Gleaner*, 28 September, 1936, p.5

65 'Minister's Sons Killed', Report, *Derby Evening Telegraph*, 22 March 1937, p.1

66 Marson, Una, 'To Joe and Ben' in *The Moth and the Star*, pp.81–83

67 Bernal, Richard L., 'The Great Depression, Colonial Policy and Industrialisation in Jamaica', *Social and Economic Studies*, Vol. 37 Nos 1 & 2, *Caribbean Economic History*, March/June 1988, pp.33–64

68 Thomas, R.O., 'Revolt in the West Indies', *The Keys*, Vol. III No. 3, 1 January 1936, p.37

69   Schwarz, *West Indian Intellectuals in Britain*; Donnell, Alison, 'Una Marson: Feminism, Anti-Colonialism and a Forgotten Fight for Freedom', p.118

70   Ibid., p.119

71   Marson, *The Moth and The Star*, p.11; Marson, *Towards the Stars*, pp.53–57

72   Her second play, *London Calling* (1937), was a comedy of manners loosely based on her experiences with Nani Ofori Atta

73   Jarrett-Macauley, *The Life of Una Marson*, p.138

74   Ibid., p.109; Snaith, *Modernist Voyages*, p.160

75   Ibid., p.141

76   Jarrett-Macauley, *The Life of Una Marson*, p.143

77   Ibid., p.146

78   Dunbar was London correspondent for the Associated Negro Press news service and later the American press, where he reported on Nazi atrocities. He was later embedded with the American 8th Army and crossed the English Channel to report on D-Day. Kaufmann, Miranda, 'Dunbar, Rudolph (1899–10 June 1988)', Dabydeen, Gilmore and Jones, *Oxford Companion to Black British History* (Oxford: Oxford University Press, 2007), pp.135–136

79   Ministry of Information film, www.youtube.com/watch?v=cjKsRGgUa-c [accessed 20 September 2024]

80   Jarrett-Macauley, *The Life of Una Marson*, p.148

81   *Daily Gleaner*, 11 May 1965, p.12; quoted in Jarrett-Macauley, *The Life of Una Marson*, p.148

82   Matera, *Black London*, p.140

83   Procter, James, 'Una Marson at the BBC', *Small Axe*, Vol. 19 No. 3, November 2015, Duke University Press, p.7. The average wage in 1942 was £320 p.a., and less for women

84   Ibid., p.7

85   Ibid., p.8. Procter quotes letter from Joan Gilbert to Cecil Madden, 14 April 1941 (BBC WAC L1/290/1) and Cecil Madden to Deputy Director of Empire Services, 14 April 1941 (BBC WAC L1/290/1)

86   Ibid., p.8. Procter quotes correspondence: Cecil Madden to Director of Empire Services, 14 April 1941 (BBC WAC L1/290/1)

87   Ibid., pp.8–9

88   Jarrett-Macauley, *The Life of Una Marson*, p.140

89   Ibid., p.140

90   Ibid., p.163

91   Ibid., p.163. From Jarrett-Macauley original interview with Dudley Thompson

92   After the war, Thompson attended Oxford as a Rhodes Scholar studying law. He later was part of the team that defended Jomo Kenyatta in 1952

when he was accused by the colonial government of instigating the Mau Mau rebellion and went on to play an active part in Jamaican political life, serving in Norman Manley's PNP

93 Jarrett-Macauley, *The Life of Una Marson*, p.143
94 Marson, Una, 'London Revisited', *Sunday Gleaner*, 28 February 1965, p.21
95 Matera, *Black London*, p.141
96 Procter disputes 11 March 1943 as the start of the broadcasts, as claimed in Jarrett-Macauley's biography, citing the BBC 'Programmes on Broadcast' files; Procter, 'Una Marson at the BBC', *Small Axe*, p.24
97 Kamau Braithwaite, Edward, *History of the Voice* (London, New Beacon Books, 1984), p.87, www.caribbean-beat.com/issue-63/london-calling#axzz8nbdxGeLZ [accessed 24 September 2024]
98 Procter, 'Una Marson at the BBC', *Small Axe*, p.18
99 Ibid., p.20. J.F. Doulton, an assistant to the Overseas Establishment Officer, relayed Marson's condition; J.F. Doulton to A.F. Whyte, 11 January 1946 (BBC WAC l1/290/1)
100 Procter, 'Una Marson at the BBC', *Small Axe*, p.22. The BBC's medical adviser Dr Whyte summarised the Maudsley Report on 25 April 1946: 'Miss Marson is suffering from schizophrenia and has delusions of persecution by a group of individuals'. Dr A.F. Whyte, 'Miss Una Marson', 3 May 1946 (BBC WAC File L1/290/1)
101 Procter, 'Una Marson at the BBC', *Small Axe*, p.24. *Caribbean Voices*, 27 May 1945 (BBC WAC script 35). June Grimble became the announcer heading up programme scripts, and mentions of Marson were rare in these early programmes
102 Procter, 'Una Marson at the BBC', *Small Axe*, p.27. Henry Swanzy diaries, entry for 13 July 1945
103 Jarrett-Macauley, *The Life of Una Marson*, p.182
104 Umoren, *Race Women Internationalists*, p.95
105 Quoted Jarrett-Macauley, *The Life of Una Marson*, p.225. Ethel Marson to Mina Ben-Zwi, May 1965, Mount Carmel Training Centre Papers, Marson file, Haifa, Israel
106 The impact of racism on mental health briefing paper 2018, legacy. synergicollaborativecentre.co.uk/briefing-papers [accessed 3 October 2024]
107 Marson, *The Moth and the Star*, p.93

Chapter Six
1 Sherwood, Marika, *Claudia Jones: A Life in Exile* (London: Lawrence & Wishart, 1999), p.58
2 Ibid., p.163. According to Sherwood's account, Levy knocked on Jones' door on Christmas Day and on Boxing Day. Increasingly worried, he broke into her apartment later on Boxing Day to discover her dead in her bed. It was determined she suffered a heart attack on the evening of

Christmas Eve. The death certificate registers the death on 31 December 1964. Deaths have to be registered within five days and the Christmas period caused delays

3   Hinds, Donald, 'The West Indian Gazette: Claudia Jones and the Black Press in Britain', *Race & Class*, Vol. 50, Issue 1, July–September 2008, Sage Journals, 2008, p.96

4   Claudia Jones Symposium, London 1996, audio British Library. Sherwood, *Claudia Jones*, p.58

5   Claudia Jones Symposium, London 1996, audio British Library. Sherwood, *Claudia Jones*, p.198

6   Jones, Claudia, 'Why a Paper for West Indians, 80,000 Good Reasons', *West Indian Gazette*, March 1958, p.1

7   'West Indian Immigrants', UK Parliament Hansard debate by Lord Elton, 20 November 1956, hansard.parliament.uk/Lords/1956-11-20/debates/057444dc-2d13-4aef-93e9-d75ed98d824a/WestIndianImmigrants [accessed 9 January 2025]

8   Peach, G.C.K., 'West Indian Migration to Britain', *The International Migration Review*, Spring 1967, Vol. 1 No. 2, pp.34–45

9   Boyce Davies, Carole, *Left of Karl Marx* (Durham and London: Duke University Press, 2007), p.74. Much later, Diane Langford, who had seen her speak in London, spoke of her 'imposing gravitas' and of her complete command of the room. Author interview with Diane Langford, 16 August 2024

10   Letter from Jones to Comrade Foster, 6 December 1955, entitled 'Autobiographical History', quoted in entirety in Boyce Davies, Carole (ed.), *Claudia Jones: Beyond Containment* (Oxford: Ayebia Clarke Publishing, 2011), p.10. Also in Claudia Jones Memorial Collection, SCMG692, Schomburg Center for Research in Black Culture, Manuscripts, Archives and Rare Books Division

11   Ibid., p.10

12   Claudia Jones, Speech at the Hotel Theresa, 21 February 1952. Johnson, Buzz, *I Think of My Mother: Notes on the Life and Times of Claudia Jones* (London: Karia Press, 1985), p.33

13   Letter from Jones to Comrade Foster, 6 December 1955, entitled 'Autobiographical History', quoted in entirety in Boyce Davies, *Claudia Jones: Beyond Containment*, p.10. Also in Claudia Jones Memorial Collection, SCMG692, Schomburg Center for Research in Black Culture, Manuscripts, Archives and Rare Books Division

14   Ibid., p.10

15   Johnson, *I Think of My Mother*, p.6

16   Baker, Ella and Cooke, Marvel, 'The Bronx Slave Market', *The Crisis*, November 1935, caringlabor.wordpress.com/2010/11/24/ella-baker-and-marvel-cooke-the-slave-market [accessed 13 August 2024]

17 Jones, Claudia, 'Lift Every Voice for Victory' (1942), in Boyce Davies, *Claudia Jones: Beyond Containment*, p.51

18 Boyce Davies, Carole, *Left of Karl Marx*, p.268 (Chapter 6, note 17)

19 Lynn, Denise, *Claudia Jones* (Cambridge: Polity Press, 2024), p.62. Quotes Louis Miller M.D., To Whom it May Concern, 19 December 1952, Box 14, Folder 7, Mary Metlay Kaufmann Papers, Sophia Smith Collection, Smith College, Northampton, Massachusetts

20 Letter from Jones to Comrade Foster, 6 December 1955, entitled 'Autobiographical History', quoted in entirety in Boyce Davies, *Claudia Jones: Beyond Containment*, p.10. Also in Claudia Jones Memorial Collection, SCMG692 , Schomburg Center for Research in Black Culture, Manuscripts, Archives and Rare Books Division

21 Ibid.

22 Martin, Douglas, 'Stretch Johnson, 85, Tap Dancer and Activist', *New York Times* obituary, 12 June 2000, p.37

23 Sherwood, *Claudia Jones*, p.37 (note 13: telephone conversation between M. Sherwood and Mr Johnson in Galveston, Texas, April 1997, p.57)

24 Boyce Davies, *Left of Karl Marx*, p.201

25 Ibid., p.105. Letter to John Gates, editor of *The Daily Worker*, 1950, published as 'Claudia Jones Writes from Ellis Island'

26 Johnson, *I Think of My Mother*, p.27

27 Lynn, *Claudia Jones*, p.99

28 Ibid., p.140; quotes Claudia Jones, 'Half the World', *The Worker*, 3 February 1952, p.8

29 Ibid., p.143

30 Ibid., p.140; Box 14, Folder 11, Mary Metlay Kaufmann Papers, Sophia Smith Collection, Smith College, Northampton, Massachusetts

31 Gurley Flynn, Elizabeth, *The Alderson Story: My Life as a Political Prisoner* (US: International Publishing Company, 1971), p.27

32 Lynn, *Claudia Jones*, p.38

33 Ibid., p.153

34 Box 1 MC692 Claudia Jones Memorial Collection, Schomburg Center for Research in Black Culture, Manuscripts, Archives and Rare Books Division

35 Sherwood, *Claudia Jones*, p.25

36 Transcript Paul Robeson. Box 1 MC692 Claudia Jones Memorial Collection, Schomburg Center for Research in Black Culture, Manuscripts, Archives and Rare Books Division

37 Original letter dated 9 December 1959 from William Z. Foster, CPUSA to Harry Pollitt, General Secretary of Communist Party Great Britain. Box 1 MC692 Claudia Jones Memorial Collection, Schomburg Center for Research in Black Culture, Manuscripts, Archives and Rare Books Division

38   Letter to Charles Cumberbatch. Box 1 MC692 Claudia Jones Memorial
      Collection, Schomburg Center for Research in Black Culture,
      Manuscripts, Archives and Rare Books Division

39   Gurley Flynn, *The Alderson Story*, p.118

40   Sherwood, *Claudia Jones*, p.189

41   Atkinson, Clarissa W., '"A Pride in Being West Indian": Claudia Jones
      and the West Indian Gazette (2012 paper)', oldestvocation.com/a-pride-
      in-being-west-indian-claudia-jones-and-the-west-indian-gazette [accessed
      10 August 2022]

42   Langford, Diane, *The Manchanda Connection* (unpublished memoir, 2007),
      p.14, abhimanyumanchandaremembered.weebly.com/manu-and-claudia.
      html; Estate late A. Manchanda [accessed 10 July 2024]

43   Atkinson, '"A Pride in Being West Indian"', oldestvocation.com/a-pride-
      in-being-west-indian-claudia-jones-and-the-west-indian-gazette [accessed
      14 August 2022]

44   Langford, *The Manchanda Connection*, abhimanyumanchandaremembered.
      weebly.com/manu-and-claudia.html; Estate late A. Manchanda [accessed
      10 July 2024]

45   Travis, Alan, 'After 44 Years Secret Papers Reveal the Truth about Five
      Nights of Violence in Notting Hill', *Guardian*, 24 August 2002, www.
      theguardian.com/uk/2002/aug/24/artsandhumanities.nottinghill-
      carnival2002 [accessed 14 August 2022]

46   Memo of interview with residents of Notting Hill, 5 September 1958,
      Warwick University Digital Collection, mrc-catalogue.warwick.ac.uk/
      records/TUC/A/10/800/31/9 [accessed 14 August 2022]

47   Gus John, interview with author, 23 September 2024

48   Travis, Alan, 'After 44 Years Secret Papers Reveal the Truth about Five
      Nights of Violence in Notting Hill', *Guardian*, 24 August 2002

49   Andrews, Kehinde, 'Claudia Jones's Transnational Radicalism', *The
      New Statesman*, 12 October 2017, www.newstatesman.com/politics/
      uk-politics/2017/10/claudia-joness-transnational-radicalism [accessed
      1 May 2022]

50   Sherwood, *Claudia Jones*, p.129. Quoted copy of original letter, Ruth
      Glass, Newcomers Centre for Urban Studies, London, 1960

51   Jones, Claudia, *The Worker*, 2 November 1958, p.6

52   Jones worked as general secretary for this organisation but may have
      dropped this duty as the *WIG* became more successful

53   Letter Ashwood Garvey to Jones. Box 1 MC692 Claudia Jones
      Memorial Collection, Schomburg Center for Research in Black Culture,
      Manuscripts, Archives and Rare Books Division

54   Lynn, *Claudia Jones*, p.183

55   Ibid., p.182

56   Hinds, 'The West Indian Gazette', *Race & Class*, p.94

57   *West Indian Gazette*, January 1960, p.3

58   Hinds, 'The West Indian Gazette', *Race & Class*, p.92

59   Pilkington, Edward, *Beyond the Mother Country: West Indians and the Notting Hill White Riots* (London: I.B. Tauris, 1988), pp.143, 144

60   Gus John, interview with author, 23 September 2024

61   Hinds, 'The West Indian Gazette', *Race & Class*. Chapter in Sherwood, *Claudia Jones*, p.142

62   Schwarz, *West Indian Intellectuals in Britain*, 'Crossing the Seas', p.12

63   Hinds, Donald, *Journey to an Illusion: The West Indian in Britain* (London: Bogie-l'Ouverture, 1966), pp.164–165

64   Diane Langford, interview with author, 16 August 2024

65   Sherwood, *Claudia Jones*, p.52

66   Diane Langford, interview with author, 16 August 2024

67   Sherwood, *Claudia Jones*, p.200

68   Gus John, interview with author, 23 September 2024

69   Hinds, 'The West Indian Gazette', *Race & Class*, pp.92–3

70   The *Gazette* was first published over eight pages and then bumped up to twelve in 1961.

71   Umoren, *Race Women Internationalists*, p.112

72   Hinds, 'The West Indian Gazette', *Race & Class*, p.95

73   Sherwood, *Claudia Jones*, p.198

74   Boyce Davies, *Claudia Jones: Beyond Containment*, Afterword by Alrick X, Cambridge, p.218

75   Jones, Claudia, 'I Spend a Night in a Notting Hill Police Station', *WIG*, February 1962, p.5

76   Sherwood, *Claudia Jones*, p.198

77   The Caribbean Carnival 1959 official souvenir programme, p.1

78   Thomson, Ian, 'Here to Stay', *Guardian*, 29 August 2009, www.theguardian.com/books/2009/aug/29/donald-hinds-journey-to-illusion [accessed 14 August 2022]

79   Hinds, 'The West Indian Gazette', *Race & Class*, p.95

80   Ibid., p.95

81   Sherwood, *Claudia Jones*, p.47

82   Letter Claudia to Manu, 25 October 1962. Marx Memorial Library, Abimanyu (Manu) Collection 1937–2015. Box MM/MM1 Correspondence between Manu and Claudia Jones

83   Letter to Eslanda Robeson, 6 June 1960, Claudia Jones Research Collection, SCMG699, Schomburg Center for Research in Black Culture, MS, Archives and Rare Books Division. Sherwood, *Claudia Jones*, p.132

84   Claudia Jones Research Collection, SCMG692, Box 1, Schomburg Center for Research in Black Culture, MS, Archives and Rare Books Division

85   Boyce Davies, *Claudia Jones: Beyond Containment*, Afterword by Alrick X, Cambridge, p.210

86 Langford, *The Manchanda Connection*, www.marxists.org/history/erol/uk.secondwave/langford.pdf [accessed 14 August 2024]

87 Jones, Claudia, 'The Caribbean Community in Britain', *Freedomways*, reprinted in Boyce Davies, *Left of Karl Marx*, p.88

88 Hinds, 'The West Indian Gazette', *Race & Class*, p.88

89 Leila Hassan Howe, interview with author, 27 September 2024

Chapter Seven

1 Bunce, Robin, and Field, Paul, *Darcus Howe: A Political Biography* (London: Bloomsbury, 2013), p.28

2 Cooper, David (ed.), *The Dialectics of Liberation* (London: Verso 2015), p.11

3 Report, 'Black Power Prophet', *New York Times*, 5 August 1966, p.10

4 Davis, Angela Y., *An Autobiography* (London: Penguin, 2022), pp.129–130

5 Joseph, Peniel E., *Stokely: A Life* (New York: Basic Civitas, 2014), p.103; *LA Times*, 25 May 1966, p.16

6 Michael X, born Michael de Freitas (also known as Abdul Malik), had been an enforcer for the notorious slum landlord Peter Rachman

7 Cooper, *The Dialectics of Liberation*, p.169

8 Carmichael stated 'a poem stolen from a black man' in his first speech at the Dialectics of Liberation Conference on 18 July 1967. These links provide greater context to that claim: scalar.lehigh.edu/mckay/if-we-must-die-in-england; winstonchurchill.org/resources/myths/churchill-quoted-radical-poet-claude-mckay; winstonchurchill.org/resources/myths/churchill-quoted-radical-poet-claude-mckay [accessed 12 September 2024]

9 Ibid., p.169

10 Anderson, Gerry, interview with Obi Egbuna; 'A Black Power Name You Will Not Forget', *Wolverhampton Express & Star*, 15 March 1971, p.6

11 Report: 'Jenkins orders "Black Power" leader probe', *Reading Evening Post*, 24 July 1967, p.1

12 Darcus Howe obituary, *The Times*, 4 April 2017, www.thetimes.com/uk/article/darcus-howe-0gkd2srpc [accessed 12 August 2024]

13 Bunce and Field, *Darcus Howe*, p.24

14 Ibid.

15 Ibid., p.32

16 Sawh had been arrested at Speakers' Corner in August 1967

17 Leila Hassan Howe, interview with author, 27 September 2024

18 Bunce and Field, *Darcus Howe*, p.34

19 *Black Dimension*, no number, undated, George Padmore Institute (GPI), JOU 3/5

20 *Black Dimension*, undated, George Padmore Institute, (GPI) JOU 35/4

21 Gus John, interview with author, 23 September 2024

22 *Black Dimension*, Vol. 1, February 1969, GPI JOU/35/1

23 Bunce and Field, *Darcus Howe*, p.36

24 Ibid., p.35

25 James was not wrong about Michael X. He fled the UK to Trinidad in February 1971 following a bizarre extortion case dubbed by media 'the Slave Collar Affair'. He set up a commune in Trinidad and was charged with the murders of two followers, whose bodies were discovered in shallow graves on the property in February 1972. He was hanged for murder in Trinidad in 1975

26 Demonstrators draped black cloth over the 'white' statues of saints in the church. UWI President Carl Blackwood railed against 'white racism', which he charged was a practice of the Catholic Church, trinidadexpress.com/news/local/black-power-storms-the-cathedral/article_53a3e46e-8d05-5d84-9d0d-b5dee252a78c.html [accessed 14 January 2025]

27 Sivanandan, A., *A Different Hunger: Writings on Black Resistance* (London: Pluto Press, 1982), p.33

28 John-Baptiste, Ashley, 'The Mangrove Nine: Echoes of Black Lives Matter from 50 Years Ago', www.bbc.co.uk/news/extra/jGD9WJrVXf/the-mangrove-nine-black-lives-matter [accessed 9 January 2025]

29 Bunce and Field, *Darcus Howe*, p.67

30 Frank Crichlow's complaint to the Race Relations Board, 23 November 1969, The National Archives, Catalogue ref. CK 2/690, www.nationalarchives.gov.uk/wp-content/uploads/2021/03/CK2-690-source-1.jpg [accessed 14 October 2025]

31 Bunce and Field, *Darcus Howe*, p.102

32 Action Group statement for the Defence of the Mangrove, 1970 (9 August written in ballpoint pen on document), issued by Anthony Mohipp, barrister at law, c/o 8 All Saints Road W11. The National Archives, Catalogue ref. HO325/143, www.nationalarchives.gov.uk/education/resources/mangrove-nine-protest/source-two [accessed 10 October 2025]

33 Bunce and Field, *Darcus Howe*, p.105

34 Ibid., p.107

35 Ibid., p.109

36 *The Scotsman*, 10 August 1970, p.1

37 *The Mirror*, 12 August 1970, p.1

38 Bunce and Field, *Darcus Howe*, p.116

39 Bunce, Robin and Field, Paul, 'Mangrove Nine: The Court Challenge Against Police Racism in Notting Hill', *Guardian*, 29 November 2010, www.theguardian.com/law/2010/nov/29/mangrove-nine-40th-anniversary [accessed 8 January 2025]

40 Farrukh Dhondy, interview with author, 17 October 2024

41 Ibid.

42   Milne, Anthony, 'The Life and Times of Darcus Howe,' *Trinidad Sunday Express Magazine*, 28 November 1982, page number obscured

43   Howe and Jones-LeCointe could dismiss only seven potential jurors each. All the defendants exercised their right to dismiss seven, so sixty-three rejected in total

44   Farrukh Dhondy, interview with author, 17 October 2024

45   Twenty-eight and thirty-three times respectively

46   Report, *Post-Mercury Series*, 19 November 1971

47   Bunce and Field, *Darcus Howe*, p.129

48   Ibid.

49   Ibid., p.136

50   Baksi, Catherine, 'Landmarks in Law: When the Mangrove Nine Beat the British State', *Guardian*, 10 November 2020, www.theguardian.com/law/2020/nov/10/landmarks-in-law-when-the-mangrove-nine-beat-the-british-state [accessed 14 October 2025]

51   Leila Hassan Howe, interview with author, 27 September 2024

52   Farrukh Dhondy, interview with author, 17 October 2024

53   Dhondy, Farrukh, *Fragments Against My Ruin: A Life* (London: Context, 2021; Verso, 2024), p.136

54   Most copies are four pages (19 February 1972 and 4 March 1972). Only two issues (June 1972 and July 1972) boast eight pages

55   *Freedom News*, 1 June 1973, p.1

56   'Fire Bomb War on Black People', *Freedom News*, 16 March 1973, p.1

57   Dhondy, *Fragments Against My Ruin*, p.146

58   Ibid., p.136

59   Report 'I Have to Turn the Prize Against Itself'; John Berger's 1972 Booker Prize speech in full: thebookerprizes.com/the-booker-library/features/i-have-to-turn-the-prize-against-itself-john-bergers-1972-booker-prize [accessed 10 October 2024]

60   Dhondy took Howe's advice after the incident (Howe was in Trinidad). According to Dhondy, Howe said: 'Bloody sign over the building. What do you want to get killed over a building?' Farrukh Dhondy, interview with author, 17 October 2024

61   Dhondy, *Fragments Against My Ruin*, p.152

62   Bunce, Robin, Field, Paul, Hassan, Leila, and Peacock, Margaret (eds), *Here to Stay, Here to Fight* (London: Pluto Press, 1988), p.3. Quotes: Report, *Guardian*, 6 November 1973

63   Bunce and Field, *Darcus Howe*, p.144

64   Wild, Rosalind E., '"Black Was the Colour of Our Political Fight": Black Power in Britain, 1955–76', PhD thesis, University of Sheffield, 2008, p.3

65   Howe, Darcus, 'From Victim to Protagonist: The Changing Social Reality', *Race Today*, January 1974. See Bunce et al., *Here to Stay, Here to Fight*, p.10

66 Bunce and Field, *Darcus Howe*, p.147
67 Dhondy, *Fragments Against My Ruin*, p.154
68 Bunce and Field, *Darcus Howe*, p.149. Report, *The Times*, 6 October 1975
69 Leila Hassan Howe, interview with author, 27 September 2024
70 C.L.R. James' marriage to Selma broke down in 1980. According to Hassan Howe, 'He said he couldn't live in Trinidad because he couldn't get the intellectual stimulus he wanted. He couldn't get the newspapers. It was hard to get his books. And he also wanted to be around young people who were active [Darcus].' Interview with author, 27 September 2024
71 Bunce et al., *Here to Stay, Here to Fight* (London: Pluto Press, 1988), p.5
72 Bunce and Field, *Darcus Howe*, p.164
73 Ibid., p.149
74 Farrukh Dhondy, interview with author, 17 October 2024
75 Bunce and Field, *Darcus Howe*, p.161
76 Trotsky's former secretary Raya Dunayevskaya coined the term and James heard it while working for Trotsky
77 Bunce and Field, *Darcus Howe*, pp.155–156
78 Ibid., p.170
79 Campbell, Duncan, '"Oval Four" Men Jailed in 1972 Cleared by Court of Appeal in London', *Guardian*, 5 December 2019, www.theguardian.com/uk-news/2019/dec/05/oval-four-men-jailed-in-1972-cleared-by-court-of-appeal-in-london [accessed 19 September 2024]
80 See specialbranchfiles.uk/2212-2; 1970 embed.documentcloud.org/documents/6204822-1970-BP-HO-376-154-BP-Intelligence-Reports/?embed=1 [accessed 7 August 2022]
81 Leila Hassan Howe, interview with author, 27 September 2024
82 *Race Today Review*, 1980, p.51
83 Milne, Anthony, 'The Life and Times of Darcus Howe', *Trinidad Sunday Express Magazine*, 28 November 1982, page number obscured
84 McQueen, Steve and Rogan, James (directors), *Uprising* (documentary BBC), Series 1 'Fire', aired 20 July 2021, www.bbc.co.uk/iplayer/episodes/m000y317/uprising [accessed 12 January 2021]
85 The George Padmore Institute New Cross Massacre Campaign, 1980–85, NCM 1/1 and 1/3
86 McQueen and Rogan, *Uprising*, Series 1 'Fire'
87 Ibid.
88 Bunce et al., *Here to Stay, Here to Fight*, p.10
89 Leila Hassan Howe, interview with author, 27 September 2024
90 Ibid.
91 Bunce and Field, *Darcus Howe*, pp.204–205
92 McQueen and Rogan, *Uprising*, Series 1 'Fire'

93   Leila Hassan Howe, interview with author, 27 September 2024
94   Mohdin, Aamna, 'The Brixton Riots 40 Years On: A Watershed Moment for Race Relations', *Guardian*, 11 April 2021, www.theguardian.com/world/2021/apr/11/brixton-riots-40-years-on-a-watershed-moment-for-race-relations [accessed 12 January 2025]
95   Leila Hassan Howe, interview with author, 27 September 2024
96   Ibid.
97   Ibid.
98   Bunce et al., *Here to Stay, Here to Fight*, pp.56–66
99   'Verdict: Not a Race Riot, but a Burst of Anger', *Guardian*, 26 November 1981, p.3
100 Bunce et al., *Here to Stay, Here to Fight*, p.6
101 Gamio, Méheut, Porter, Gebrekidan, McCann and Apuzzo: 'Haiti's Lost Billions', *New York Times*, 20 May 2022, www.nytimes.com/interactive/2022/05/20/world/americas/enslaved-haiti-debt-timeline.html [accessed 14 January 2025]
102 Bunce and Field, *Darcus Howe*, p.228
103 Howe, Darcus, 'My Battle with Prostate Cancer', *Guardian*, 17 November 2009, www.theguardian.com/lifeandstyle/2009/nov/17/darcus-howe-surviving-prostate-cancer [accessed 13 September 2024]
104 Howe had a further two children, Rap and Clare, from a second marriage. Hassan Howe raised his son Amiri and their daughter Zoe
105 Report: 'Darcus' Final Farewell: "A Real Revolutionary … I Miss Him"', *The Voice*, 27 April 2017, www.voice-online.co.uk/news/uk-news/2017/04/27/darcus-final-farewell-a-real-revolutionaryi-miss-him [accessed 12 September 2024]
106 Bunce and Field, *Darcus Howe*, p.2
107 Ibid.
108 Leila Hassan Howe, interview with author, 27 September 2024
109 Ibid.

Conclusion

1   Speech given by C.L.R. James in London, 1967, www.marxists.org/archive/james-clr/works/1967/black-power.htm [accessed 13 January 2025]; Wild, '"Black Was the Colour of Our Fight"', p.3
2   Thomas, Theodore, *Hard Truth* (London: Lawrence & Symcox, 1894), p.60
3   *Lux*, 27 August 1892; Schneer, *London 1900*, p.210
4   The 2020 Pulitzer Prize Winner in Special Citations and Awards, Ida B. Wells (2020), www.pulitzer.org/winners/ida-b-wells [accessed 24 March 2025]
5   Matera, *Black London*, p.93

6   Howe, Darcus, 'From Victim to Protagonist: The Changing Social Reality', *Race Today*, January 1974. See Bunce et al., *Here to Stay, Here to Fight*, p.10

7   UCL, The Black People's Day of Action 1981 online exhibition, 22 February 2021, www.ucl.ac.uk/racism-racialisation/events/ black-peoples-day-action-1981-online-exhibition [accessed 8 February 2025]

ACKNOWLEDGEMENTS

I started this book in the summer of 2021 – at a point when my eldest child was in his first year of secondary school; he is now about to take his GCSEs. This book has taken considerable time, funds and energy, but what has kept me going is that the stories of these journalists needed to be told.

I am forever grateful to Arts Council England for awarding me a Developing Your Creative Practice grant in 2022. I was able to take some time off work and go on a research trip to the Schomburg Archives in New York. I am also indebted to the Society of Authors for awarding me a grant in spring 2024 – again this was invaluable funding, giving me the time and space to complete the book.

Archives, libraries and their dedicated and patient staff, both here and in the US, were instrumental to this project. I would like to thank the Arthur Gillett Trust; the Library of the Society of Friends; Geoffrey Thomas Ross and William Alan Schlaack on the digitisation services desk at the University of Illinois' History, Philosophy and Newspaper Library; the British Library; the Bodleian Library of Commonwealth and African Studies at Rhodes House; the Institute of Race Relations; the National Archives; Lambeth Archives; the Marx Memorial Library; the Schomburg Center for Research in Black Culture in New York (many thanks to my cousin Shanti Rywkin and her husband Richard for accommodating me and my family during our stay); and particularly Sarah Garrod and the staff of the George Padmore Institute, who went above and beyond the call of duty in accommodating my requests. I would also like to thank the Rev. Chris Howson at the University of Sunderland, who along with university staff was involved in establishing

Celestine Edwards' blue plaque in the city; further thanks to Alex Wilson at Villon films for the archival footage of Stokely Carmichael and Kevin Ring of *Beat Scene* magazine.

Huge thanks to my agent David Godwin, whose keen eye recognised the value and worth in my writing early on, and The History Press' Claire Hartley for her and her team's support and endorsement of the project.

I was lucky enough to be part of the London Library Emerging Writer cohort, 2022–23. The books, periodicals and archive services provided have been a vital resource, as has been the support of my fellow writers and programme director Claire Berliner. I would also like to thank Dr Michael Pourfar, my fellow non-fiction 'buddy' that year, who read the chapters of *INK!* in its earliest incarnations and was a source of constant motivation. I have benefited from being part of the SI Leeds family of writers – I was awarded second prize in 2018 and was a judge for the 2020 competition. The Prize Director Fiona Goh is tremendously supportive of new writers and for the past seven years has been a consistent champion of my work, as has the writer Irenosen Okojie, whom I met through the prize and who has been generous with both her time and support.

Similarly, my friend Carrie Gibson has been a constant well of encouragement and advice. I also offer my deepest gratitude to my friend Barbara Harper, who generously read, edited and commented on the whole manuscript. Her wise and insightful input improved the project considerably and I am eternally grateful for her help.

For the friends, colleagues and family members who showed interest and support, I thank you. The kindest word can sustain someone through moments of dark doubt and struggle, especially when funds are scarce, and time is of the essence.

And finally to my family – to Steve, Freddie and Ashtyn – *INK!* could not have come into being without your love, generosity and support.

INDEX

Note: *italicised* page references denote illustrations